STUDY GUIDE

for use with

ECONOMICS OF
SOCIAL ISSUES

Twelfth Edition

Ansel M. Sharp
University of the South

Charles A. Register
Mississippi State University

Paul W. Grimes
Mississippi State University

IRWIN

Chicago • Bogotá • Boston • Buenos Aires • Caracas
London • Madrid • Mexico City • Sydney • Toronto

©Richard D. Irwin, a Times Mirror Higher Education Group, Inc. company,
1974, 1976, 1978, 1980, 1982, 1984, 1986, 1988, 1990, 1992, 1994, and 1996

Printed in the United States of America.

ISBN 0–256–16076–7

1 2 3 4 5 6 7 8 9 0 WCB 2 1 0 9 8 7 6 5

A Note to Students

This *Study Guide* is designed to complement your exploration of the *Economics of Social Issues,* Revised Edition. The consistent pursuite of the material presented here will help you learn basic economic concepts in a systematic fasion. Each chapter provides you with a set of learning objectives, an application article, question, and problems which will lead you throught the material presented in the text. Working through the *Study Guide* will test your understanding of basic economic concepts and your ability to apply economice reasoning to important issues that face our modern society. Each chapter of the *Study Guide* consists of several sections which are described below.

Learning Objectives. The learning objectives are brief statements of expected learning outcomes. They require you define, list, distinguish among, explain, and evaluate. You should do what they suggest in writing.

The arrangement of the learning objectives follows the content sequence of the chapter. Therefore, the first objective is <u>not</u> necessarily more important that any of the other objectives.

Some learning objectives are marked with an asterisk (*). They include economic concepts that are critical to economic understanding. You will use these concepts again as you study other economic issues in the text. You should allocate more time to these learning objectives.

The objectives are not meant to be ends in themselves. They are designed to help you identify quickly the important chapter content. In this way, they should aid you in using your study time efficiently and guide you to a satisfactory performance.

Chapter Orientation. This section of the *Guide* highlights the chapter content. In addition, it indicates, as does the chapter, that the learning objectives are interrelated and how they are interrelated. You may find it helpful to read the "Chapter Orientation" immediately after reading the learning objectives and before reading the chapter. Both sections of the *Guide* should help you focus your reading of the chapter upon its main points.

Consider This. This section of the *Guide* provides additional content that complements, illustrates, or expands upon the textbook content. Each "Consider This" is followed by a series of questions to help you relate the issues to the economic content of the chapter.

Study Questions. You should use the study questions to check your understanding of the chapter's content. They parallel very closely the learning objectives.

Self-Test. This section the *Guide* contains a crossword puzzle, true-false questions, multiple-choice questions, and problems that you can use to assess your attainment of the learning objectives. You should do the self-test without reference to the textbook chapter or the "Answers to the Self-Test."

Answers to the Self-Test. Answers to the question of the self-test are provided in this section of the *Guide*. If you score 90 percent or better on the self-test, you probably have a good understanding the chapter's content.

Note that all the chapters in the *Study Guide* follow the same organizational structure. You will find the chapters in this guide to be most helpful if you work through the material sequentially. For example, you should review the learning objectives and read the chapter orientation prior to studying the "Consider This" application article. Once you feel fonfident in your understanding of the relevant concepts and how they can be applied, you should move on and answer the "Self-Test" questions and problems. Remember that this *Study Guide* is designed to complement the textbook and is not intended to be a substitute for it. You should always read and study the relevant chapter in the textbook before working through the guide material.

Much of the material contained in this edition was originally prepared by DeVon L. Yoho of Ball State University. Special thanks are extended to Tia Schultz and Ellen Cleary, Developmental Editors for their help in bringing this project to completion.

Good Luck!

Paul W. Grimes,
Mississippi State University

Contents

Chapter

1 **Human Misery.** The Most Important Issue of Them All 1-1
   Consider This: 1-2
   Self-Test 1-4
   Answers to Selt-test 1-11
   Appendix: Graphic Tools of Analysis 1-12
   Self-Test 1-16
   Answers to Self-Test 1-18

2 **Economic Systems, Resource Allocation, and Social Well-being.**
   Lessons from the Fall of the Soviet Union 2-1
   Consider This: 2-2
   Self-Test 2-5
   Answers to Selt-Test 2-11

3 **Economics of Higher Education.** Who Benefits and Who Pays the Bills? 3-1
   Consider This: 3-3
   Self-Test 3-6
   Answers to Selt-Test 3-12

4 **Economics of Crime and Its Prevention.** How Much Is Too Much? 4-1
   Consider This: 4-2
   Self-Test 4-4
   Answers to Selt-Test 4-12

5 **Pollution Problems.** Must We Foul Our Own Nests? 5-1
   Consider This: 5-2
   Self-Test 5-4
   Answers to Selt-Test 5-12

6 **Health Issues.** Is It Worth What It Costs? 6-1
   Consider This: 6-2
   Self-Test 6-7
   Answers to Self-Test 6-14

7 **Poverty Problems.** Is Poverty Necessary? 7-1
   Consider This: 7-2
   Self-Test 7-6
   Answers to Self-Test 7-14

8 **Discrimination.** The High Cost of Prejudice 8-1
   Consider This: 8-2
   Self-Test 8-7
   Answers to Self-Test 8-15

9 **The Economics of Big Business.** Who Does What to Whom? 9-1
   Consider This: 9-2
   Self-Test 9-5
   Answers to Selt-Test 9-11

10   **Airline Regulation and Deregulation.** Who Gains from Regulation?   10-1
       Consider This: 10-2
       Self-Test   10-4
       Answers to Selt-Test   10-9

11   **The Economics of Professional Sports.** What Is the Real Score?   11-1
       Consider This: 11-2
       Self-Test   11-5
       Answers to Selt-Test   11-11

12   **Protectionism Versus Free Trade.**   Can We Restrict Ourselves into Prosperity?   12-1
       Consider This: 12-2
       Self-Test   12-5
       Answers to Selt-Test   12-11

13   **Unemployment Issues.** Why Do We Waste Our Labor Resources?   13-1
       Consider This: 13-3
       Self-Test   13-6
       Answers to Selt-Test   13-14

14   **Inflation.** How to Gain and Lose at the Same Time   14-1
       Consider This: 14-2
       Self-Test   14-5
       Answers to Selt-Test   14-11

15   **Government Expenditures and Tax Issues.** Who Wins and Who Loses? ..   15-1
       Consider This: 15-2
       Self-Test   15-5
       Answers to Selt-Test   15-11

16   **The Big National Debt.** Is It Bad?   16-1
       Consider This: 16-2
       Self-Test   16-5
       Answers to Selt-Test   16-11

Chapter 1

● # Human Misery

The Most Important Issue of Them All

LEARNING OBJECTIVES

After studying this issue, you should be able to:

1. State the reasons for a growing awareness of the world poverty problem.

2. *Explain the fundamental economic problem facing all societies.

3. *Explain what a production possibilities curve measures, what points lying inside and outside the curve mean, and what a shift of the curve indicates.

4. *Calculate and explain opportunity cost using a production possibilities curve.

5. Define gross domestic product (GDP), per capital GDP, and per capital real GDP.

6. Calculate and interpret price indices.

7. Explain how an economy can provide rising living standards over time.

8. Evaluate the impact of population growth and density on living standards.

9. Evaluate alternative government antipoverty policies.

● ### CHAPTER ORIENTATION

As you read the chapter try to discover what has caused people's recent concern for world poverty, what causes world poverty, and how it can be alleviated. To investigate these concerns you will need to know the determinants of living standards as well as a few other basic economic concepts.

Economics is the study of how people cope with scarcity. Our wants are virtually infinite but the resources that we use to satisfy our wants are limited. It is this inequality between wants and resources that forces persons to choose. When resources—labor, capital—are used to satisfy one want, they are unavailable for use in the satisfaction of other wants.

The production possibilities curve can be used to illustrate decision making as a consequence of scarcity. Given our limited resources, we can have more of one thing only by giving up some of something else. What is given up is the opportunity cost of our choice. You must develop an appreciation for the proper labeling of a production possibilities curve. Only real quantities of goods and services appear on the axes. Resources used in the production of consumer goods are not available for use in the production of capital goods—plant, equipment, and net changes in inventories. Or, as another example of labeling, resources used in the production of loaves of bread cannot be used in the production of quarts of milk.

Pay particular attention to the assumptions on which a production possibilities curve is based. Your understanding of them will enable you to explain the impact of unemployed resources and economic growth on output combinations and to explain why some combinations of real output (consumer goods plus capital goods) are unattainable.

When you are familiar with the technical aspects of production possibilities curves, you will want to relate production possibilities curves to Gross Domestic Product (GDP) and then relate per capita real GDP to the measurement of living standards. How do we measure living standards?

Armed with the knowledge of a few basic economic concepts you can begin to analyze the world poverty problem. To break out of the poverty trap a country must improve its resource base, efficiency, and technology. The rate of growth in the economy's real GDP must exceed the rate of growth of its population. Can governments help solve the world poverty problem?

CONSIDER THIS:

World Poverty Could Soar[1]

A fifth of the world's population lives in grinding poverty and the number of poor could rise to 1.5 billion by the year 2000 with the biggest burden falling on women and children, a British charity said on Friday. A report on world poverty trends by the development group Actionaid painted a grim picture of a growing global underclass of people in the poorest regions of the world, barely subsisting and vulnerable to disease and early death.

It said that 1.1 billion people "out of a world population of around 5.5 billion" are now in absolute poverty, defined by the World Bank as living on $420 a year or less.

The problem was particularly acute in Latin America and Africa, where incomes had fallen sharply over the last 20 years, it said. Based on current economic trends, the poverty figure could reach at least 1.5 billion by the end of the century unless there is a massive global effort to target aid at basic needs such as food security, to boost the economies of developing countries and ease the Third World debt burden, it said.

Africa, already stricken by famine, civil war and falling commodity prices, is likely to see poverty rise at an even sharper rate. Sub-Saharan Africa was said to have the bleakest prospects, with the number of poor expected to rocket from 184 million to 304 million on what the charity called optimistic economic growth forecasts.

The report said that over the last two decades, significant progress had been made to improve living standards for thousands of people but the gap between the world's richest and the poorest was growing. If action is not taken now to bridge this gap then the millions who exist in grinding poverty will continue to slip through the net, it said.

Going by current trends, the burden of poverty will fall on those least able to bear it "women, children, ethnic minorities, those who are ill, disabled and landless, it said. The number of women in absolute poverty had almost doubled over the last two decades, the report said.

Actionaid, Britain's fourth largest development charity, was founded 21 years ago. It received four million pounds ($5.8 million) last year from the Overseas Development Administration, the British government agency that distributes state aid, for its work among poor communities in 19 countries.

Consider These Questions:

1. What are some of the consequences for individuals who live in absolute poverty according to Actionaid?

2. Research by the World Bank indicates that more than a billion people live on less than $420 a year. How does this compare to per capita GDP in the United States?...in Nigeria?

3. Why is poverty "particularly acute in Latin America and Africa?"

4. What groups bear the heaviest burden of poverty? What economic factors explain why?

---

[1]World Poverty Soar by End-Century, Charity Says, *The Reuter Asia-Pacific Business Report*, March 19, 1993, Reprinted with permission.

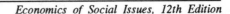

STUDY QUESTIONS

1. Country A's per capita real GDP is considerably greater than Country B's per capita real GDP. Clearly, Country A has overcome the fundamental economic problem. Evaluate.

2. Can the economic activity of people satisfy all the wants of human beings? Explain.

3. Draw a production possibilities curve for the choice between capital goods and services and all other goods and services. Label the diagram fully and discuss what a production possibilities curve measures. What do points lying inside and outside of the curve mean? What does a shift of the curve indicate? What causes it?

4. If, for an economy, 20,000 calculators must be given up for 4,000 microcomputers, what is the opportunity cost of a microcomputer?

5. In what sense is per capita real GDP a limited measure of an economy's standard of living?

6. What measures of economic performance are helpful in determining the impact of population growth on living standards?

7. What are the economic roots of world poverty?

8. Is world poverty caused by high rates of population growth and/or population density? Explain.

9. "Governments must solve the world poverty problems." Evaluate. What can governments do to help eliminate world poverty?

10. In the space below, draw a production possibilities curve for an economy choosing between capital and consumption goods. Show what should happen over time as technology improves in the production of both type of goods.

PUZZLE Complete the following crossword puzzle.

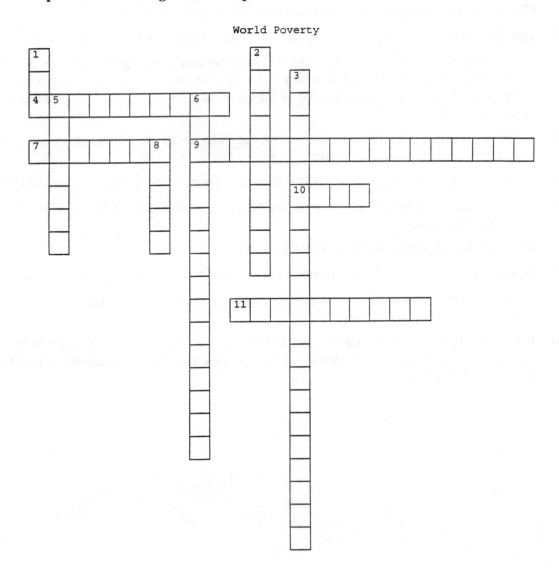

World Poverty

Across

4. The process of using technology to combine and transform resources to make goods and services.
7. All non-human resources used in production.
9. A set of numbers reflecting price level changes relative to a given base year. (3 words)
10. Nations with relatively low living standards due to low levels of labor quality, capital, and technology. (initials)
11. The means and methods available for combining resources to make goods and services.

Down

1. The market value of all final goods and services produced within an economy during one year. (initials)
2. Extraction of the greatest possible value of output from a given set of inputs.
3. Capital used by the economy as a whole rather than by individual firms. (3 words)
5. Gross Domestic Product corrected for changes in the price level relative to a base year.
6. The value of alternatives given up when a choice is made.
8. All human efforts of mind and muscle used in production.

TRUE-FALSE QUESTIONS Circle T (true) or F (false)

T F 1. One quarter of the world population survive on no more than $1.00 per day.

T F 2. The basic economic problem of all societies is that human wants exceed the resources available to satisfy them.

T F 3. If it is on its production possibilities curve, an economy is using its available resources inefficiently.

T F 4. For an economy producing output combinations on its production possibilities curve, the cost of an increase in the output of a good or service is the resources used to produce the output.

T F 5. GDP is defined as the total value of an economy's annual output of goods and services in final form.

T F 6. Per capita real GDP is a perfect measure of an economy's living standard despite the unequal distribution of its output among the population.

T F 7. If production is unchanged from one year to the next but the price index increases, real GDP will increase.

T F 8. A country's living standard will improve over time if population increases at a faster rate than real GNP.

T F 9. If an economy is to provide rising living standards over time, it must experience improvements in labor force quality, capital accumulation, and technological development.

T F 10. There is considerable evidence that population growth by itself has impinged significantly on the living standards of most developed countries.

T F 11. The economically advanced countries of the world provide economic assistance to LDCs in the form of loans and grants of money, and technical assistance.

T F 12. A product manufactured in Mexico by an American company is counted as part of the U.S. GDP.

T F 13. When GDP in current dollars is corrected for inflation, the result is called Real GDP.

T F 14. Population pressures are the single most important cause of world poverty today.

T F 15. Capital resources which are shared by the entire economy, such as highways and communication networks, are called "social overhead capital."

MULTIPLE-CHOICE QUESTIONS Select the one best answer.

1. Which of the following is a capital resource?
    a. An IBM computer.
    b. The services of an economist.
    c. Money.
    d. All of the above except (b).

2. With regard to human wants and economic resources, which one of the following statements is correct?
    a. Human wants are limited or scarce relative to the economic resources available for satisfying them.
    b. Human wants are unlimited while the economic resources available are scarce.
    c. Both human wants and human resources are unlimited, but nonhuman resources are limited.
    d. Both human wants and human resources are limited, but nonhuman resources are superabundant.

The following diagram applies to Questions 3-5.

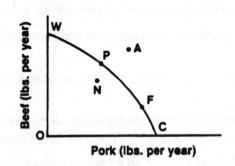

The diagram represents all that an economy can produce, in this case beef, pork, or some combination of them, per year.

3. The curve WC is known as a:
   a. demand curve.
   b. production possibilities curve.
   c. budget line.
   d. None of the above.

4. Which point represents underemployment of resources?
   a. F
   b. N
   c. P
   d. W

5. With given quantities of resources and constant technology, which combination of beef and pork is currently unattainable?
   a. F
   b. N
   c. A
   d. W

6. Which point represents an efficient use of resources?
   a. N
   b. A
   c. P
   d. O

Questions 7 and 8 below refer to the following diagram.

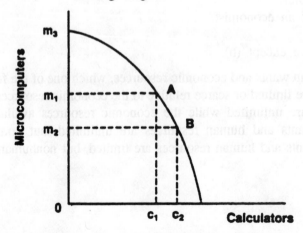

7. If none of an economy's scarce resources are to be used to produce calculators, then:
   a. by giving up $0c_2$ of calculators, m_2m_3 additional units of microcomputers can be produced.
   b. an increase of m_1m_3 of microcomputers could be obtained by giving up $0c_1$ of calculators.
   c. $0m_3$ of microcomputers could be produced.
   d. All of the above.

8. The opportunity cost of producing additional calculators, c_1c_2, is:
   a. $0m_2$ of microcomputers.
   b. m_2m_3 of microcomputers.
   c. m_2m_1 of microcomputers.
   d. $0m_1$ of microcomputers.

9. The opportunity cost of a video disk player is measured by the:
   a. money costs of resources bought and/or hired to produce it.
   b. value of other goods and services that must be given up to obtain it.
   c. amount of labor required to produce it.
   d. All of the above.

10. The production possibilities curve illustrates the basic principle that:
    a. an economy's capacity to produce increases in proportion to its population size.
    b. if all the resources of an economy are used efficiently, more of one good can be produced only if less of another good is produced.
    c. an economy will automatically seek that level of output at which all of its resources are employed.
    d. the production of more of any one good requires no sacrifice of other goods employed.

11. Per capita real GDP:
    a. measures an economy's standard of living.
    b. has typically increased over the years.
    c. indicates the comparative economic performances of countries.
    d. All of the above.

12. To correct a current dollar GDP for inflation:
    a. divide GDP in current dollars by the price index for that year.
    b. multiply GDP in current dollars by the price index for that year.
    c. divide real GDP by the price index for that year.
    d. divide current dollar GDP by real GDP.

13. To provide rising living standards over time, an economy should:
    a. improve the quality of the labor force.
    b. enhance capital accumulation.
    c. raise levels of technology.
    d. All of the above.

14. The standard of living would decline if:
    a. real GDP declined and population increased.
    b. per capita real GDP declined.
    c. real GDP increased but population increased relatively more.
    d. All of the above.

15. Which one of the following statements correctly indicates the impact of population growth on living standards?
    a. Without exception, population growth by itself has reduced living standards significantly.
    b. There is considerable evidence that population growth by itself has impinged significantly on the living standards of most developed countries.
    c. Population growth and the standard of living are unrelated.
    d. A few countries may have experienced a decreased standard of living essentially as a result of population growth.

16. The greatest obstacle to economic development in LDCs is:
    a. exploitation by multinational corporations.
    b. illiteracy.
    c. political instability.
    d. None of the above.

17. An LDC government can help in the capital accumulation process by:
    a. creating new capital resources directly.
    b. taxing away the returns that accrue from capital accumulation.
    c. pursuing monetary and fiscal policies conducive to economic stability.
    d. None of the above.

18. Which of the following would be included in United States GDP but would not be included in GNP?
    a. A Nissan pickup built in Tennessee.
    b. A bottle of white wine produced in France.
    c. A General Motors car manufactured in Canada.
    d. A bale of cotton grown in Mississippi.

19. International students from LDC's who decide to remain in the United States to work after college contribute to the:
    a. Capital Flight.
    b. Brain Drain.
    c. Development of social overhead capital.
    d. Inequality of the U.S. income distribution.

20. Developed countries jointly help LDC's by extending them low interest loans through this organization:
    a. The U.S. Congress.
    b. The United Nations.
    c. The World Bank.
    d. CARE.

21. Incomes in LDC's tend to be:
    a. More equally distributed than in DC's.
    b. Almost equally distributed.
    c. Less equally distributed than in DC's.
    d. Larger than in DC's.

22. Which of the following is the best example of social overhead capital?
    a. an automobile factory in Detroit.
    b. the Interstate Highway system.
    c. a family farm in Kansas.
    d. Disneyland.

23. The term "private property rights" refers to:
   a. individual ownership and control of resources.
   b. governmental ownership and control of resources.
   c. communal rights to the economic development of resources.
   d. development of individual rights to economic growth.

24. Which of the following would shift the production possibilities curve for an LDC?
   a. technological development.
   b. capital accumulation.
   c. improvements in labor force quality.
   d. All of the above.

25. The expression, "There ain't no such thing as a free lunch" refers to what important economic concept?
   a. diminishing returns.
   b. price index numbers.
   c. opportunity costs.
   d. production possibilities.

PROBLEMS

1. Assuming that an economy produces two goods X and Y only:
   a. plot its production possibilities curve on the graph using the following schedule:

Product X (1000)	Product Y (1,000)
90	0
88	10
85	20
80	30
74	40
66	50
57	60
47	70
35	80
20	90
0	100

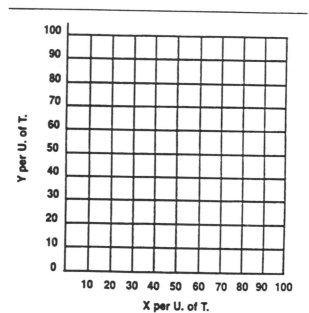

b. How much X must be given up to increase the output of Y from 40,000 to 50,000?
c. Indicate a combination of X and Y that is (1) produced inefficiently, (2) not currently attainable.
d. If the economy is able to produce an additional 10,000 units of X at each output level of Y,
   1) draw the new production possibility curve on the graph above.
   2) explain what might have caused the shift in the production possibilities curve.

2. Using the following table, answer the following questions.
   a. For the years 1970 through 1993, current dollar GDP (increased/decreased).
   b. In what years did real GDP decline?
   c. For the years 1980-1993, population (increased/decreased).
   d. What happened to per capita GDP between 1989 and 1990?

Table 1-2
Gross Domestic Product, United States, current dollars and real, 1970-1992

(1) Year	(2) Current Dollars (Billions)	(3) Implicit Price Deflator	(4) Real or 1987 Dollars (Billions)	(5) Population (Millions)	(6) GDP per Capita 1987 Dollars
1970	$1,010.7	35.2	$2,873.9	205.1	$14,012
1971	1,097.2	37.1	2,955.9	207.7	14,232
1972	1,207.0	38.8	3,107.1	209.9	14,803
1973	1,349.6	41.3	3,268.6	211.9	15,425
1974	1,458.6	44.9	3,248.1	213.9	15,185
1975	1,585.9	49.2	3,221.7	216.0	14,915
1976	1,768.4	52.3	3,380.8	218.0	15,508
1977	1,974.1	55.9	3,533.3	220.2	16,046
1978	2,232.7	60.3	3,703.5	222.6	16,637
1979	2,488.6	65.5	3,796.8	225.1	16,867
1980	2,708.0	71.7	3,776.3	227.7	16,585
1981	3,030.6	78.9	3,843.1	229.8	16,724
1982	3,149.6	83.8	3,760.3	232.1	16,201
1983	3,405.0	87.2	3,906.6	235.5	16,589
1984	3,777.2	91.0	4,148.5	237.6	17,460
1985	4,038.7	94.4	4,279.8	239.3	17,885
1986	4,268.6	96.9	4,404.5	241.6	18,231
1987	4,539.9	100.0	4,539.9	243.8	18,621
1988	4,900.4	103.9	4,718.6	246.4	19,150
1989	5,250.8	108.5	4,838.0	248.8	19,445
1990	5,522.2	113.2	4,877.5	251.3	19,409
1991	5,677.5	117.8	4,821.0	252.7	19,078
1992	5,942.2	120.9	4,915.0	255.4	19,244
1993	6,374.0	124.2	5,132.0	258.2	19,876

Note: Discrepancies in calculations due to rounding.
Source: Economic Report of the President, February 1991, p. 288 and February 1993, p. 348; and February 1994, p. 26.

ANSWERS TO SELF-TEST

PUZZLE

Across

4. Production
7. Capital
9. Price Index Numbers
10. LDCs
11. Technology

Down

1. GDP
2. Efficiency
3. Social Overhead Capital
5. Real GDP
6. Opportunity Costs
8. Labor

TRUE-FALSE QUESTIONS

1. T	4. F	7. F	10. F	13. T
2. T	5. T	8. F	11. T	14. F
3. F	6. F	9. T	12. T	15. T

MULTIPLE-CHOICE QUESTIONS

1. a	7. c	12. a	17. c	22. b
2. b	8. c	13. d	18. a	23. a
3. b	9. b	14. d	19. b	24. d
4. b	10. b	15. d	20. c	25. c
5. c	11. d	16. c	21. c	
6. c				

PROBLEMS

1. a.

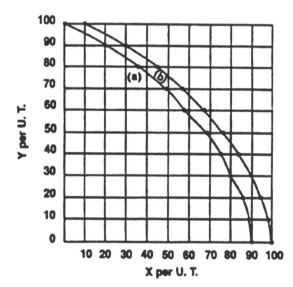

   b. 8,000 units of X must be given up.
   c. 1) Any combination below the production possibilities curve.
       2) Any combination outside the production possibilities curve.
   d. 1) See (b) on graph.
       2) The shift in the product possibilities curve, economic growth, is caused by improvements in the quality of the labor force, investment in capital goods and improved technology.

2. a. increased
   b. 1974-75, 1980, 1982
   c. increased
   d. It fell.

APPENDIX: Graphic Tools of Analysis

LEARNING OBJECTIVES

After studying this appendix, you should be able to:

1. Explain why economists use graphs.
2. Construct a graph showing the relationship between two variables and explain the relationship in writing.
3. Distinguish between direct (positive) and inverse (negative) relationships.
4. Identify and explain three typical economic graphs.

If you are already familiar with the use of graphs and thus can accomplish the learning objectives, you will want to omit the following and do the self-test.

CONSIDER THIS:

Graphs, a Tool of Analysis

What is a graph? A graph is an illustration picturing how two sets of numbers are related to one another. Graphs are an efficient means of relating a great deal of information. A good graph reveals things which might otherwise be very difficult to grasp.

There is nothing difficult about graphs. They are shorthand ways of presenting information that could be described more laboriously in written or tabular form. The table below contains two sets of numbers—one set for the variable Y and another for the variable X. Each XY pair in the data set is identified with a capital letter, e.g., for D, X=8 and Y=4. From the data of Table 1A-1 you should note that variables X and Y are inversely related—as X increases, Y decreases. Without the tabular form, we would have been able to communicate sufficient information to establish the inverse relationship between X and Y but it would have involved more space and effort. Like the tabular form, a graph indicates the relationship between two variables but does so visually. Much more information can be communicated with considerably fewer resources and the information is more readily comprehensible as a graph.

Table 1A-1

	X	Y
A	2	7
B	4	6
C	6	5
D	8	4
E	10	3

The information in tabular form may be presented as a graph. The lines placed at right angles to each other are called the coordinate axes. The X value is measured along the horizontal axis, while the vertical axis is marked off into units for measuring the Y value. In the space between the axes, the XY pairs may be plotted. For example, point E is plotted in the space by counting 10 units to the right along the horizontal axis and by counting up 3 units parallel to the Y axis. When all points are plotted they are usually connected by a smooth line or curve. Using the graph, Figure 1A-1, you can see at a glance that as the X value increases, Y value decreases. We know then that X and Y are inversely related.

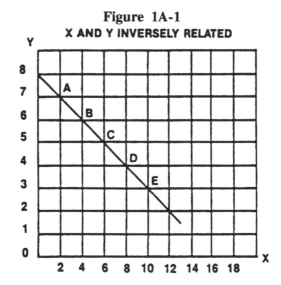

Figure 1A-1
X AND Y INVERSELY RELATED

On the other hand, Figure 1A-2 indicates at a glance a situation in which the variables X and Y are directly related since X and Y increase together.

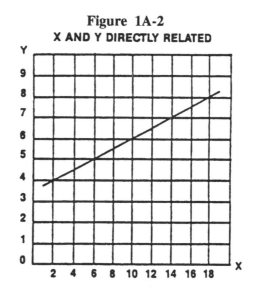

Figure 1A-2
X AND Y DIRECTLY RELATED

Economists use graphs with many different kinds of labels on the coordinate axes. The relationship between price and quantity demanded is frequently graphed by economists. Figure 1A-3 presents the relationship between the price of wheat and the number of units demanded at any give price for the data of Table 1A-2. As is clear at a glance, price and quantity demanded are inversely related. As a matter of convention, the vertical axis measures price and the horizontal axis measures quantity.

Table 1A-2
A demand Schedule for Wheat

Price (dollars)	Quantity (bushels per month)	Price (dollars)	Quantity (bushels per month)
$10	1,000	$5	6,000
9	2,000	4	7,000
8	3,000	3	8,000
7	4,000	2	9,000
6	5,000	1	10,000

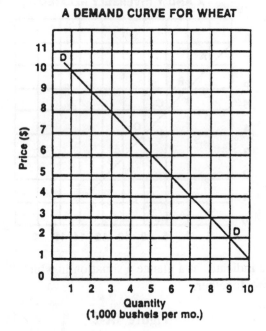

A DEMAND CURVE FOR WHEAT

Often you will find the relationship between price and quantity supplied drawn on the same graph with a demand curve as in Figure 1A-4. This is an acceptable practice since the axes of both graphs are labeled the same—price on the vertical axis, quantity on the horizontal axis. When demand and supply are combined on the same graph, you can see at a glance that the quantity demanded equals the quantity supplied at a single price.

Figure 1A-4

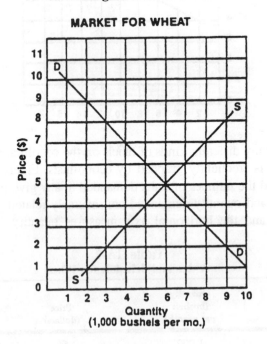

MARKET FOR WHEAT

Another commonly used graph in basic economics depicts a production possibilities curve like that of figure 1A-5. A production possibilities graph presents the relationship between the quantities of two products that an economy can produce. The intersection with the vertical axis indicates the maximum number of loaves of bread that the economy can produce if all resources are employed efficiently and no other products are produced. The horizontal axis intercepts under the same assumptions as above; indicates the maximum number of quarts of milk the economy can produce. All points on and to the left of the production possibilities curve between these extremes indicate the combinations of bread and milk the economy can produce. Combinations of products lying to the right of the curve are unattainable.

Figure 1A-5

PRODUCTION POSSIBILITIES CURVE FOR AN ECONOMY

Economists frequently use graphs to indicate how an economic magnitude changes over time. Figure 1A-6, National Health Expenditures as a % of the GDP in Selected Years, is drawn with time on the horizontal axis and percent of GDP on the vertical axis. At a glance you can see that national health expenditures have grown faster than the gross domestic product and is expected to do so.

Figure 1A-6

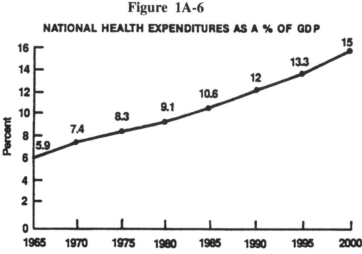

NATIONAL HEALTH EXPENDITURES AS A % OF GDP

You will find that economists, often in texts and even more often in lecture, use abstract graphs to express general principles. When the general form of the economic relationship is known but the exact numbers are not known or are not critical to the discussion, the numbers along the axes may not be specified. The abstract graph of the agricultural product market, Figure 1A-7, captures what we know generally about demand, supply, market price, and market forces. It is unnecessary to specify price and quantity numbers. Graphs with numbers on the axes are used to summarize specific known information.

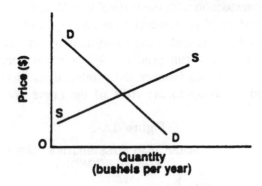

Figure 1A-7
AGRICULTURAL PRODUCT MARKET

By now it should be clear that graphs are a highly efficient communication tool and relatively easy to understand. With a knowledge and appreciation of graphic methods, you will undoubtedly find the study of economics easier and more meaningful.

STUDY QUESTIONS

1. Select a graph from any chapter of the text and, without reference to the text discussion, write a brief paragraph explaining it. In a separate paragraph, explain why economists use graphs.

2. Hypothesize the relationship between earned economic points and earned math points for quizzes taken the same day and construct an abstract graph of the relationship. Be sure to state your assumptions.

3. Using the graph selected for Question 1, determine the relationship between the two variables.

4. Using the text, locate two examples of each of the three typical economic graphs. Without reference to the text discussion, write a brief paragraph explaining one graph from each category.

SELF-TEST

TRUE-FALSE QUESTIONS Circle T (true) or F (false)

T F 1. Economists make extensive use of graphs because they are interested in abstract relationships between Xs and Ys.

T F 2. If two variables are directly related, they both can increase but they both cannot decrease.

T F 3. If the relationship between two variables can be illustrated on a graph as a curve falling to the right, then the relationship between the variables is inverse.

T F 4. The variables, grade point average and hours studying, are likely to be inversely related.

T F 5. since economics is concerned with decision making, economists may well use a graph with the axes labeled consumer goods and capital goods.

MULTIPLE-CHOICE QUESTIONS Select the one best answer

1. Graphs are used by economists to:
    a. clarify the relationship between the two variables.
    b. impress students with their expertise.
    c. convey a lot of information efficiently.
    d. both (a) and (c).

2. If two variables are inversely related:
   a. both can increase but they both cannot decrease.
   b. one can go up only if the other goes up.
   c. when one increases, the other decreases, and vice versa.
   d. when one increases, the other increases, and vice versa.

3. Which of the following sets of variables is an economist likely to graph?
   a. Price/quantity
   b. Time/income
   c. Quantities of goods X and Y
   d. All of the above.

4. Which of the following sets of variables is likely to be inversely related?
   a. Price and quantity supplied
   b. Temperature and attendance at the swimming pool
   c. Time (years) and the number of color television sets owned by households.
   d. None of the above.

PROBLEMS

1. Plot the following pairs of X and Y values on the graph below and connect the points.

X	Y
0	9
10	8
20	7
30	6
40	5
50	4
60	3
70	2
80	1

How are X and Y related?

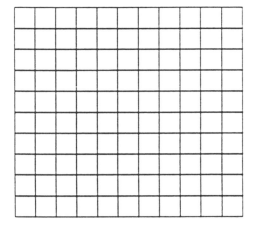

2. Plot the per capita real GDP data for the years 1972-1993 from Table 1-2, in the text.

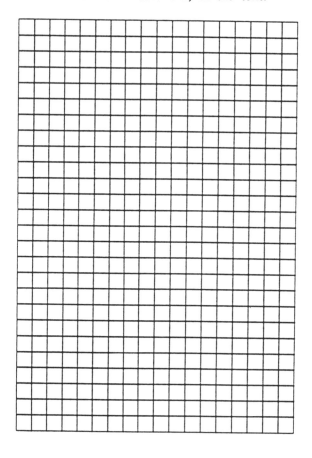

3. Hypothesize the relationship between temperature and attendance at the municipal swimming pool and construct an abstract graph of the relationship.

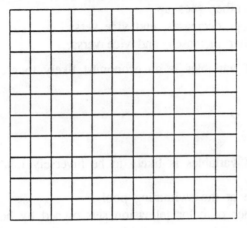

ANSWERS TO SELF-TEST

TRUE-FALSE QUESTIONS

1. F
2. F
3. T
4. F
5. T

MULTIPLE-CHOICE QUESTIONS

1. d
2. c
3. d
4. d

PROBLEMS

1. The variables X and Y are inversely related.

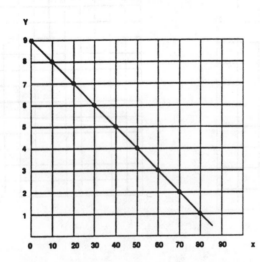

2. Per Capita GDP.

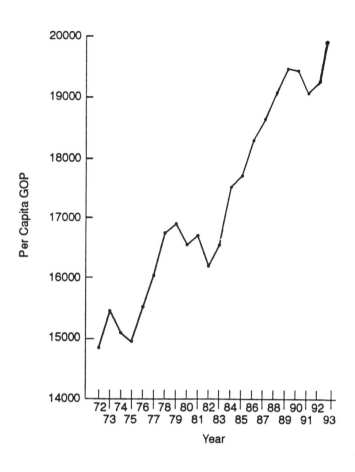

3. Temperature and attendance, at the municipal swimming pool are probably directly related—as the temperature rises attendance increases. As temperatures rise above 100 degrees attendance may fall— the relation becomes inverse.

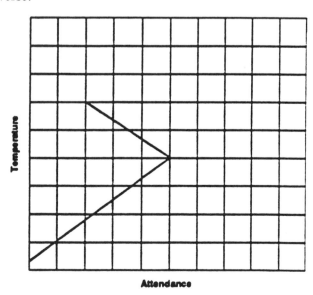

Chapter 2
Economic Systems, Resource Allocation, and Social Well-Being

Lessons from the Fall of the Soviet Union

LEARNING OBJECTIVES

After studying this issue, you should be able to:

1. Identify the distinguishing characteristics of pure market, mixed, and pure command economies.

2. Understand and explain the mechanisms whereby scarce resources are allocated within different economic systems.

3. *Discuss the importance of voluntary exchange in a market setting with respect to social well-being.

4. List and explain the characteristics of purely competitive, purely monopolistic, and imperfectly competitive markets in a market economy.

5. Define demand and supply.

6. *Explain and illustrate with graphs the law of demand and the relationship between price and quantity supplied.

7. *List the determinants of demand and supply and illustrate their effects on equilibrium price and quantity exchanged.

8. *Distinguish between a change in demand and a change in quantity demanded and between a change in supply and a change in quantity supplied and illustrate the differences graphically.

9. Explain and illustrate with a graph how the equilibrium price and equilibrium quantity exchanged are determined in a competitive product market.

10. Explain and illustrate using graphs the effects of changes in demand, changes in supply or both on equilibrium price and quantity exchanged.

11. Understand how central planners in the former USSR controlled and allocated resources without the use of markets.

12. Explain how the economic and social results of a command economy led to the fall of the Soviet Union.

CHAPTER ORIENTATION

This chapter introduces you to the some of the most important concepts that you will study in economics. The way in which we organize our economic institutions influences each of our lives in uncountable ways. By examining different types of economic systems you will come to understand the importance of resource allocation in the determination of social well-being. All economies must determine what goods and services will be produced and who will benefit from that production. Our mixed economic system which relies heavily on markets is contrasted to the command system of the former Soviet Union. The economic analysis of how the Soviet system worked yields important insights into the downfall of the USSR.

In order to appreciate the drawbacks of a command economy, it is first necessary to understand how market economies answer the basic economic questions. This involves the study of the forces of supply and demand.

Demand refers to a set of prices and the quantity demanded at each price in the set given that all other factors affecting demand are constant. Thus, demand cannot change unless one or more of the nonprice determinants of demand changes. A change in demand is caused by a change in consumer tastes, a change in consumer income, a change in the prices of substitutes and complements, a change in consumer expectations, and a change in the number of buyers in the market.

A change in quantity demanded is caused by a change in price. Note that this definition follows directly from the way in which demand is defined. As indicated by objective 5, you will be expected to know and use this distinction. A similar distinction exists for supply and quantity supplied. Thus supply refers to a set of prices and the quantity supplied at each price in the set, while quantity supplied refers to one price in the set of prices.

With a good command of the concepts, demand and supply, you should have little difficulty understanding competitive market price determination. Product prices are determined by the interaction of the forces of demand and supply. The equilibrium market price and quantity exchanged are maintained by market forces. All prices above the equilibrium price result in a surplus. The surplus creates an incentive for sellers to cut price. All prices below the equilibrium price result in a shortage. The shortage creates an incentive for individual buyers to bid up the price. At the equilibrium price there is no incentive, shortage or surplus, for price to rise or fall.

Changes in demand and/or changes in supply may alter the equilibrium price and the quantity exchanged. You will have less difficulty with these relationships if you recognize that correct definitions of demand and supply are critical. If demand increases while supply is constant, the equilibrium price increases. However, if supply is also increasing, then the impact on equilibrium price is indeterminate since the supply increase alone would decrease equilibrium price. Therefore, for an increase in demand *and* supply, the equilibrium price may increase, decrease, or remain unchanged. You should examine the other combinations of demand and supply changes to determine the impact on equilibrium price and quantity exchanged.

It is important to understand how markets respond to changing economic circumstances. Be sure to remember that in a market system with private property rights, all market transactions reflect voluntary exchange and therefore will maximize social well-being.

Because the Soviet system was based on central planning, the market forces of supply and demand did not generate an allocation of resources which resulted in maximum social well-being. Central planners could not respond to the changing economic environment in the same way that markets do. Consumers in the former Soviet Union were often frustrated with limited choices and major shortages of many goods and services which Westerners take for granted. These problems contributed greatly to the collapse of the USSR.

CONSIDER THIS:

Economic Freedom and Political Freedom

Milton Friedman's clarification of the relationship between economic freedom and political freedom will be particularly helpful to you as you study the remaining social issues even if you disagree with some or all of his remarks.[1]

What would you add to or delete from his statement? Why?

> It is widely believed that politics and economics are separate and largely unconnected; that individual freedom is a political problem and material welfare an economic problem; and that any kind of political arrangements can be combined with any kind of economic arrangements. The

---

[1] Abridged from Milton Friedman, *Capitalism and Freedom*, pp. 7-15. Copyright by the University of Chicago Press. All rights reserved. Reprinted by permission of the author and publisher.

chief contemporary manifestation of this idea is the advocacy of "democratic socialism" by many who condemn out of hand the restrictions on individual freedom imposed by "totalitarian socialism" in Russia, and who are persuaded that it is possible for a country to adopt the essential features of Russian economic arrangements and yet to ensure individual freedom through political arrangements....

Such a view is a delusion....

Historical evidence by itself can never be convincing. Perhaps it was sheer coincidence that the expansion of freedom occurred at the same time as the development of capitalist and market institutions. Why should there be a connection? What are the logical links between economic and political freedom?....

The basic problem of social organization is how to coordinate the economic activities of large numbers of people. Even in relatively backward societies, extensive division of labor and specialization of function is required to make effective use of available resources. In advanced societies, the scale on which coordination is needed, to take full advantage of the opportunities offered by modern science and technology, is enormously greater. Literally millions of people are involved in providing one another with their daily bread, let alone with their yearly automobiles. The challenge to the believer in liberty is to reconcile this widespread interdependence with individual freedom.

Fundamentally, there are only two ways of coordinating the economic activities of millions. One is central direction involving the use of coercion—the technique of the army and of the modern totalitarian state. The other is voluntary cooperation of individuals—the technique of the marketplace.

The possibility of coordination through cooperation rests on the elementary—yet frequently denied—proposition that both parties to an economic transaction benefit from it, provided the transaction is bilaterally voluntary and informed....

Indeed, a major source of objection to a free economy is precisely that it does this task so well. It gives people what they want instead of what particular group thinks they ought to want. Underlying most arguments against the free market is a lack of belief in freedom itself.

The existence of a free market does not, of course, eliminate the need for government. On the contrary, government is essential both as a forum for determining the "rules of the game" and as an umpire to interpret and enforce the rules decided on. What the market does is to reduce greatly the range of issues that must be decided through political means, thereby to minimize the extent to which government need participate directly in the game. The characteristic feature of action through political channels is that it tends to require or enforce substantial conformity. The great advantage of the market, on the other hand, is that it permits wide diversity.

Consider These Questions:

1. Friedman refers to the belief that individual freedom can be maintained in a socialist economy as a "delusion." How does this comment relate to the breakup of the former Soviet Union?

2. Based on your study of markets, how do they insure the "voluntary cooperation of individuals" as maintained by Friedman?

3. Do you believe, as Friedman does, that markets will always provide people with what they want? Why or why not?

4. To what extent does our political system fulfill the economic role for governments outlined by Friedman?

STUDY QUESTIONS

1. Outline the differences between a pure market, a mixed, and a pure command economy. Can you identify nations that seem to fit these different categories. How would you classify the United States? Why?

2. Evaluate the role of private property rights in a pure market economy. How do we enforce private property rights in our economy? Provide examples.

3. What is required for a market to exist? What rules govern how markets operate? Explain.

4. Evaluate this statement - "Households in the former Soviet Union may have had few modern consumer goods and services, but everyone had a job and no one was homeless."

5. Use supply and demand to discuss the last economic transaction you undertook. Example: Buying lunch in school cafeteria.

6. Select a product, classify its market structure, and support your classification. Example: aspirin.

7. Draw a hypothetical demand curve for video discs.
   a. Choose a price at random and identify the quantity that will be purchased per unit of time at that price.
   b. What happens to quantity demanded if the price increases?
   c. What is the law of demand?
   d. Show what happens to quantity demanded for the price selected for (a) above if consumer incomes increase. Is this a change in demand or a change in quantity demanded? Explain.
   e. What happens to the demand curve for video disks if the price of video disk players decreases? Explain.

8. Construct a hypothetical supply curve for microcomputers.
   a. Select a price and determine the quantity of microcomputers that suppliers will offer for sale per unit of time at that price.
   b. How will suppliers respond to a decrease in price? Why?
   c. What happens to the supply of microcomputers if the price of crude oil increases? Explain.
   d. Show what happens to quantity supplied at the price selected for (a) above if a change in techniques of production increases efficiency. Is this a change in supply or a change in quantity supplied? Explain.

9. Use a diagram of a hypothetical market for gasoline to show and explain the determination of the equilibrium price and quantity.

10. "Killing frost strikes peach groves in the Midwest." What does this headline indicate about the probable effect on:
    a. quantity demanded?
    b. quantity supplied?
    c. demand?
    d. supply?
    e. equilibrium price?
    f. elasticity of demand?
    g. elasticity of supply?

PUZZLE   Complete the following crossword puzzle.

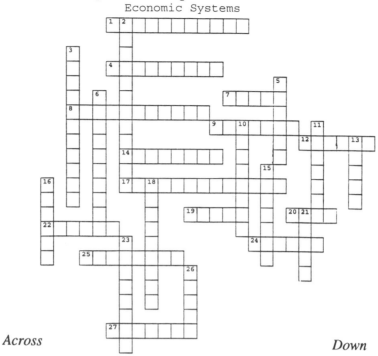

Across

1. Market structures between purely competitive and purely monopolistic are known as _____ competitive markets.
4. The "C" in CPSU.
7. In a pure command economy, all economic resources are owned and controlled by the _____.
8. In a market, where quantity supplied is equal to quantity demanded.
9. The general directives of the former Soviet Union's State Planning Commission.
12. Quantities of a product that sellers are willing to sell at various prices, other things being equal.
14. Planners in the USSR imposed a _____ tax to siphon-off excess demand when shortages developed.
17. An increase in the price of one good leads to a fall in the demand for another good when the two goods are _____.
19. A change in the price of a product is illustrated as a movement _____ the product's demand curve.
20. The official name of the former Soviet Union. (Initials)
22. A pure _____ economy is based on private property rights and decentralized economic decision making.
24. In 1928 this Soviet leader established the vast system of centralized economic planning.
25. A change in price results in a change in _____ supplied.
27. A pure _____ economy is characterized by state ownership and control of resources and centralized decision making.

Down

2. The opposite extreme of a purely competitive market.
3. In a _____ market price is allowed to move up and down and there are no obstacles to firms entering or leaving the market.
5. The quantity of a product that consumers are willing to purchase at various prices, other things equal.
6. Coke and Pepsi are _____ goods.
10. Occurs when price is below the market equilibrium price.
11. Occurs when price is above the market equilibrium price.
13. Founder of the Soviet Union.
15. Within a market economy, resources are owned and controlled by _____ parties.
16. The demand rises for a _____ good when consumer incomes rise.
18. Markets operating on their own ensure that production is carried to the point where social well-being is _____.
21. A change in consumers' tastes will cause a demand curve to _____.
23. A good is said to be _____ if its demand falls as consumer incomes rise.
26. A _____ economy has some elements of both a market economy and a command economy.

TRUE-FALSE QUESTIONS Circle T (true) or F (false)

T F 1. The two primary characteristics of a pure market economy are private property rights and centralized decision making.

T F 2. State ownership and control of most economic resources is characteristic of a pure command economy.

T F 3. The United States is a pure market economy.

T F 4. The former Soviet Union's economic system was closer to a pure command economy than to a pure market economy.

T F 5. Social well-being is maximized when markets are allowed to allocate scarce resources.

T F 6. Most modern economies around the world today are either pure market or pure command systems.

T F 7. When buyers and sellers interact and engage in exchange, a market is said to exist.

T F 8. A purely competitive market is said to exist if there is more than one seller.

T F 9. A demand curve represents the various quantities of a product that consumers are willing to purchase at various prices, all else equal.

T F 10. Demand curves slope upward to the right and supply curves slope downward to the right.

T F 11. Most markets for goods and services in the United States are imperfectly competitive.

T F 12. The market for microcomputers is a purely competitive market because some of the sellers can influence market price.

T F 13. Supply of a product means the quantity per unit of time placed on the market by sellers at the present price, other things being equal.

T F 14. An increase in the price of Coke will increase the demand for Pepsi if Coke and Pepsi are complementary goods.

T F 15. When an economist says that the demand for a product has increased, this means that consumers are now willing to purchase more of the product at each possible price.

T F 16. A "change in supply" is shown graphically by a movement along the supply curve.

T F 17. Given the supply curve for microcomputers, an economic recession will tend to lower the market price of computers.

T F 18. At the market clearing price, buyers have incentives to bid up product price.

T F 19. As long as the shortages of a product exist, a seller has an incentive to cut price below that at which others sell.

T F 20. Both the equilibrium price and quantity exchanged must decrease when demand and supply both decrease.

T F 21. The demand curve for a normal good shifts to the right when consumer income rises.

T F 22. Central planners in the former Soviet Union used a turnover tax to eliminate shortages.

T F 23. Social well-being is easier to maximize in a command economy than in a pure market economy.

T F 24. Soviet consumers had fewer goods and services due to the poor decisions that they made as owners of their economy's resources.

T F 25. Market systems cannot fail to yield the optimal outcomes for society.

Economics of Social Issues, 12th Edition

MULTIPLE-CHOICE QUESTIONS Select the one best answer

1. Private property rights and decentralized decision making are primary characteristics of which type of economic system?
   a. pure command economy.
   b. pure communist economy.
   c. pure democratic economy.
   d. pure market economy.

2. Economies that combine elements of both the pure market and pure command economies are called what?
   a. blended systems.
   b. mongrel systems.
   c. mixed systems.
   d. monarchies.

3. A purely monopolistic market
   a. has only one seller.
   b. has only one buyer.
   c. has many sellers.
   d. has no control over price.

4. The law of demand implies
   a. consumers are not responsive to changes in the price of products.
   b. consumers will buy more of a product at higher prices than at lower prices, all else equal.
   c. consumers will buy less of a product at higher prices than at lower prices, all else equal.
   d. sellers are willing to offer more of their products for sale at higher prices than at lower prices, all else equal.

5. A change in the price of a product will result in
   a. a shift in the demand curve for the product.
   b. a change in demand for the product.
   c. a change in quantity demanded for the product.
   d. the formation of a new demand curve for the product.

6. If consumer incomes rise and the demand curve for Product X shifts to the left, Product X must be
   a. an inferior good.
   b. a normal good.
   c. a superior good.
   d. a complementary good.

7. Which of the following will cause a change in quantity supplied?
   a. a change in the costs of production.
   b. a change in price.
   c. the number of sellers in the market.
   d. seller expectations.

8. Which of the following would cause the supply curve to shift?
   a. a change in price.
   b. changes in the cost of production.
   c. a shift in the demand curve.
   d. an increase in the number of buyers in the market.

9. The market for pencils in the U.S. is likely to be competitive because:
   a. there are many buyers and sellers.
   b. suppliers can manipulate the prices.
   c. the government regulates the price of pens.
   d. sellers can not enter the market easily.
   e. None of the above.

10. Demand for a product refers to the quantities per time period that:
    a. buyers will take at all possible income levels, other things being equal.
    b. sellers will place on the market at all possible alternative prices, other things being equal.
    c. buyers will take at all possible alternative prices, other things being equal.
    d. consumers want.

Answer questions 11-12 on the basis of the following schedules:

Schedule A		Schedule B	
Price	Bushels	Price	Bushels
$0.25	30	$0.25	42
.50	35	.50	35
.75	42	.75	30
1.00	50	1.00	26
1.25	59	1.25	23
1.50	69	1.50	21

11. Referring to Schedules A and B, which statement is correct?
    a. Schedule A is a demand schedule and Schedule B is a supply schedule.
    b. Not enough information is provided to determine which is the demand schedule and which is the supply schedule.
    c. Schedule A is a supply schedule and Schedule B is a demand schedule.
    d. Both are demand schedules.

12. According to Schedules A and B, which statement is correct?
    a. The equilibrium price is $0.50 and the quantity exchanged is 35 bushels.
    b. The equilibrium price is $1.00 and the quantity exchanged is 50 bushels.
    c. The equilibrium price is $0.75 and the quantity exchanged is 30 bushels.
    d. Not enough information is provided to determine an equilibrium position.

13. The supply of popcorn would likely decrease if the price of:
    a. fertilizer decreased.
    b. regular corn increased.
    c. popcorn increased.
    d. popcorn seed decreased.
    e. All of the above.

14. During a recent winter, the orange crop was severely damaged by freezing weather. As a result:
    a. the demand for oranges decreased and the equilibrium price decreased.
    b. the demand for oranges decreased and the equilibrium price increased.
    c. the supply of oranges decreased and the equilibrium price increased.
    d. the supply of oranges decreased and the equilibrium price decreased.

15. Suppose that the demand for pizza decreases. The decrease in the demand for pizza may be due to:
    a. a shift in consumer tastes and preferences toward pizza.
    b. a shift in consumer tastes and preferences away from pizza.
    c. a decline in the price of pizza.
    d. an increase in the price of pizza.
    e. an excessive supply of pizza.

16. Many mathematics and science teaching positions in public schools cannot be filled; this indicates a price for mathematics and science teachers:
    a. that assures quality education.
    b. that clears the market.
    c. below the equilibrium price.
    d. above the equilibrium price.

17. The price of gasoline in a competitive market is $1.20 per gallon. At that price buyers want to buy 1,000 gallons weekly and sellers want to sell 2,000 gallons weekly. The price will tend to:
    a. fall below $1.20; and buyers will tend to buy less than 1,000 units.
    b. fall below $1.20; and suppliers will tend to offer less than 2,000 units.
    c. rise above $1.20; and suppliers will tend to offer more than 2,000 units.
    d. rise above $1.20; and suppliers will tend to offer less than 2,000 units.

Questions 18-19 below refer to the following diagram for pencils:

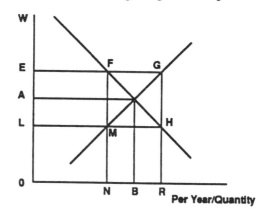

18. The equilibrium price is measured by distance:
    a. 0E.
    b. 0L.
    c. HG.
    d. 0A.

19. At price level OL there will be:
    a. a shortage equal to NR.
    b. a surplus equal to 0B.
    c. a shortage equal to 0B.
    d. a surplus equal to NR.

20. What is the distinction between a shortage and a scarcity?
    a. Prices free to adjust to changing demand and supply eliminates scarcity.
    b. The increasing relative scarcity of a good or service automatically leads to a shortage.
    c. A shortage exists whenever a good or service is scarce.
    d. Resources have been and continue to be scarce and thus there exists a shortage.
    e. None of the above.

21. If ice cream and yogurt are substitutes and the supply of yogurt increases with demand unchanged, then:
    a. the price of ice cream would decrease.
    b. the price of ice cream would increase.
    c. the supply of ice cream would decrease.
    d. the demand for ice cream would decrease.
    e. Both (a) and (d).

22. The equilibrium quantity of gasoline exchanged would decrease:
    a. if the supply of gasoline increases.
    b. if consumer incomes increase.
    c. if the supply of crude oil increases.
    d. All of the above.
    e. None of the above.

23. If the demand for housing increases and supply decreases:
    a. the quantity bought and sold will increase, but the effect upon price will be indeterminate.
    b. the quantity bought and sold will decrease, but the effect upon price will be indeterminate.
    c. the price will rise, but the effect upon the quantity bought and sold will be indeterminate.
    d. the price will fall, but the effect upon the quantity bought and sold will be indeterminate.
    e. the equilibrium price will rise and the quantity bought and sold will rise.

24. In the former Soviet Union, resources were allocated based on
    a. the market forces of supply and demand.
    b. the decisions of private owners of resources.
    c. predetermined socially optimal outcomes.
    d. the Gosplan determined within the hierarchy of central planners.

25. Which of following is true about a command economy?
    a. It is more difficult to maximize social well-being in a command economy than in a market economy.
    b. Consumers have fewer choices of goods and services in a command economy than in a market economy.
    c. A command economy is less responsive to the changing economic environment than a market economy.
    d. All of the above.

PROBLEMS

1. The demand curve and supply curve for video discs are as follows:

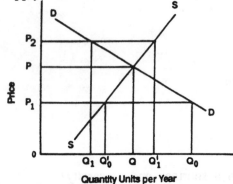

   a. How much would be placed on the market per day at price P_1? At price P_2?
   b. How much will be demanded at price P_1? At price P? At price P_2?
   c. Which of the prices will generate a surplus? How much is the surplus?
   d. Which of the prices will generate a shortage? How much is the shortage?
   e. Which of the prices is an equilibrium price? Why?

2. Examine the price and quantity schedules used for Multiple Choice questions 11 and 12. (Hint: You may want to sketch the curves associated with the schedules.) Answer the following questions:
   a. What is the equilibrium price?
   b. What is the equilibrium quantity?
   c. If price were $1.00 per bushel would a surplus or shortage exist? What would be the size of the surplus or shortage?
   d. If price were $0.25 per bushel would a surplus or shortage exist? What would be the size of the surplus or shortage?

ANSWERS TO SELF-TEST

PUZZLE

	Across		*Down*
1.	Imperfectly	2.	Monopolistic
4.	Communist	3.	Competitive
7.	State	5.	Demand
8.	Equilibrium	6.	Substitute
9.	Gosplan	10.	Shortage
12.	Supply	11.	Surplus
14.	Turnover	13.	Lenin
17.	Complementary	15.	Private
19.	Along	16.	Normal
20.	USSR	18.	Maximized
22.	Market	21.	Shift
25.	Quantity	23.	Inferior
27.	Command	26.	Mixed

TRUE-FALSE QUESTIONS

1.	F	8.	F	14.	F	20.	F
2.	T	9.	T	15.	T	21.	T
3.	F	10.	F	16.	F	22.	T
4.	T	11.	T	17.	T	23.	F
5.	T	12.	F	18.	F	24.	F
6.	F	13.	F	19.	F	25.	F
7.	T						

MULTIPLE-CHOICE QUESTIONS

1.	d	8.	b	14.	a	20.	e
2.	c	9.	a	15.	c	21.	e
3.	a	10.	c	16.	c	22.	e
4.	c	11.	c	17.	b	23.	c
5.	c	12.	a	18.	d	24.	d
6.	a	13.	b	19.	a	25.	d
7.	b						

PROBLEMS

1. a. Q'_0. Q. Q'_1.
   b. Q_0. Q. Q_1.
   c. P_2. Q_1 Q'_1.
   d. P_1. Q'_0 Q_0.
   e. P. There are no forces that will cause it to change.

2. a. Equilibrium price = \$0.50
   b. Equilibrium quantity = 35 Bushels
   c. Surplus, 24 Bushels
   d. Shortage, 12 Bushels

Chapter 3
Economics of Higher Education

Who Benefits and Who Pays the Bills?

LEARNING OBJECTIVES

After studying this issue, you should be able to:

1. Identify the problems in higher education.

2. List and explain the major "products" of higher education and identify the incidence and relative size of each.

3. Explain, using the opportunity cost concept and production possibility curve, why higher education is not a free good.

4. Identify the largest cost component of higher education and who pays it.

5. Explain why it is important to recognize both the explicit and implicit costs of producing higher education.

6. Explain and illustrate diagrammatically the outcome of charging all students the same tuition.

7. *Define, illustrate, and use the concept of price elasticity of demand.

8. Explain the present method of allocating higher education services and analyze the argument that a market allocation of higher education services would do a better job of determining service level.

9. State the arguments for a state-supported higher education system and assess the relative creditability of them against the argument that those who benefit are the ones who should pay the costs.

10. Identify and evaluate an alternative to the present institutional structure of higher education and explain its implications for the poor.

CHAPTER ORIENTATION

As you study this issue you may find it helpful to recognize how the concept of scarcity is involved. Because of scarcity it is necessary to study the services of higher education, their incidence, and to study the means by which resources are brought together for the production of higher education services. Also, because of scarcity, it is necessary to study the efficiency and distribution consequences of the production process. Given that it is desirable to reduce relative scarcity, it is important that not one additional unit of resources be used in the production of a given level of educational services than is required by the existing technology. Inefficient production is wasteful and will increase relative scarcity.

Your key to a clearer understanding of the economics of higher education is to recognize educational institutions as production units or business firms. They use scarce resources—labor and capital—to produce an output—educational services. In this respect, they are like all other business firms.

Educational institutions are multiproduct business firms. Their most important output is the development of "human capital." In this way and through direct consumption benefits, students gain from a higher education. But others may benefit as well from higher education. When such externalities exist, society is presented with the choice between underproduction of higher education services or with government intervention in the market to promote the optimal amount of scarce resources used in the production of higher education. How can these externalities be captured without limiting individual choices—economic freedom?

This chapter introduces you to cost concepts. The basis of economic costs is the opportunity cost principle. You must understand it and the concepts of explicit and implicit costs.

It may come as quite a surprise to you to learn that the largest cost component of your higher education is not what you pay out of your pocket or for that matter what taxpayers pay from their pockets. What, then, is the largest component? Your income loss while in school is the largest component. No wonder it is overlooked. You never see it, nor does anyone else, but it is nonetheless a cost of your education. Your time and ability have alternative uses. To use them in their next best alternative would generate income. You forgo that income and society forfeits the output that income represents. If the rate of return on education is not to be overstated, the opportunity cost of higher education must be calculated.

With these cost concepts and the other economic principles at your command, you are ready to analyze the problems of higher education. You will want to determine the explicit and implicit costs to a society of providing educational services and who pays them.

Elasticity may give you some difficulty initially. If you recognize that price elasticity is related to the law of demand and/or supply as a natural extension of what we might want to know about the relationship between price and quantity, elasticity will be considerably easier to remember and understand.

Remember the law of demand tells us that price and quantity are inversely related, i.e., as price increases quantity demanded decreases. Elasticity indicates "how responsive quantity demanded is to a change in price." Although the variables are different, the notion is the same as observing that on hot days the number of persons entering a swimming pool increases. Doesn't it seem reasonable that the manager of the pool might want to know how responsive attendance is to a given change in temperature? That relationship is also an elasticity concept but it differs slightly from price elasticity. Perhaps you can think of another situation not involving price and quantity demanded or supplied in which elasticity would be of interest for purposes of decision-making.

Price elasticity of demand provides information useful in making decisions. Suppose the hospital board of directors in a midwestern city finds, after having moved into a new building, that expenses exceed income. They examine the situation and discover that the hospital has an occupancy rate of 40 percent. After a minimum amount of discussion the board decides to raise room rental rates. They do not discuss price elasticity. But if they expect revenues to rise as a result of the rate increase, what are they assuming regarding price elasticity? They must be assuming that for the change in price, quantity demanded is inelastic—total revenue will increase in this situation only if the quantity demanded expressed as a percentage change falls less than the percentage increase in price. Total revenue is equal to price times quantity sold. The law of demand tells us that as price increases the quantity demanded decreases and, as an extension of this relationship, elasticity tells us how responsive quantity-demanded will be to the price increase. It could be that the hospital board will make the problem worse. If demand is elastic, total revenue will fall. Caution: we do *not know* that demand for hospital rooms is elastic, we are only hypothesizing. Using the determinants of elasticity as discussed in the reading assignment, you should be able to explain the effects of a price increase if demand is elastic, or the effects of a price increase if demand is inelastic.

Finally, in applying your economic tools of analysis to problems of higher education, you should examine critically the institutional structure we have today and the means of financing it. Do they give us the kinds of educational services we desire as a society? Are they responsive to changing societal needs? Are they conducive to supply the economically correct amounts of educational services? Is "free" or "low-tuition" higher education an affective way to help the children of the poor.

An alternative higher education institutional structure might make greater use of the price system in the production of higher educational services. With the tuition rates large enough to cover all the explicit costs of providing educational services, many of the problems facing higher education might be reduced significantly if not eliminated.

CONSIDER THIS:

Students Protest Tuition Increases[1]

University of California regents voted yesterday to impose double-digit student fee increases for the third consecutive year, touching off a student takeover of an auditorium at the Davis campus, where the university leaders had cast their votes.

The regents, including Governor Wilson, voted 20 to 1 to raise fees 22 percent effective next fall, a $550-per-year increase that would bump the cost of an undergraduate education for a California resident to an average $3,036 per year, excluding room, board, books and incidentals. After the regents ended their meeting at Freeborn Hall, about 300 students chanting Fight back! broke through a line of campus police and occupied the auditorium. Five people were arrested on charges including inciting to riot and battery against a police officer.

The latest increase represents a near-doubling of fees in three years at the nine-campus system, which serves more than 150,000 students. The regents imposed a 10 percent increase of $148 in 1990 and a 40 percent increase of $650 last year. Wilson said the university was compelled to make some tough decisions because of the economy and a state system in which 85 percent of the budget is already earmarked before it gets to him.

University President David Gardner also backed the increase. We are keenly aware that the cost of attending UC is going up dramatically, he told the regents. But he said student fees at UC campuses are still comparable to those at other four-year public universities. Fees also have generally lagged behind increases in the average Californian's income, Gardner said.

Lieutenant Governor Leo McCarthy was the lone opposing vote among board members on what he called the whopping student fee increase. It's inescapable to me that there are a lot of middle-class kids who are going to be adversely impacted, he said, adding that he believes significant damage would be done to the "public nature of the university."

Gardner, who is retiring in October, noted that even though students may be paying more, they will be getting more, rather than paying more and getting less. He took an uncharacteristic swipe at a competing state higher education system, labeling as inexplicable the disparity in the fee increases at the community-college level compared with the UC and California State University levels. Earlier this week, California State University trustees raised fees at its 20 campuses by 40 percent. I find it exceedingly difficult to comprehend the rationale that leads to fees at the University of California going up $1,200 (in two years) and fees at the California Community Colleges going up $20, Gardner said.

Although the regents said they had no choice but to increase student fees, considering the 1.5 percent university budget increase proposed by Wilson, students warned of being forced to quit school or being pitted against each other as a result of higher costs. Imagine the disruption that can occur when one group of students is seen as supporting another group of students, particularly when there is a perception that traditionally underrepresented students receive financial aid, Marisela Marques, president of the UC Student Association, told the boar. In this way, high fees, even coupled with financial aid, fuels the fires which are threatening our campus communities, Marques said.

About 350 demonstrators remained in Freeborn Hall last night, saying that they would occupy the building until the Legislature convenes Tuesday in Sacramento. They said they would then seek meetings with lawmakers and urge them to overturn the regents' vote.

---

[1] Diane Curtis, "Regents Raise Fees 22%—UC Students Protest," *The San Francisco Chronicle*, January 18, 1992, p. A1. Copyright San Francisco Chronicle. Reprinted by permission.

Campus speakers demanded the resignation of student regent Diana Darnell, a graduate student at the University of California at San Francisco, who tearfully voted for the fee increase. Darnell reasoned that despite the hardships it would cause for students, it was needed to maintain UC's high academic quality.

At a news conference, board chairwoman Meredith Khachigian said the regents would have preferred to give students more time to plan for such increases. We certainly regret this decision, she said. University officials estimate that it costs about $11,000 a year for a California resident to enroll full-time. Fees are used to pay for such student services as counseling, financial aid and general administration. University officials say much of the student fee increase will be used to support the libraries.

The fee-increase proposal was included in the university's overall $2.1 billion spending plan, which was approved by the regents. Besides imposing the fee increase, the budget proposal freezes general staff, administration and faculty salaries, although merit increases for members of the faculty and staff will be allowed.

The budget proposal also requires a 25 percent cut in financing in the office of the president, adds early retirement incentives, finances replacement of obsolete equipment and provides a 3 percent increase in nonsalary budget. Gardner said the plan preserves access for all qualified students next year "and does so without eroding quality."

Consider These Questions:

1. Using the information reported, can you identify and calculate the explicit costs of attending the University of California?

2. How do the explicit costs of attending a University of California campus compare to the explicit costs of attending a California State University campus or a California Community College? Provide an economic argument why the costs vary between these systems of higher education.

3. Why will students actively protest increases in the explicit costs of college when it is only a fraction of the total cost of their higher education?

4. Do you feel the student protest described above was justified? Why or why not? Use economic arguments to defend your position.

5. Identify *your* own personal explicit and implicit costs of attending college. Have you made a rational economic choice?

STUDY QUESTIONS

1. "Educational services should be free." Which of the problems facing higher education is expressed by this statement?

2. Jill enjoys the numerous opportunities for interactions with college classmates. Rachel, Jill's classmate, commute to campus, does not know Jill, and does not take part in other aspects of university life. What "product" of higher education is best illustrated by this description? Is the incidence of this "product" of higher education different for Jill and Rachel? Explain. Does the incidence of this "product" of higher education differ from other "products?"

3. Using the scarcity and opportunity cost concepts and a production possibility curve, illustrate and explain why higher education is not a free good.

4. Sam Econosmith recently decided not to return to the university next fall. You may assume that Sam is a rational decision maker. As a student of economics, what would you conclude characterized Sam's decision?

5. Barbara Jones has worked as an accountant for the last two years. She earns $32,000 a year. Next fall she plans to enroll in law school. What is likely to be the highest cost of her decision? What is the incidence of the cost?

6. Assume that the return on an investment in human capital is 15 percent. Would it make any difference to your investment decision to find out that the calculation did not include the implicit cost of a higher education? Why?

7. Recently the mass media have reported numerous incidents of university students unable to enroll in several majors including computer science. Explain, using graphs, how this is an expected outcome of charging all students the same tuition.

8. Devin Mock and thousands of other students will enroll in colleges and universities this fall. To what extent will the educational services available to Devin and other students be responsive to their demands? Explain. Will the level of education services tend to be efficient? Explain.

9. Can a strong case be made that students and their families should pay the full cost of a higher education? That the state should subsidize higher education? Explain.

10. Would charging students the full explicit cost of providing higher educational services alter educational outcomes? Why? Does it preclude helping children of the poor obtain higher education services? Explain.

PUZZLE   Complete the following crossword puzzle.

Higher Education

Across

2. The value of the goods and services that must be given up to obtain any other good or service. (2 words)
3. A measure of responsiveness of consumer demand to changes in price. (2 words)
7. Those who receive benefits without paying the costs of production. (2 words)
8. Benefits from consumption that accrue to persons other than those doing the consuming. (3 words)
9. Costs of production incurred by the purchase of resources by the producing unit. (2 words)

Down

1. Costs of production imposed on persons or economic units other than those doing the producing. (3 words)
4. The productive power of labor resulting from education and training. (2 words)
5. Costs of production incurred by producing a unit for the use of self-owned, self-employed resources. (2 words)
6. Payments made to persons or economic units that are not for services currently provided. (2 words)

TRUE-FALSE QUESTIONS Circle T (true) or F (false)

T F 1. Determining the extent to which taxpayers should pay the costs of producing higher education services is one of the problems of higher education.

T F 2. Society receives easily identifiable and measurable social spillover benefits from higher educational services.

T F 3. Education is a "free" good because the resources used in obtaining it are not scarce.

T F 4. The resources used in higher education must ordinarily be paid an amount equal to or greater than their remuneration in their next best alternative use.

T F 5. The opportunity costs principle states that the cost of producing a unit of products is the value of the resources used to produce it in their next best alternative use.

T F 6. The foregone earnings of students and their families is the largest explicit cost of higher educational services.

T F 7. The implicit costs of higher educational services are approximately the same for private as for public institutions.

T F 8. The annual economic costs to society of educational services is approximately equal to the sum of each institution's annual budget, each student's foregone annual income, and each student's annual miscellaneous educational expenses.

T F 9. A fixed cost to students for a year of educational services, regardless of the field of study the student desires to pursue, leads to crowding in some fields of study and excess capacity in others.

T F 10. If the value of a unit of educational services is worth less to society than it costs to produce it, then output should be increased.

T F 11. The optimum amount of higher education is that at which costs per credit hour to students is the least.

T F 12. If the production of higher educational services generates substantial spillover benefits, then to assure an efficient allocation of resources students must pay the full explicit cost of their education.

T F 13. State support of higher education tends to redistribute income from taxpayers to the children of the poor.

T F 14. Given no spillover benefits, charging tuition rates large enough to cover all the explicit costs of providing educational services would result in an efficient output of educational services.

T F 15. Institutions of higher education would tend to be more responsive to the demands of students and their families if tuition rates covered all the explicit costs of providing educational services.

T F 16. Increases in tuition and student fees will always increase the revenues of colleges and universities.

T F 17. The price elasticity of demand measures the responsiveness of consumers to changes in price.

T F 18. The demand for accounting education is most likely more inelastic than the demand for secretarial education.

T F 19. The most substitutes available, the more elastic the demand for any product or service.

T F 20. The price elasticity of demand is equal to the percentage change in price divided by the percentage change in quantity demanded.

T F 21. The productive power of labor resources is called human capital.

T F 22. An accurate measure of opportunity costs must include both explicit and implicit costs.

T F 23. Most of the benefits of higher educational services accrue to society.

T F 24. Tuition and lab fees would be considered an implicit cost of a college education.

T F 25. A free rider is someone who receives the benefits of a good or service without paying the costs of production.

MULTIPLE-CHOICE QUESTIONS Select the one best answer

1. Colleges and universities face many problems, including:
   a. what kinds of services to provide.
   b. how much service to provide.
   c. who should pay for the service provided.
   d. what is the appropriate institutional structure.
   e. All of the above.

2. The educational services produced by institutions of higher education include:
   a. direct consumption benefits.
   b. investment in human capital.
   c. social spillover benefits.
   d. All of the above.

3. Social spillover benefits of education may include:
   a. an increase in the student's lifetime earning power.
   b. more intelligent participation on the part of voters in the democratic process.
   c. greater contributions of citizens to the life of the community.
   d. All of the above.
   e. Only (b) and (c) above.

4. The direct consumption benefits of a student's higher education are:
   a. the benefits received from attending classes for which the student is unprepared.
   b. those benefits that accrue to the society apart from the direct benefits that accrue to the individual receiving the education.
   c. the immediate benefits received from social life, entertainment, and interaction with other students.
   d. that part of one's education received from on-campus courses.

Questions 5 and 6 below refer to the following diagram.

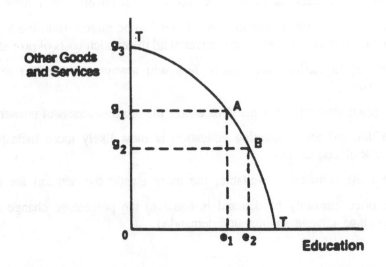

5. If none of a country's scarce resources are to be used to produce educational services, then:
   a. $0g_3$ of other goods and services could be produced.
   b. an increase of g_1g_3 of other goods and services could be obtained by giving up $0e_1$ of education.
   c. by giving up $0e_2$ of education, g_2g_3 additional units of other goods and services can be produced.
   d. All of the above.

6. The opportunity cost of producing an additional unit of education, e_1e_2, is:
   a. $0g_2$ of other goods and services.
   b. g_2g_3 of other goods and services.
   c. g_2g_1 of other goods and services.
   d. $0g_1$ of other goods and services.

7. The opportunity cost of a unit of educational services is measured by the:
   a. amount of money it takes to produce it.
   b. amount of labor required to produce it.
   c. the value of another good or service that must be given up to obtain it.
   d. the money costs of resources bought and/or hired to produce it.

8. The largest cost component of higher education is:
   a. foregone income.
   b. tuition and fees.
   c. government appropriations and explicit costs.
   d. None of the above.

9. Given the plant, equipment, and the staff of a college or a university, the explicit costs to the student of education provided by it will:
   a. be higher if it is private than if it is public.
   b. be lower if it is private than if it is public.
   c. be the same whether it is public or private.
   d. rest primarily on the state.

10. The explicit costs of a student's higher educational services in a state university with low tuition are paid for by:
    a. students and their families.
    b. taxpayers.
    c. donors.
    d. All of the above.

11. The implicit costs of higher education are usually:
    a. borne entirely by students and their families.
    b. borne entirely by the taxpayer.
    c. paid for by doctors.
    d. shared by all of the above.

12. If institutions of higher education used a differential pricing scheme for different majors, they could:
    a. increase their efficiency.
    b. increase their responsiveness to their customers.
    c. eliminate shortages and surpluses.
    d. All of the above.

13. Institutions of higher education using a differential pricing scheme instead of the same prices for different majors would:
    a. increase tuition and fees for majors more in demand.
    b. experience less of a decrease in enrollment for major with deceasing demands.
    c. experience less of an increase in enrollment for majors with increasing demands.
    d. All of the above.

14. State support of higher education tends to make educational institutions more responsive to the desires of:
    a. taxpayers.
    b. students and their families.
    c. the legislative body that makes the appropriations.
    d. society.

Questions 15 and 16 below refer to the following diagram.

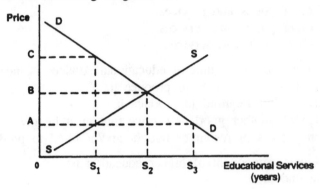

15. If OS_2 years of educational services are provided in the society, the value of a unit of it to students is:
    a. 0A
    b. 0B
    c. 0C
    d. AC

16. The cost of OS_1 years of education services:
    a. exceeds its value indicating that services should be reduced.
    b. is less than its value indicating that services should be expanded.
    c. equals its value indicating that services should be maintained at the present level.
    d. insufficient information to tell.

17. If higher education provides spillover benefits to society and student costs are subsidized, the equilibrium quantity of educational services provided will be:
    a. the socially optimum amount.
    b. more than the socially optimum amount.
    c. less than the socially optimum amount.
    d. inefficient unless all high school graduates can obtain four years of "free" higher education.

18. If we are really serious about making higher educational opportunities available to the children of the poor, an efficient way to do so is to:
    a. drop all entrance requirements to colleges and universities.
    b. subsidize all students in state colleges and universities by means of legislative allocations to those institutions.
    c. subsidize directly students from poor families, then require all students to pay the full costs of their education.
    d. increase the amount of funds appropriated by legislatures to state colleges and universities.
    e. Both (c) and (d).

19. Assume the demand for engineering education is inelastic. To increase revenues, an engineering college could:
    a. increase implicit costs.
    b. lower tuition and fees.
    c. raise tuition and fees.
    d. limit enrollments of new students.

20. Big State University increased its tuition and fees last year and enrollment fell such that total revenues from tuition and fees decreased. The demand for higher education at BSU is:
    a. price elastic.
    b. price inelastic.
    c. unitary elastic.
    d. a social spillover benefit.

PROBLEMS

1. A person earning $25,000 per year as a civilian is drafted into military service. As a soldier, he earns $10,000 per year. What is the opportunity cost of this soldier to the society? Explain.

2. You plan to attend public college and live in a dormitory. Your task is to calculate your costs and the costs to others who plan to attend for one year. The following information is available to you (use only these figures, realistic or unrealistic as they may be). Consider these data carefully, then answer the questions.*
    a. Tuition: $1,395/year
    b. Textbooks and school supplies: $375/year
    c. Faculty and administrative salaries and other university expenses budgeted by the Board of Trustees and funds provided by the state legislature: $7,146/student/year.
    d. Contributions to the university from alumni, private foundations, and other sources: $459/student/year
    e. You can normally work and earn $950/month when not in school. But now, except for summer, you go to school full time, nine months per year
    f. A Board of Trustees scholarship: $300/year
    g. It costs $135/month to live at home
    h. Dormitory fees: $175/month
    *Note: The formulation of the incidence of higher education costs is somewhat different from the treatment in the text.

    A. How much will it cost you, as a student, to attend college for an academic year? Indicate the components of your cost and categorize as implicit or explicit.

    B. How much will it cost state taxpayers to send you to college? Indicate the cost components.

    C. How much will it cost society to send you to college? Indicate the cost components.

3. Assume that Old State University raises from $4,000 per year to $5,000 per year. As a result (assuming nothing else changes), enrollment falls from 20,000 students to 18,000 students.

   A. Calculate the change in tuition revenue experienced by OSU.

   B. Calculate the price elasticity of demand.

   C. Is the demand for an OSU education price elastic or price inelastic?

ANSWERS TO SELF-TEST

PUZZLE

Across		*Down*	
2.	Opportunity Costs	1.	Social Spillover Costs
3.	Price Elasticity		
7.	Free Riders	4.	Human Capital
8.	Social Spillover Benefits	5.	Implicit Costs
		6.	Transfer Payments
9.	Explicit Costs		

TRUE-FALSE QUESTIONS

1.	T	6.	F	11.	F	16.	F	21.	T
2.	F	7.	T	12.	F	17.	T	22.	T
3.	F	8.	T	13.	F	18.	T	23.	F
4.	F	9.	T	14.	T	19.	T	24.	F
5.	T	10.	F	15.	T	20.	F	25.	T

MULTIPLE-CHOICE QUESTIONS

1.	e	6.	c	11.	a	16.	b
2.	d	7.	c	12.	d	17.	a
3.	e	8.	a	13.	d	18.	c
4.	c	9.	c	14.	c	19.	c
5.	a	10.	d	15.	b	20.	a

PROBLEMS

1. $25,000. His civilian output valued at $25,000 is foregone to produce $10,000 in military output.

2. A. Student's Costs

    Explicit Costs

Tuition Less Scholarship		$ 1,095
Texts and Supplies		375
Monthly Dorm Fee	$175	
Less 9 Months' Home Living	135	
	$40 x 9 Months	360
		$ 1,830
Implicit Costs		8,550
Foregone Income ($950 x 9)		8,550
Total		$10,380

    B. State Taxpayers' Costs

Salaries and Expenses	$ 7,146
Scholarship	300
Total	$ 7,446

    C. Society's Costs

Student's Components	$10,380
Taxpayers' Components	7,446
Contributions	459
Total	$18,285

3. A. Year 1 Tuition Revenue: $4,000 x 20,000 = $80,000,000
   Year 2 Tuition Revenue: $5,000 x 18,000 = $90,000,000

   B. Percentage Change in Enrollment: 2,000/20,000 = 10%
   Percentage Change in Tuition: $1,000/$4,000 = 25%

   C. Price Inelastic.

Chapter 4
●Economics of Crime and Its Prevention

How Much Is Too Much?

LEARNING OBJECTIVES

After studying this issue, you should be able to:

1. Define and classify criminal activities.

2. Distinguish between immorality and illegality.

3. List and evaluate the causes of crime.

4. Illustrate, using a production possibilities curve, the costs of crime in opportunity cost terms.

5. Explain how crime and crime prevention affect the size of GDP.

6. Explain why crime prevention is a collectively consumed good.

7. Evaluate the government's role in the solution of the "free rider" problem.

8. *Discuss the costs and benefits of crime prevention and explain how an efficient level of crime prevention is determined.

9. *Define the equimarginal principle and use is to determine the efficient use of resources budgeted for crime prevention activities.

10. Explain, using graphs, the effects of changing the legal status of a good or service on its demand, supply, quantity demanded, quantity supplied, market (equilibrium) price, quality, and relative elasticity of demand and supply.

CHAPTER ORIENTATION

In attacking the crime issue, as in attacking any other issue, your first task is to learn as precisely as you can what it is. So you should define crime and learn the classifications of criminal activities.

Using economic analysis, you should be better able to understand the costs of crime—at least conceptually, the costs of crime, according to the opportunity cost doctrine, are best measured by the loss in GDP that occurs because crime exists and because resources are used for crime prevention activities rather than for the production of other goods and services. Adequate and accurate data on the cost of crime do not exist.

Crime prevention activities provide an introduction to the concept of collectively consumed goods and services. The provision of these goods and services by private groups usually results in a "free rider" problem which governments are in a unique position to solve.

Because of scarcity we cannot have as much of everything as we want. Two questions must be answered. How much total crime prevention activity should we have? How much of each of the different facets of crime prevention activity should we have? The second question involves the equimarginal principle.

More crime prevention activity may mean less education, for example, if we have full employment. Therefore, we must decide how to allocate units of resource inputs. Resources should be allocated to crime prevention activities as long as they add more to total benefits from crime prevention than to total costs. Note that costs, as used here, are opportunity costs—the value of the education given up in order to have more crime prevention activity. The decision rule is: increase crime prevention activity until marginal benefits

(MB) equal marginal costs (MC). When the amount added to total benefits (i.e., marginal benefits) equals the amount added to total costs (i.e., marginal costs) the resource input is allocated efficiently. No waste is involved in the allocation. Be sure you understand the concepts of marginal benefits and marginal costs and how these are used to determine the "correct" level of services.

To determine the most efficient mix of different facets of crime prevention, the equimarginal principle is used. Answering the first question determined the efficient size of the total budget for crime prevention activities. The budget is a constraint. The goal is to acquire the most quantity and quality of crime prevention possible given the budget constraint; i.e., the resources available. The goal is met when the last dollar spent on any one facet of crime prevention yields the same addition to the benefits of crime prevention as the last dollar spent on the others. This relationship may also be expressed as:

$$\frac{MBd}{MCd} = \frac{MBa}{MCa} = \frac{MBc}{MCc} = \frac{MBr}{MCr}$$

where the MB of detection (d) equals the MC of detection, the MB of apprehension (a) equals the MC of apprehension, the MB of conviction (c) equals the MC of conviction, and the MB of rehabilitation/punishment (r) equals the MC of rehabilitation/punishment. In addition the sum of the amounts spent on detection, apprehension, conviction, and rehabilitation/punishment must not exceed the amount budgeted. Thus, the equimarginal principle provides information on how the total budget for crime prevention should be allocated among its component parts.

Economic analysis provides little information on the morality of the purchase and sale of items like drugs, alcohol, and abortions. It is useful, however, in predicting what the effects will be on demand, supply, price, and quantity exchanged when these are made legal or illegal as the case may be.

CONSIDER THIS:

Criminals to be billed[1]

Criminals will soon be billed for the cost of their arrests under an unusual plan approved unanimously by the Fremont, California City Council. The new fee, which is authorized under state law but is rarely adopted by cities, will apply only to people who have been arrested by Fremont police, booked into the Santa Rita county jail and found guilty. The city finance department will send out bills ranging from $89.85 to $134.10, the amount the county now charges the city for each jail booking. Fremont officials hope to raise $15,100 annually through the new fee.

Consider These Questions:

1. Will convicted criminals in Fremont be billed for the entire economic cost of their criminal activity? Define and illustrate the costs of crime other than those of making arrests.

2. What are some of the more conventional ways that governments finance collectively consumed public goods? Provide examples.

3. Do you feel that making convicted criminals pay for the costs of their arrests will deter crime? Why or why not? Provide an economic argument.

---

[1]"Criminals to be Billed for Cost of Arrests," *The San Francisco Chronicle*, May 19, 1993, p. A13. Copyright San Francisco Chronicle. Reprinted by permission.

STUDY QUESTIONS

1. Consider the following activities. Which are criminal acts? Which are immoral acts? Explain. Classify those which are criminal acts.
    a. marijuana smoking
    b. speeding
    c. prostitution
    d. gambling
    e. murder
    f. theft
    g. air pollution

2. Selling liquor by the drink except in a private club setting is illegal in some states. Is it also immoral? Provide another illustration of this distinction.

3. Does the general public's concern about crime seem well-founded? Why or why not?

4. "Money is the root of all evil." Evaluate this statement in terms of the causes of crime.

5. Review the assumptions and structure of a production possibilities curve. Remember that it is a way of illustrating opportunity costs. Illustrate and explain the economic cost of crime in opportunity cost terms.

6. If GDP is lower with crime prevention activities that it would be without them, are the crime prevention activities an economic service?

7. Can governmental units exclude you from the benefits of crime prevention activities? Why or why not?

8. The production of collectively consumed goods and services gives rise to the "free rider" problem. Should the government be asked to correct this problem? Explain. Can the government accomplish the task? Explain.

9. What are the costs and benefits of crime prevention activity? How does scarcity force attention to the level of crime prevention activity? How does society decide how much crime prevention activity to undertake?

10. Assume that one unit of crime prevention costing $60,000 keeps $240,000 worth of GDP from being destroyed by criminal activities. A second unit yields total benefits to the community of $180,000.
    a. Calculate the marginal benefits for both units of crime prevention.
    b. Does it pay the community to acquire the second unit of crime prevention if it also costs $60,000?
    c. How many $60,000 crime prevention units should the community purchase? Explain.

11. Suppose that reducing the expenditures on the incarceration of criminals by a dollar increases criminal activity and causes the community to lose $1.10. Increasing police protection by that dollar makes the community better off by $2.60. Is the community better off as a result of the reduced expenditure on incarceration? Explain.

12. Diagram and discuss the effects of making the sale of "Saturday Night Special" handguns illegal. Do the economic effects of such legislation support the usual arguments for gun control? Explain. What might happen to the demand for other types of guns? Could this change in demand affect the expected outcome of gun control? Explain.

PUZZLE Complete the following crossword puzzle.

Crime and Its Prevention

Across

1. Goods and services that benefit the consumer and provide social spillover benefits to others are _____ consumed.
5. The change in total costs resulting from a one unit change in the output of a good or service. (2 words)
6. _____ consumed goods and services directly benefit only those persons who consume them.
8. _____ - _____ analysis is used to evaluate the economic worth of an activity and the extent, if any, to which it should be carried on.

Down

2. The change in total benefits yielded by an activity from a one unit change in the amount of the activity carried on. (2 words)
3. Holds when the marginal benefit of a dollar spent on any input is the same as for that spent on any other input. (2 words)
4. _____ consumed goods and services yield benefits to the group and no single individual can single out his/her specific benefit.
7. Goods and services of a collectively consumed nature provided by governmental units. (2 words)

TRUE-FALSE QUESTIONS Circle T (true) or F (false)

T F 1. Governments can remedy the free rider problem by providing collectively consumed public goods.

T F 2. All immoral activities are crimes.

T F 3. The total crime rate in the United States decreased from 1980 through 1984 but it has increased since then.

T F 4. The standards of social values of a society are an important determinant of criminal activities.

T F 5. Poverty coupled with frustrated economic and social aspirations may cause some individuals to engage in criminal activities.

T F 6. The net economic cost of crime to the society is the difference between what GDP would be if there were neither criminal nor crime prevention activities and what GDP currently is, given present criminal and crime prevention activities.

T F 7. Theft usually results in a large net economic cost to society as well as to the individual victims.

T F 8. If crime prevention activities raise GDP above the level that it would be in their absence then such activities may be considered an economic good or service.

T F 9. The optimum amount of crime prevention activities will ordinarily be generated by private crime prevention organizations.

T F 10. Governments can solve the free rider problem by requiring all who receive benefits of a collective consumed good or service to pay appropriate taxes for it.

T F 11. Private businesses usually are more efficient producers of collectively consumed goods than are governments.

T F 12. The marginal benefits of crime prevention are defined as the change in total benefits resulting from a one-unit change in the amount of crime prevention activity.

T F 13. The marginal cost of crime prevention is the change in total cost resulting from a one-unit change in the production of the service.

T F 14. From the economic welfare point of view, crime prevention activities should be expanded if their marginal costs exceed their marginal benefits.

T F 15. The complete suppression of crime is unlikely because the benefits of some additional unit of crime prevention activity will not be worth what it costs.

T F 16. Crime prevention activities should be expanded until total benefits are maximized.

T F 17. In any city with a fixed crime prevention budget, additional suppression of gambling will usually be achieved at the expense of an increase in other kinds of criminal activities like robbery and assault.

T F 18. The equimarginal principle applied to crime prevention states that expenditures on different components of crime prevention should be so allocated that the last dollar spent on each results in the same addition to the benefits of crime prevention.

T F 19. If the marginal benefits of a dollar's worth of police activities is less than the marginal benefits of a dollar's worth of court activities, then society would be better off by the transfer of expenditure from police activities to court activities.

T F 20. If marijuana were made legal, it can be expected that there will be an increase in price, a decrease in supply, and a decrease in the quantity exchanged.

T F 21. National defense is collectively consumed.

T F 22. Governments can effectively remedy the free rider problem through coercion.

T F 23. The optimal level of crime prevention activity is found by setting total social benefits equal to total social costs.

T F 24. Criminal activities in the aggregate lower Gross Domestic product.

T F 25. Cost-benefit analysis suggests that all criminal activity can be eliminated if the proper amount of crime prevention activity is provided by society.

MULTIPLE-CHOICE QUESTIONS Select the one best answer

1. Acts that are illegal or criminal are:
    a. generally, but not always moral acts.
    b. designated as such by legislative bodies.
    c. restricted to actions against property.
    d. All of the above.

2. As a criminal act, burning trash within the city limits:
    a. would be classified as a crime against property.
    b. is also clearly immoral.
    c. is contrary to the general welfare of the society.
    d. All of the above.

3. Criminal activity stems from many sources, including:
    a. poverty coupled with low levels of expectations
    b. unrestrained passion or emotions.
    c. unduly high standards of social values.
    d. None of the above.

4. Crime prevention activities:
    a. lower GDP below what it would be without them.
    b. can be considered an economic good or service.
    c. use productive resources.
    d. All of the above.
    e. Both (b) and (c).

Question 5 is based on the following diagram:

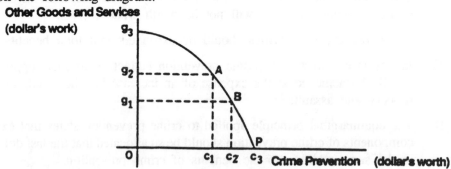

5. Suppose society is currently at point A, then the cost of producing an additional unit of crime prevention, c_1c_2, is:
    a. $0G_1$ of other goods and services.
    b. g_1g_2 of other goods and services.
    c. g_1g_3 of other goods and services.
    d. $0G_2$ of other goods and services.

6. The annual economic costs of criminal activities are best measured by:
   a. the value of goods stolen and destroyed by criminals.
   b. the costs of all law enforcement activities.
   c. what criminals could have earned in their best alternative employments.
   d. foregone GDP that results from them.

7. Crime prevention activities:
   a. are an individually consumed service.
   b. are a collectively consumed service.
   c. can be provided in the optimum amount by competitive private enterprises through the market-price system.
   d. yield benefits primarily to the individuals who consume them.

8. Collectively consumed goods:
   a. benefit directly only those individuals who consume them.
   b. yield identifiable benefits to those that consume them.
   c. may be easier to produce than individually consumed goods because of the "free rider" problem.
   d. None of the above.

9. Which one of the following is an example of a collectively consumed good or service?
   a. Crime prevention.
   b. National defense.
   c. Communicable disease control.
   d. Smog control.
   e. All of the above.

10. The government is a predominantly private enterprise economic system:
    a. is responsible for the production of individually consumed as well as collectively consumed and semicollectively consumed goods and services.
    b. tends to leave the bulk of individually consumed goods and services to private business.
    c. plays a relatively important role in the provision of semicollectively consumed and collectively consumed goods and services.
    d. Both (b) and (c).

11. Voluntary associations to provide collectively consumed goods:
    a. can effectively handle the free-rider problem.
    b. can require all who benefit from a collectively consumed good to pay for it.
    c. tend to fall apart because of the incentives that induce some people to become free riders.
    d. All of the above.

12. The costs of crime prevention are:
    a. estimates of how much better off the suppression of crime makes society.
    b. essentially intangible.
    c. much more difficult to estimate than the benefits.
    d. None of the above.

13. Assume one unit of crime prevention activity would yield benefits to the community of $300,000 and cost $120,000. The community:
    a. would be better off not providing one unit of crime prevention.
    b. would provide at least one unit of crime prevention since the net benefits are $180,000.
    c. would provide two units of crime prevention if the total net benefits are less than $180,000.
    d. could provide four units of crime prevention if the marginal cost of the fourth unit exceeds its marginal benefit.

14. A social spillover cost of crime is illustrated by:
    a. the inability of a victim of assault to do work following the assault.
    b. the value of property destroyed in the course of a robbery.
    c. the anxiety or decrease in well-being that people feel in going about their business in areas where crime rates are high.
    d. the diversion of resources from making butter to making guns.

Answer Questions 15 through 18 on the basis of the following information.

The estimates of the total costs and total benefits of crime prevention are as follows:

Units of Crime Prevention	Total Costs	Total Benefits
1	$ 10,000	$ 40,000
2	22,500	75,000
3	37,500	105,000
4	55,000	130,000
5	75,000	150,000
6	97,500	165,000
7	122,500	175,000

15. The marginal benefits of the sixth unit of crime prevention is equal to:
    a. $10,000.
    b. $15,000.
    c. $22,500.
    d. $25,000.
    e. $67,500.

16. The total net benefits at three units of crime prevention is equal to:
    a. 0.
    b. $12,500.
    c. $15,000.
    d. $67,500.
    e. $75,000.

17. At which level of crime prevention are the total net benefits maximum?
    a. 3 units.
    b. 5 units.
    c. 6 units.
    d. 7 units.
    e. 4 and 5 units.

18. The "correct" level of crime prevention is:
    a. 3 units.
    b. 5 units.
    c. 6 units.
    d. 7 units.

19. Suppose that a dollar reduction in the crime detection activity results in a $1.40 loss to the community as a result of an increase in criminal activity. The reduction in crime detection is:
    a. inappropriate since it results in a net loss of $1.40.
    b. appropriate if the dollar when spent for rehabilitation activities makes the community better off by more than $1.40.
    c. appropriate since the marginal benefits of the last dollar spent on crime detection of $1.40 is equal to the loss due to the reduction.
    d. None of the above.

Answer Questions 20 and 21 on the basis of the following information concerning the marginal benefits from utilizing various numbers of policemen and patrol cars in the prevention of crime.

Units	Marginal Benefits from Employing One More Policeman	Marginal Benefits From Utilizing One More Patrol Car
1	$ 60,000	$ 54,000
2	54,000	45,000
3	48,000	36,000
4	42,000	28,000
5	34,000	24,000
6	28,000	20,000
7	24,000	18,000

The cost of each policeman is $14,000; the cost of each patrol car is $12,000. The total budget is $92,000.

20. What is the most efficient allocation of the crime prevention budget?
    a. 2 policemen, 1 patrol car
    b. 5 policemen, 3 patrol cars
    c. 4 policemen, 3 patrol cars
    d. 5 policemen, 1 patrol car
    e. 6 policemen, 5 patrol cars

21. If the police department gets an additional allocation of $52,000, how should the money be divided between policemen and patrol cars?
    a. 2 more policemen and 2 more patrol cars
    b. 3 more policemen and 2 more patrol cars
    c. 1 more policeman and 3 more patrol cars
    d. 2 more policemen and 1 more patrol car

Answer Questions 22-25 on the basis of the following diagram:

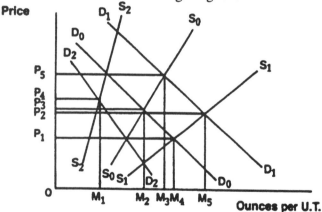

22. If D_0D_0 and S_0S_0 are the demand and supply curves for illegal marijuana, which one of the following represent the market equilibrium price and quantity?
    a. P_3, M_2
    b. P_2, M_5
    c. P_4, M_1
    d. P_5, M_3
    e. P_1, M_4

23. If marijuana were legalized, the demand curve would:
    a. increase to D_1D_1
    b. increase to D_2D_2
    c. decrease to D_1D_1
    d. decrease to D_2D_2
    e. stay the same.

24. Which one of the following would most likely represent the market equilibrium price and quantity after the legalization of marijuana?
    a. P_3, M_2
    b. P_2, M_5
    c. P_4, M_1
    d. P_5, M_3
    e. P_1, M_4

25. Suppose a price control of OP_3 were imposed when marijuana were legalized. As a result:
    a. more marijuana is demanded and supplied than before its legalization.
    b. a shortage of marijuana will occur.
    c. a surplus of marijuana will occur.
    d. Both (a) and (b).
    e. Both (a) and (c).

PROBLEMS

1. As a member of the Bigtown City Commission, you are presented the data below on the costs and benefits of crime prevention activities in that city. Crime prevention activities are measured in $50,000 units.

Units of Crime Prevention	Total Benefits	Marginal Benefits	Total Costs	Marginal Costs	Total Net Benefits
1	$ 200,000	_____	$ 50,000	_____	_____
2	350,000	_____	100,000	_____	_____
3	450,000	_____	150,000	_____	_____
4	500,000	_____	200,000	_____	_____
5	525,000	_____	250,000	_____	_____
6	540,000	_____	300,000	_____	_____

   a. Complete the table above by computing the:
      (1) marginal benefits of the various levels of crime prevention activities.
      (2) marginal costs of the various levels of crime prevention activities.
      (3) net total benefits of the various levels of crime prevention activities.

   b. What is the *rule* for determining the "correct" amount to spend on crime prevention activities?

   c. Based upon this information, the "correct" dollar amount for the City Commission to appropriate to the Police Department is $_____.

2. The research staff of a state penitentiary provides the warden with the following information concerning the benefits from hiring various numbers of guards, psychologists, and teachers.

Marginal Benefits from Correctional Services
Provided by Employing One More

Number Employed	Guard	Psychologist	Teacher
1	$ 60,000	$ 180,000	$80,000
2	54,000	120,000	70,000
3	48,000	60,000	60,000
4	42,000	30,000	50,000
5	36,000	20,000	40,000
6	24,000	10,000	30,000
7	12,000	5,000	20,000
8	6,000	2,000	10,000

The cost of each guard is $6,000; the cost of each psychologist is $30,000; and the cost of each teacher is $10,000.

If the warden has $146,000 to spend on the labor services of guards, psychologists, and teachers, he should allocate his budget to employ:

_____ guards at a total cost of $_____.
_____ psychologists at a total cost of $_____.
_____ teachers at a total cost of $_____.
Total Expenditure $_____.

3. The research staff of the Police Department provides the Chief of Police with the following information concerning the benefits from utilizing various numbers of policemen, patrol cars, and helicopters.

Marginal Benefits from Crime Prevention Services Provided

Units	Policemen	Patrol Cars	Helicopters
1	$64,000	$30,000	106,000
2	56,000	25,000	53,000
3	48,000	20,000	23,000
4	40,000	15,000	13,000
5	32,000	10,000	3,000
6	24,000	5,000	1,000
7	16,000	4,000	500
8	8,000	3,000	100

The cost of each policeman is $8,000; the cost of each patrol car is $5,000; and the cost of each helicopter is $53,000.

a. Complete the above table by computing the marginal benefit per dollar spent on policemen, patrol cars, and helicopters.

b. What is the correct size of the crime prevention budget? _____

c. What is the *rule* for determining the "correct" allocation of the crime prevention budget?

d. Based upon the above information, the Chief of Police should allocate his budget to utilize:

_____ policemen at a total cost of $_____.
_____ patrol cars at a total cost of $_____.
_____ helicopters at a total cost of $_____.
Total Expenditures = $_____.

ANSWERS TO SELF-TEST

PUZZLE

Across		Down	
1.	Semicollectively	2.	Marginal Benefits
5.	Marginal Costs	3.	Equimarginal Principle
6.	Individually	4.	Collectively
8.	Cost-Benefit	7.	Public Goods

TRUE-FALSE QUESTIONS

1.	T	6.	T	11.	F	16.	F	21.	T
2.	F	7.	F	12.	T	17.	T	22.	T
3.	T	8.	T	13.	T	18.	T	23.	F
4.	T	9.	F	14.	F	19.	T	24.	T
5.	T	10.	T	15.	T	20.	F	25.	F

MULTIPLE-CHOICE QUESTIONS

1.	b	8.	d	14.	c	20.	c
2.	c	9.	e	15.	b	21.	a
3.	b	10.	d	16.	d	22.	a
4.	e	11.	c	17.	e	23.	a
5.	b	12.	d	18.	b	24.	b
6.	d	13.	b	19.	b	25.	e
7.	b						

PROBLEMS

1. a.

Units of Crime Prevention	Marginal Benefits	Marginal Costs	Total Net Benefits
1	$ 200,000	$ 50,000	$ 150,000
2	150,000	50,000	250,000
3	100,000	50,000	300,000
4	50,000	50,000	300,000
5	25,000	50,000	275,000
6	15,000	50,000	240,000

    b. Marginal benefits equal marginal costs
    c. $200,000 (4 units x $50,000 per unit)

2. 6 at $36,000; 2 at $60,000; 5 at $50,000; $146,000

3. a.

Units	Policemen	Patrol Cars	Helicopters
1	$8	$6	$2
2	7	5	1
3	6	4	0.43
4	5	3	0.25
5	4	2	0.06
6	3	1	0.02
7	2	0.80	0.01
8	1	0.60	0.00

b. $200,000 (Hint: Apply the equimarginal principle).

c. Marginal benefits per dollar spent on each should be the same.

d.
    8 at $ 64,000
    6 at   30,000
    2 at <u>106,000</u>
 Total = $200,000

Chapter 5
●Pollution Problems

Must We Foul Our Own Nests?

LEARNING OBJECTIVES

After studying this issue, you should be able to:

1. Explain the circumstances under which nature's recycling processes are inadequate.

2. Explain why pollution occurs.

3. Explain why pollution from the production of a good results in the product being underpriced from a social point of view and why this leads to an inefficient allocation of resources.

4. Illustrate, using a production possibilities curve, the cost of pollution control.

5. Explain, using cost-benefit analysis, why a zero level of pollution would be inefficient.

6. Explain how resources available to reduce pollution should be allocated among the common forms of pollution.

7. Evaluate the three main types of governmental pollution control policies, given their effects on resource allocation, relative scarcity, and economic goals.

8. Explain how property rights in a pollution rights market may be used to control environmental damage.

CHAPTER ORIENTATION

Pollution takes many forms—all of them undesirable. It is the industrial waste-filled lakes and streams, the dust-and-fume-filled air of our cities, the noise of the city during rush hour, the run-off from Smith's feedlot, and much more. Why don't we eliminate it?

Most economists would knowingly allow some pollution to occur, even though it could be eliminated. To others who argue that pollution should be reduced by whatever degree our technology makes possible, such a position is untenable. But is it?

Actually, the economists's position is quite defensible. After studying this issue, you should be able to defend a policy of nonzero pollution while at the same time arguing that pollution is undesirable. You will be able to do this only if you understand that the environment is a resource capable of processing pollutants and that the cost of pollution control may exceed its benefits far above the zero pollution level.

Pollution control is not free. Real resources will be used up in the production of a cleaner environment. If society is to have a cleaner environment, it will have to give up other goods and services. How much are you willing to give up of other things in order to have a cleaner environment?

In addition to the opportunity cost of pollution, another important question arises. Who should pay for pollution abatement? An efficient allocation of resources requires that the consumer of the product generating the pollution should pay. Why? When the product price does not reflect its total cost of production, too many units of it will be purchased and too many resources will be used in its production. Resources are misallocated and relative scarcity is not reduced. The polluter by polluting passes some of the cost of production on to those who do not purchase the product. These people in a sense subsidize the product users. The market fails to allocate resources efficiently because the price generated by the market understates the true cost of production.

This chapter provides you with the opportunity to reinforce and apply in a new context concepts and principles learned in preceding chapters. The economic tools of analysis provide valuable aid in determining what antipollution policies are likely to be most efficient and most effective.

CONSIDER THIS:

Pricing Pollution[1]

The small and misunderstood sale of pollution rights by the US Environmental Protection Agency and the Chicago Board of Trade last week was the latest step in the evolution of a market. Pricing pollution is no different from pricing bonds, according to Nobel laureate Professor Ronald Coase of the University of Chicago. His work on determining economic costs of social problems forms the basis of the EPA's market-based pollution reduction programme.

"People basically think they need something physical to trade. The point is you never, ever trade in physicals. You always only trade the rights to something. Once that's understood, it becomes much easier to see trading in intangibles," Professor Coase says.

He says the great advantage of a market-based system for allocating pollution is that it achieves a set level of pollution reduction at the lowest possible cost. Eventually, information from that market can become a valuable public-policy tool. "Over the long run, it allows us to determine what the costs of pollution are, and will allow the EPA to balance better the costs and benefits of pollution control."

For industry, a secondary market for pollution permits would communicate the real costs of emissions, forcing producers to factor those costs into the price of their goods. Even environmentalists like the concept. They can use their dollars to buy pollution rights and retire them.

The pollution permits scheme will falter, however, if a liquid secondary market does not develop soon. Only a handful of the permits have traded privately, and last week's auction also failed as a secondary market. All the permits sold had been donated by the EPA, not contributed by utility owners.

The EPA is late in launching its on-line system for clearing secondary trades, forcing counterparties to construct expensive contracts. Regulatory and tax uncertainties also stifle the market.

Some investment bankers say the needs of electric utilities are so diverse, that custom-tailored transactions are likely to win out over mass-market trading systems.

This view conflicts with that of Mr. Richard Sandor, a principal inventor of financial derivatives and now an advocate for a CBOT futures market in air pollution permits. He expects the pollution-rights market to mimic the architecture of the credit markets: screen and telephone-based cash trading; dynamic, customised off-exchange derivative trading, and an on-exchange futures market as the ultimate public pricing and risk-management vehicle.

Mr. Sandor is willing to be patient—like the bond markets, he expects pollution market synergies to take two decades to achieve. It may take longer.

Nevertheless, Chicago's deep-pocketed trader-entrepreneurs have historically been willing to back applications of the latest pricing theories.

The CBOT is starting a low-cost electronic bulletin board to highlight allowance bids and offers, and will hold periodic auctions to provide necessary spot market infrastructure.

The CBOT has competition in this area, because other exchanges—floor and screen-based—also view pollution rights as a potentially lucrative new venture.

---

[1]Laurie Morse, "Risk and Reward: Chicago Attempts to Put a Price on Pollution," *Financial Times*, April 5, 1993. Reprinted with permission.

Even if trading fails to blossom, the existence of the permits has provided an economic alternative to more expensive pollution abatement techniques. They have intrinsically brought down costs of environmental compliance.

Regulators are already working to adapt the concept to other forms of pollution—including nitrogen oxide, a chemical precursor to the noxious air pollutant, ozone, and to some water pollutants. Prof. Coase would like to see his ideas applied to broadcasting, where he advocates market-based allocation of radio frequencies and other common carriers. Prof. Coase's theories are becoming increasingly popular, perhaps because of the growing realization that the most plentiful of resources—even air and water—are finite and thus have a determinable and defendable value.

Consider These Questions:

1. Why is pricing pollution "no different from pricing bonds"? Use the economic theory learned in class to answer this question.

2. What is meant by a "secondary market" for pollution permits? Can you explain why utility owners may not offer their permits for sale? What is necessary for them to sell their permits?

3. Discuss why a market allocation of pollution permits may be more efficient than other means of allocation.

4. Do you feel the price of pollution permits will rise or fall over time? Why? How will price changes effect the incentives for utilities to pollute the environment?

STUDY QUESTIONS

1. Pollution takes many forms. Identify a form of pollution and a set of circumstances for which nature's recycling processes as a natural resource is inadequate. Adequate. Is it important that nature's recycling processes be utilized fully? Explain.

2. "Pollution consists of loading the environment with wastes that are either not completely recycled, are not recycled fast enough, or are not recycled at all." What do you add to the environment as pollutants? Why do you continue to do so?

3. What forms of pollution are associated with strip mining? If coal users do not fully pay these costs, is the allocation of resources to the production of coal efficient? Explain using graphs. Why is efficiency a concern? Explain.

4. Are the resources used to control pollution the opportunity cost of pollution? Explain. Using Figure 6-3 in the text, determine the opportunity cost of an increase in pollution control.

5. "Most economists would knowingly allow some pollution to occur, even though it could be eliminated." Explain.

6. Assume the Environmental Protection Agency research findings indicate that a one-dollar reduction in water pollution expenditure results in a loss due to additional pollution of $.37. The study also finds that an additional dollar spent on smog control increases benefits by $.23. Given the available information, select the pollution reduction activity that would be allocated a one-dollar change in funding. Explain your choice.

7. "A reduction in economic freedom is a necessary cost of pollution control." Evaluate.

8. Compare direct and indirect pollution control measures. What are the advantages and disadvantages of indirect controls?

9. Can air pollution be controlled by selling air property rights to persons, then allowing owners of air to sell pollution rights to would-be polluters? Explain.

PUZZLE Complete the following crossword puzzle.

Pollution Problems

Across

4. Costs of production imposed on persons other than those doing the producing are called social _____ costs.
7. The transformation of wastes into raw materials that are again usable.
8. Marginal _____ measures the change in total cost due to a one unit change in output.
10. Consists of the air, water, and land around us. Our habitat.
12. The marginal _____ measures the change in total benefits due to a change in total output.
13. In 1990, established a pollution rights market for sulfur dioxide emissions by electric utility companies. (3 words)

Down

1. Unrecycled waste dumped into the environment by man.
2. Government issued licenses to pollute are bought and sold by business firms in a pollution rights _____.
3. A curve showing maximum output in a two-product economy, given the economy's resources and technology. (Initials)
5. In making a choice, the value of the foregone activity is called the _____ cost.
6. The greatest possible value of output from a given set of economic resources.
9. _____ consumed goods and services yield benefits to the consuming group and no individual can identify their specific benefits.
11. Cost-Benefit _____ evaluates the economic worth of an activity.

TRUE-FALSE QUESTIONS Circle T (true) or F (false)

T F 1. Natural recycling processes will prevent all wastes from accumulating in the environment.

T F 2. The absence of property rights creates an incentive to pollute certain segments of the environment.

T F 3. Automobile owners can dump combustion gases into the air without charge because of the collectively consumed nature of the air.

T F 4. Pollution occurs when wastes added to the environment are not completely recycled, are not recycled fast enough, or are not recycled at all.

T F 5. A manufacturing firm that is permitted to pollute freely tends to produce larger quantities of its product than society really wants relative to quantities of other products.

T F 6. When producers are able to pollute the environment without any cost to themselves, a divergence between the costs to the firm and the opportunity costs of production tends to develop.

T F 7. Polluters impose spillover costs on nonpolluters inducing nonpolluters to underuse environmental services.

T F 8. When the manufacturer of a product is able to pollute without charge, the price of the product will reflect the firm's private costs but not the full opportunity costs of production.

T F 9. Requiring electrical utility companies to install smoke stack scrubbers will shift the supply curve for electricity upward and to the left.

T F 10. The costs of pollution control to a society are measured by the value of the goods and services that must be sacrificed in order to put the control into effect.

T F 11. The term "marginal benefits" of any specific kind of economic activity means the change in total benefits per unit change in the amount of the activity being carried on.

T F 12. As the level of an air pollution control activity increases, marginal costs and marginal benefits both increase.

T F 13. To obtain the proper level of pollution control from the viewpoint of economics, it is necessary to weigh the total benefits of pollution control against the total costs and if total benefits exceed total costs to increase the amount of control.

T F 14. Zero pollution can be achieved by engaging in pollution control activities until marginal benefits equals marginal costs.

T F 15. From an economic standpoint, society always should make expenditures on pollution control wherever pollution exists.

T F 16. If the marginal benefits from a dollar's worth of smog control is greater than the marginal benefits of a dollar's worth of water treatment, the society would be better off by the transfer of expenditure from smog control to water treatment.

T F 17. A tax per unit of polluted discharge should be decreased if the amount of polluted discharge permitted by the tax is such that marginal benefits of cleaning exceed the marginal costs of cleaning.

T F 18. Taxing the polluting activity of a firm tends to move the firm toward bearing the real costs of producing their products; hence, tends to reduce the amount of pollution that occurs.

T F 19. A tax per unit of polluted discharge will induce the firm to reduce its polluting activity if the amount of the tax is less than the marginal costs of cleaning the discharge.

T F 20. If a city government assigns property rights over a certain block of air to a polluter, the cost of reducing air pollution will be borne by the polluter.

T F 21. The production of anti-pollution goods and services increases Gross Domestic Product.

T F 22. Taxes on environmental discharges are the most common governmental control of pollution in the U.S. today.

T F 23. In a pollution rights market, firms buy and sell government issued licenses to pollute the environment.

T F 24. The Clean Air Act of 1990 established a pollution rights market for sulfur dioxide emissions by electric utility companies.

T F 25. Through the use of a pollution rights market, government could reduce the level of pollution by issuing more licenses and thereby disperse the degree of environmental damage.

MULTIPLE-CHOICE QUESTIONS Select the one best answer

1. Nature's recycling processes:
   a. may be insufficient when wastes accumulate too fast.
   b. require variable lengths of time, depending on what is being recycled.
   c. determine the capacity of the environment to yield environmental services.
   d. transform some wastes into raw materials that are again usable.
   e. All of the above.

2. Consumers and producers use the environment as a dumping ground because:
   a. no one has property rights in the environment being polluted.
   b. the environment being polluted is collectively consumed.
   c. existing property rights are not enforced.
   d. All of the above.

3. Pollution:
   a. is a problem of relatively recent origin.
   b. occurs when recycling processes fail to prevent wastes from accumulating in the environment.
   c. results mostly from unnecessary production and consumption.
   d. continues to occur because people have not taken action to prevent it.
   e. can be controlled at no great cost.

4. If a profit-maximizing producer dumps wastes into the air, river, or ocean, and if the disposal of these wastes has adverse effects on others:
   a. the private and opportunity costs of disposal are identical and zero.
   b. there is a spillover cost imposed by the action.
   c. there is no pollution problem.
   d. (a) and (c) above.

Answer Questions 5–8 based on the following diagrams for an upstream paper industry and a downstream power industry.

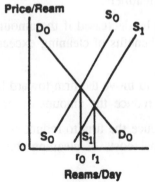

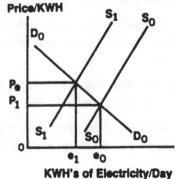

5. If the upstream paper industry is allowed to dump its waste free of charge into the river instead of otherwise disposing of them:
   a. the supply of paper by the industry will decrease from S_1S_1 to S_0S_0.
   b. the supply of paper by the industry will increase from S_0S_0 to S_1S_1.
   c. the paper industry will shift its waste disposal costs to downstream industries.
   d. the quantity of paper produced will increase from r_0 to r_1 reams per day.
   e. All of the above except (a).

6. If the upstream paper industry is allowed to dump its waste into the river:
   a. the supply of electricity will decease from S_0S_0 to S_1S_1.
   b. the quantity of electricity produced will decrease from e_0 to e_1 KWH/day.
   c. the supply of electricity will increase from S_1S_1 to S_0S_0.
   d. the quantity of electricity produced will increase from e_1 to e_0.
   e. Both (a) and (b).

7. If the upstream paper industry dumps its waste into the river:
   a. too much of the economy's resources will be devoted to producing paper.
   b. the value that society places on the last r_0r_1 reams of paper produced will be greater than the additional costs of producing them.
   c. society's net welfare could be increased by devoting more resources to producing paper.
   d. All of the above.

8. If the upstream paper industry dumps its waste into the river:
   a. too little of the economy's resources will be devoted to producing electricity.
   b. the value (Pe) that society places on the last KWH of electricity produced (e_1) exceeds the additional costs of producing it (P_1).
   c. the additional water-cleaning cost of the power industry of producing the last KWHs of electricity (e_1) will be P_1P_0 dollars per KWH.
   d. All of the above.

9. If an upstream paper industry pollutes water used by a downstream power industry forcing the latter to clean the water it uses, then:
   a. both will be induced to overproduce.
   b. the paper industry will be induced to underproduce and the power industry will be induced to overproduce.
   c. the paper industry will be induced to overproduce and the power industry will be induced to underproduce.
   d. both will be induced to underproduce.
   e. neither will be induced to overproduce or underproduce.

10. In the process of polluting the environment, polluters:
    a. impose spillover costs on others.
    b. incur costs above what they would be in the absence of pollution.
    c. overuse environmental services at the expense of other users.
    d. use environmental services efficiently.
    e. Both (a) and (c)

Question 11 is based on the following diagram.

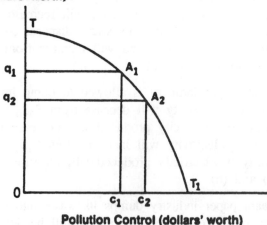

Other Goods and Services
(dollars' worth)

Pollution Control (dollars' worth)

11. The economy can have $0c_1$ dollar's worth of pollution control by giving up:
    a. $0q_1$ of other goods and services.
    b. q_1q_2 of other goods and services.
    c. q_1T of other goods and services.
    d. None of the above.

12. To determine the amount of pollution that would be permissible:
    a. the costs of keeping the environment clean must be considered.
    b. the benefits of pollution control activities must be considered.
    c. society should weigh the benefits of pollution control against its costs.
    d. All of the above.

Questions 13-15 are based on the following table. The total costs and total benefits of air pollution control in Smog City are listed as follows:

Reduction in Pollution Level		Total Benefits	Total Costs
1st	10%	$ 100,000	$ 50,000
2nd	10%	190,000	100,000
3rd	10%	270,000	150,000
4th	10%	340,000	200,000
5th	10%	400,000	250,000
6th	10%	450,000	300,000
7th	10%	490,000	400,000
8th	10%	515,000	450,000
9th	10%	530,000	500,000
10th	10%	530,000	550,000

13. The marginal benefits of the fifth 10 percent increment in the total amount of control are:
    a. $340,000.
    b. $140,000.
    c. $70,000.
    d. $60,000.
    e. $50,000.

14. The marginal costs of each 10 percent increment in the total amount of control are:
    a. $90,000.
    b. $80,000.
    c. $70,000.
    d. $60,000.
    e. $50,000.

15. The optimum level of control is to reduce the pollution in the air by:
    a. 50 percent.
    b. 60 percent.
    c. 70 percent.
    d. 90 percent.
    e. 100 percent.

16. As the level of pollution control increases, marginal benefits:
    a. decline because total pollution is smaller and an additional unit of pollution control has less value.
    b. decline because society values the additional unit of pollution more than the last unit.
    c. rise because marginal costs increase as the level of pollution control increases.
    d. rise because each additional unit of pollution control has more value.

17. A pollution control activity should be expanded until:
    a. the total benefits equal the total cost of the activity.
    b. the marginal benefits equal the marginal costs of the activity.
    c. pollution is eliminated.
    d. the total benefits of the activity are maximized.

18. The pollution control budget should be allocated among pollution control activities so that:
    a. the average dollar spent on any one activity yields the same addition to the benefits of pollution control as the average dollar spent on the others.
    b. the last dollar spent on any one activity yields the same addition to the benefits of pollution control as the last dollar spent on the others.
    c. the marginal benefits from a dollar's worth of activity one will equal the marginal benefits of a dollar's worth of activity two and the marginal benefits of a dollar's worth of all other activities.
    d. Both (b) and (c).
    e. None of the above.

Questions 19 and 20 are based on the following diagram. The farm depicted in the diagram produces strawberries. To extract maximum yields from its acreage, it uses chemical fertilizers, some of which are washed into a city reservoir designed to impound water for drinking. It costs the city $40 in cleaning costs for every ton of strawberries produced.

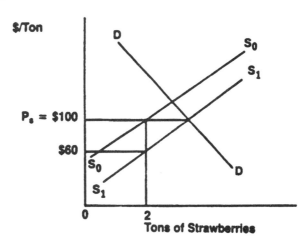

19. If a strawberry farmer is forced to absorb the full opportunity costs of producing strawberries:
    a. the supply of strawberries by the farm can be represented by S_0S_0.
    b. the supply of strawberries by the farm can be represented by S_1S_1.
    c. the farmer will produce two tons of strawberries per year.
    d. the farmer's total receipts from sales will be $200.
    e. All of the above except (a).

20. The imposition of a tax equal to $_____ per ton would be necessary to induce this farmer to produce the socially optimal number of tons of strawberries.
    a. $140
    b. $100
    c. $80
    d. $60
    e. $40

21. Those who incur spillover costs from pollution may find it to their advantage to:
    a. have the government enact legislation compelling the polluters to take antipollution measures.
    b. bribe the polluters to control their pollution.
    c. have the government tax any pollution at a rate that increases with the amount of pollution generated.
    d. All of the above.
    e. (a) and (c) only.

Questions 22-24 are based on the following diagram.

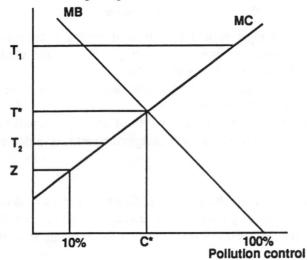

22. A tax of T_1 per unit of pollution will result in:
    a. too much pollution control effort.
    b. too much of the economy's scarce resources devoted to pollution control.
    c. too little pollution control effort.
    d. too little of the economy's scarce resources devoted to pollution control.
    e. Both a and b.

23. Given that C* is the desired amount of pollution control, the required tax per unit of pollution is:
    a. T*
    b. T_1.
    c. T_2.
    d. T*-Z.

24. For units of pollution control less than C* the firm:
    a. will eliminate its discharge and avoid the tax because the MC of pollution control is less than the tax.
    b. will continue its discharge and pay the tax because the MC of pollution control is greater than the tax.
    c. is indifferent and may do either a or b.
    d. pays the tax and eliminates its discharge.

25. Economists often advocate minimum use of direct controls and maximum use of market mechanisms and the price system in fighting pollution for the following reason(s):
    a. the price system tends to be more efficient because it would use the equimarginal principle.
    b. the price system tends to be more equitable in that it would allow people to pollute more in proportion to the benefit they gain from polluting.
    c. the price system tends to make people pay in proportion to the cost which they impose on others by polluting.
    d. All of the above.

PROBLEMS

1. Suppose you are a member of the State Pollution Control Board. The Board receives the following information concerning the benefits and costs of reducing the pollution in Big Lake by 10 percent increments.

Polluted Water	Reduction in Pollution Level		Total Benefits of Controls	Marginal Benefits	Total Costs of Control	Marginal Costs
↑	1st	10%	$100,000	_____	$ 1,000	_____
	2nd	10%	180,000	_____	3,000	_____
	3rd	10%	240,000	_____	6,000	_____
	4th	10%	280,000	_____	11,000	_____
	5th	10%	300,000	_____	19,000	_____
	6th	10%	316,000	_____	29,000	_____
	7th	10%	328,000	_____	41,000	_____
	8th	10%	336,000	_____	56,000	_____
	9th	10%	340,000	_____	81,000	_____
↓	10th	10%	341,000	_____	111,000	_____

Pollution-Free Water

   a. Complete the table by computing the marginal benefits and the marginal costs of controlling pollution.
   b. As a member of the Pollution Control Board, what would you recommend as the economically designed level of control to be achieved? _____ to reduce pollution in the lake by _____%.

2. Use the information in Problem 1 to answer the following questions.
   a. What tax per unit of pollution is required to achieve the desired level of pollution control?
   b. What tax rates will result in MB < MC for the amount of pollution control?

ANSWERS TO SELF-TEST

PUZZLE

Across	Down
4. Spillover	1. Pollution
7. Recycling	2. Market
8. Cost	3. PPC
10. Environment	5. Opportunity
12. Benefit	6. Efficiency
13. Clean Air Act	9. Collectively
	11. Analysis

TRUE-FALSE QUESTIONS

1. F	6. T	11. T	16. F	21. T
2. T	7. T	12. F	17. F	22. F
3. T	8. T	13. F	18. T	23. T
4. T	9. T	14. F	19. F	24. T
5. T	10. T	15. F	20. F	25. F

MULTIPLE-CHOICE QUESTIONS

1. e	8. d	14. e	20. e
2. d	9. c	15. b	21. d
3. b	10. e	16. a	22. e
4. b	11. c	17. b	23. a
5. e	12. c	18. d	24. a
6. e	13. d	19. a	25. d
7. a			

PROBLEMS

1. a.

Reduction in Pollution Level		Marginal Benefits	Marginal Costs
1st	10%	100,000	1,000
2nd	10%	80,000	2,000
3rd	10%	60,000	3,000
4th	10%	40,000	5,000
5th	10%	20,000	8,000
6th	10%	16,000	10,000
7th	10%	12,000	12,000
8th	10%	8,000	15,000
9th	10%	4,000	25,000
10th	10%	1,000	30,000

   b. $41,000; 70 percent

2. a. $12,000, for all tax rates per unit of pollution less than $12,000 the amount of pollution reduction will be less than the desired level.

   b. All tax rates above $12,000.

Chapter 6
Health Issues

Is It Worth What It Costs?

LEARNING OBJECTIVES

After studying this issue, you should be able to:

1. List the factors that explain the growth in expenditures for personal health services and explain why the rising costs of health-care may not necessarily be a problem.

2. Identify the special characteristics of health services and explain how they contribute to the health-care debate.

3. List the major economic problems of the healthcare industry and relate them to scarcity.

4. Explain what effects of the low elasticity of demand for health services on the costs of health care.

5. Explain why the demand for health services has been increasing and illustrate, using a graph, how such increases contribute to the rising costs of health care.

6. Explain how the elasticity of supply of physician services contributes to the rising costs of health care.

7. Explain, using the principle of diminishing marginal returns, why the short-run supply curve of hospital services is upward sloping.

8. List the factors affecting the supply of hospital services and discuss how they affect supply.

9. Evaluate the efficiency and equity of the U.S. health care system and explain what could be done to improve the system.

10. State and discuss the goals and basic issues associated with a national health insurance program and evaluate alternative national health insurance proposals.

CHAPTER ORIENTATION

This social issue offers you an opportunity to apply much of what you have learned in previous chapters. For example, demand and supply analysis is used to examine issues pertaining to the rising costs of medical care.

For the consumer, most markets are characterized by uncertainty—none so much as the market for medical services. Rational consumer decision making is hindered by the lack of objective information on medical services. Although consumers could do more to acquire additional information, they certainly have not been helped by the suppliers of health services. Recent Supreme Court decisions have removed many professional restrictions on advertising and other methods of supplying information to the consumer.

Inefficiency in the supply of health services increases relative scarcity. In addition, it leads to a misallocation of resources and, as is also apparent to the consumer, higher prices. This issue will help you understand why inefficiency exists and what can be done to reduce the inefficiency associated with the supply of health services.

What would you expect to happen to the price of any good or service assuming demand increases rapidly for it? Given supply or assuming supply does not increase as fast as demand, the price of the good would rise. This description of changes in demand and supply explains the behavior of prices of many health services. Demand for health services has risen because of increases in income of consumers, increases in tastes and preferences, and increases in federal expenditures. In contrast, supply of many health services have been slow to respond, and in the care of physicians' services, supply increases are held in check by restrictions to entry into the field.

The principle of diminishing marginal returns is a very important economic concept. It can be used to explain why the short-run supply curve of goods and services (e.g., hospital services) is upward sloping. The table below should help you better understand the principle of diminishing marginal returns.

Capital is assumed constant at three units. As the quantity of labor increases, the total product (the amount of output) increases. Marginal product is the amount added to total product resulting from the use of one more unit of the variable input (labor). Note that marginal product first increases (17 to 20) and then decreases (20 to 12). Thus, when increasing amounts of a variable factor are used with a given amount of a fixed factor, eventually each additional unit of the variable factor will add less to total product than did the previous unit. This relationship is called the principle of diminishing marginal returns.

When each additional worker adds the same amount to cost and a decreasing amount to output, then the cost per unit of output must eventually increase. Given increasing per unit costs, the firm would be willing to sell additional output only at a higher price; therefore, the short-run supply curve is upward sloping.

National health insurance proposals have been made to achieve certain goals. Find out what these goals are. Although national health insurance proposals have common aims, they differ as to the extent of patient payment, sources of finance, and the role of private insurance companies and governments. Whether you support one proposal as compared to another one will likely depend upon your position in regard to these differences.

Rising health care costs are essentially symptomatic of the health care industry problems. The economic goals of efficiency and equity require careful analysis and evaluation of policies designed to increase the supply of health care services, decrease demands, or regulate costs. The reform approach to improving the economic performance of the healthcare industry would eliminate the traditional fee-for-service practice.

Variation of Output with Capital Fixed and Labor Variable

Quantity of Capital (K)	Quantity of Labor (L)	Marginal Product (MP)	Total Product (Output)
3	0	0	
3	1	17	17
3	2	37	20
3	3	49	12
3	4	60	11
3	5	66	6
3	6	68	2

CONSIDER THIS:

Dissecting Health Care Costs[1]

The voluntary price controls favored by Hillary Rodham Clinton's health-care task force may not be able to restrain the nation's total medical spending.

The task force favors negotiating short-term voluntary controls on the prices charged by doctors, hospitals, insurance companies, drugmakers and others in the health-care industry. Now in the final phase of decision making, the task force is expected to recommend later this month sweeping changes in the USA's health-care system.

[1]Michael Clements, "Dissecting Health-Care Dollars—Rising Costs Reflect Many Influences," *USA Today,* May 5, 1993. Reprinted with permission.

But prices are only one reason the nation's health-care bill has nearly quadrupled since 1980 and will top $900 billion this year. Excess medical inflation, the rate medical prices rise above general inflation, accounted for only 2.9% of the 11.6% increase in health-care spending in 1991. The rest was caused by general inflation, 4.2%; population growth, 1%; and other factors, 3.4%. Those include the number and types of medical services performed and are influenced by factors such as the aging of the population and advances in medical technology.

"If medical inflation doesn't go up but your doctor does six more procedures, your costs are going to go up," says George Borkow, chief financial officer of United Healthcare, which owns or manages 20 health-maintenance organizations in 15 states. "(Prices) are only part of the equation, and utilization is the bigger part."

Medical inflation is growing at an annual rate of 6%, down from 9.7% at the start of 1991. In March, costs rose 3%, the lowest monthly rise in nine years. But overall spending for health care still outpaces increases in medical prices. Despite slowing medical inflation, employers this year are paying 9% to 12% more per employee for health care. That follows a similar increase last year, when health-care spending consumed 14% of the gross domestic product.

Why is there such a large gap between the medical- inflation rate and what employers pay? Because the Consumer Price Index measures only the change in typical prices consumers pay. For example, the average doctor visit cost $46 last year, says the American Medical Association, vs. $30 in 1986. The CPI does not count the number of office visits, prescriptions, X-rays, lab tests or surgeries done in the USA.

Likewise, there's little relationship between the price a consumer pays for a gallon of gasoline and the nation's spending on fuel. If people drive more, fuel use rises, and so does total spending, even if the pump price stays the same.

And that's the key to the current problem: Americans are seeing doctors more frequently than they did a few years ago, and they are having more procedures performed.

The average American saw a doctor nearly six times in 1991, vs. five in 1985, according to the National Center for Health Statistics. Between 1980 and 1991, coronary-bypass operations for men rose from 108,000 to 296,000, diagnostic ultrasounds for women rose from 114,000 to 652,000, and CAT scans rose from 306,000 to more than 1.4 million.

Besides the rising volume, new medical technology also is boosting prices. "People want to use all of the technology that's available," says Ken Price, an anesthesiologist in Lake Charles, La. "If a CAT scan is available, if an MRI is available, they want it done."

One example of the cost of medical advances: A two-year study of 41,000 heart-attack patients released last week showed that patients who received TPA, a genetically engineered drug marketed by Genentech under the brand name Activase, had a 14% higher survival rate than those receiving the generic drug streptokinase. But Activase costs $2,200 a dose—11 times the $200 cost for a dose of streptokinase.

"As new approaches become available, they are used in more and more patients," says Richard Ostuw, chief health-benefits actuary for Towers Perrin. "In the current system, something new is used if there is a hope it will benefit, without regard to cost."

Patients and their families usually support a doctor's recommendation of expensive tests or drugs. "The demand for medical services is unlike the demand for gasoline," Borkow says. If the cost of driving one car rises too high, "we can always go to a smaller car. But when it's your father who's dying, it's different."

And doctors have their own reason for using more and more expensive medical services—defensive medicine to protect themselves from malpractice suits. "Ninety-nine percent of the doctors I know do not order tests to make money," Price says. "They do it to cover their behinds."

Any move by the Clinton administration to persuade the medical industry to impose voluntary price controls could backfire, says Warren Greenberg, a professor of health economics at George Washington University in Washington. Price controls could lead to even more use of medical services, canceling much of the savings. Doctors, for example, might schedule more office visits per day or require more follow-up visits to make up for price restraints.

Rising costs aside, the slowing rate of medical inflation buys reformers a little time to help get total spending under control. But not a lot of time because the slowdown in medical-care inflation is largely due to an overall slowdown in inflation, which has reduced pressure on doctors, hospitals and drug companies to raise prices.

In 1990, when the overall inflation rate was 6.1%, the medical inflation rate was 9.6%. Now, general inflation is about 3% and medical inflation 6%.

Still, voluntary price controls are a tempting idea for the administration because of evidence that the health-care industry can restrain prices at will. Some economists think political pressure from the Clinton administration may have contributed to March's nine-year low for medical inflation.

Take drug pricing, for example. In February, President and Hillary Rodham Clinton denounced the pharmaceutical industry for profiteering at the expense of U.S. consumers. Under White House pressure, drugmakers such as Merck pledged to keep prices down. The medical-care-commodities group, which includes prescription drugs, rose a mere 0.2% in March.

But if the medical-care industry is voluntarily restraining prices, it may inadvertently be making a point it doesn't want highlighted right now. "The fact that (providers) can shift their pricing behavior so easily shows there is a problem," says Donald Ratajczak, head of economic forecasting at Georgia State University. "This is not a free market at work."

Even so, voluntary restraints can't work indefinitely. Eventually, prices could lurch upward to make up for the restraint, recapturing income sacrificed during the price slowdown. A period of voluntary price controls by hospitals in 1977-78 was followed by four years of 10% to 12% increases in medical-services inflation.

The task force's idea is to use short-term, voluntary price controls—backed up by the threat of mandatory controls—to bridge the transition from the current system until the administration's radically new health-care system is in place. The new system is expected to rely on managed care and incentives to control the amount and type of medical services used by Americans, thereby controlling total costs.

Ultimately, prices and cost are only part of what economist Allen Sinai of Boston Co. Economic Advisors calls "the toughest public-policy problem we've ever had."

"There's more to the medical-care problem than just the cost—including the 37 million uninsured, including the inability to get insurance coverage unless you're in perfect health," Sinai says. "There are 20 big policy questions on health care, and inflation is only part of it."

Dissecting health-care dollars National expenditures for health care have quadrupled since 1980. They are expected to top $900 billion this year despite a slowdown in inflation.

Where Health Spending Goes

	Billions
Total health costs	$903
Hospital care	359
Physician services	167
Nursing home care	74
Drugs	71
Administration/insurance	48
Other services	45
Dental services	41
Public health	24
Other personal health care	20
Research and development	16
Vision products	14
Home health care	12
Construction	12

Consider These Questions:

1. How has medical inflation compared to general inflation in recent years? Why?

2. How does the number of doctor's office visits influence the cost of health care? How is this figured into the measurement of medical inflation? Explain.

3. How has technology influenced the cost of health care? Do we use high-tech equipment and procedures too often? What economic rule could be applied to determine when to undertake a specific medical activity?

4. Do you feel voluntary restraint on medical costs by health care providers is an effective means to lower medical inflation? Why or why not?

STUDY QUESTIONS

1. The general public objects to the rising costs of health care. The mass media often carry articles about the rising costs of health care. Although we may object to rising health care costs, is it necessarily a problem? What factors explain the rise in health care costs?

2. Many public schools refuse to enroll students who have not been immunized for certain communicable diseases. What special characteristics of health services is indicated by this policy? Cite an example for each of the other special characteristics of health services.

3. Are rising prices and costs of health care services the major economic problems in the health care industry? Explain. Does scarcity determine the major economic problems in the health care industry? Explain.

4. Compare the relative price elasticities of demand for the specific medical services listed below:
    a. physical examination.
    b. open-heart surgery.
    c. laboratory test for blood sugar.
    d. office call for cold symptoms.

    Are the costs of these health care services affected by their elasticities of demand? Explain.

5. Why has the demand for health services been increasing? Illustrate, using a graph, how such increases affect the costs of health care. If supply is inelastic, will demand increases have a greater or smaller effect on price? Explain.

6. If an increase in the demand for physician services in the short run impacts primarily on the price of physician services, what is the short-run elasticity of supply of physician services?

7. Is the short-run supply curve of hospital services upward sloping to the right? Explain.

8. What factors determine the supply of hospital services and how do they change supply?

9. What changes could make the health-care system more efficient and equitable.

10. What seems to be the goals and basic issues to be met by a national insurance program? Discuss and evaluate one of the alternative national insurance proposals.

● PUZZLE Complete the following crossword puzzle.

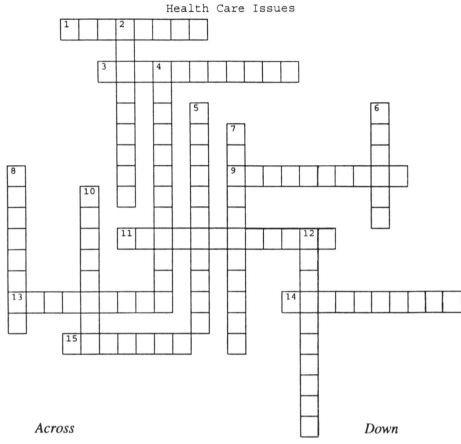

Health Care Issues

Across

1. An institution where the sick or injured receive health care.

3. A _____ payment system makes payments to doctors and hospitals based on a predetermined fee schedule for diagnostic diseases.

9. _____ of supply measures the responsiveness of quantity offered of a product to a change in the price.

11. Health insurance coverage of long-term and acute-cost illnesses.

13. Increases in the price level which reduce purchasing power.

14. Advances in health care _____ improve the quality and quantity of hospital services.

15. Fee-for-_____ is the concept that a seller is paid an amount based on the price and quantity of services provided.

Down

2. _____ income is equal to total income divided by the population. (2 words)

4. _____ effect occurs when a buyer responds to a price increase by switching consumption to a now relatively lower priced alternative.

5. The principle of _____ returns indicates that increments of a variable resource used with fixed resources will lead to smaller and smaller increments in product output.

6. _____ and preferences are buyers' psychological desires for goods and services.

7. Tastes and _____ are buyers' psychological desires for goods and services.

8. A public health program administered by the state governments and targeted for the poor.

10. Federal health program for the aged and disabled which covers the major costs of physician and hospital services.

12. The purchase of real assets, such as land, buildings, equipment, machines, and raw and semi-finished materials.

TRUE-FALSE QUESTIONS Circle T (true) or F (false)

T F 1. Consumers of health-care services pay for approximately 50 percent of total health care costs directly out of their own pocket.

T F 2. As a supplier of health services, a physician has nothing to do with how many health services are demanded.

T F 3. Consumers are as well informed about medical care services as they are about most goods and services that they buy.

T F 4. There are social spillover benefits involved in the consumption of some health services.

T F 5. Producing health-care services efficiently is one of the major problems in the health-care industry.

T F 6. The elasticity of demand for special medical-care services may vary. For example, the demand for a life-saving surgery may be highly price inelastic.

T F 7. The demand for health services has increased because of technological advancements that have lowered the cost and raised the quality of health services.

T F 8. Less-than-full cost pricing to the individual consumer of health services tends to increase the demand for health-care services.

T F 9. The demand for medical services will be substantially affected by changes in relative prices because there are many good substitutes for medical services.

T F 10. In the long run, the supply curve of physicians is inelastic.

T F 11. If supply is price inelastic, an increase in demand for physicians in the short run will increase prices relatively more than quantity of physicians.

T F 12. The American Medical Association, although alleged to have control over the supply of physicians, actually exerts no control over the supply of physicians.

T F 13. Given increasing per unit costs, a firm would be willing to sell additional output only at a higher price.

T F 14. If new medical technology is introduced, then the same quantity of hospital services will be supplied only at a higher price.

T F 15. Hospitals, by joining together in a given area and specializing in certain services, could likely provide better services at lower costs.

T F 16. The U.S. health care system has shortcomings with respect to the efficient supply of service but not the equitable distribution of the services.

T F 17. Most Americans have health insurance coverage that will pay for almost all of the cost of an ordinary and a prolonged illness.

T F 18. A program of national health insurance providing universal coverage would shift almost the entire financial burden of health care costs to the government, and redistribute income from taxpayers to the users of health services.

T F 19. Consumers with health insurance coverage tend to acquire an efficient quantity of health-care services.

T F 20. Under a prospective plan based on a negotiated schedule of fixed fees, incentives would be provided for health-care services to be supplied in an efficient manner.

T F 21. The most significant factor contributing to the growth in health care expenditures in recent years is price inflation.

T F 22. National health expenditures have grown at a slower rate than Gross Domestic Product during the 1990's.

T F 23. Medicare is the federal health care program for the children of single parents who receive Aid to Families with Dependent Children (AFDC).

T F 24. The number of Americans without health insurance increased from 15 million to about 40 million between 1980 and the mid-1990's.

T F 25. Like many of the industrialized nations of Europe, the United States has a national health insurance program. It is administered by the Health Security Administration.

MULTIPLE-CHOICE QUESTIONS Select the one best answer

1. Most of the growth in spending on personal health care services is due to:
   a. substantial increases in the quality of services offered.
   b. general and medical care inflation.
   c. population growth.
   d. increased consumer incomes.

2. Personal health care costs would tend to rise if:
   a. the supply of health services increases more than the demand for health services.
   b. the demand for health services increases more than the supply of health services.
   c. the supply of health services increases and demand decreases.
   d. the demand for health services decreases and supply remains unchanged.

3. The demand for health-care services is influenced by:
   a. physicians who are suppliers as well as demanders of health-care.
   b. consumers who lack adequate information.
   c. people who benefit from health-care services but do not pay for the service.
   d. the unpredictability of illness.
   e. All of the above.

4. The health care industry's major problem is:
   a. inefficiency in the supply of health services.
   b. too many physicians.
   c. inequity in the distribution of health-care services.
   d. Both (a) and (c).

5. Elasticity of demand for health services tends to be low because:
   a. as prices decline the quantities demanded increase.
   b. increased per capita income decreases demand.
   c. there are few substitutes for health services.
   d. All of the above.

6. If the demand for health services is inelastic, this implies that:
   a. a given percentage increase in price is accompanied by a smaller percentage change in quantity demanded.
   b. the demand for health services is increasing relative to the supply of health services.
   c. an increase in the supply of health services.
   d. a decrease in the demand for health services.

Answer Questions 7–9 using the following diagram showing the supply and demand for health services.

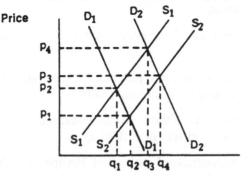

Health Services per Month

7. If D_1D_1 and S_1S_1 are the initial demand and supply curves for health services, the equilibrium price and quantity will be:
   a. p_2 and q_2, respectively.
   b. p_1 and q_1, respectively.
   c. p_2 and q_1, respectively.
   d. p_1 and q_2, respectively.

8. The increase in demand from D_1D_1 to D_2D_2 might be due to any of the following *except:*
   a. an increase in per capita income.
   b. increased coverage provided by Medicare and Medicaid.
   c. more efficient utilization of human and capital resources in the health services industry.
   d. new health products and services being offered.

9. The increase in supply from S_1S_1 to S_2S_2 might be due to any of the following *except:*
   a. more efficient utilization of human and capital resources in the health services industry.
   b. relaxation of restrictions placed upon the types of medical services that may be performed by paramedics.
   c. improved medical technology.
   d. a rise in the prices of resources relative to their productivity in producing health services.

10. Increases in the supply of physicians have been restricted by:
    a. limited medical facilities and entrance quotas.
    b. the long training period required to become an M.D.
    c. limited numbers of hospitals providing intern training.
    d. All of the above.

11. The supply of physicians is:
    a. inelastic in the short run and thus an increase in the short-run demand for physicians will have an impact primarily on prices.
    b. inelastic in the long run and thus an increase in demand is expected to increase the number of physicians.
    c. elastic in the long run and thus an increase in demand is expected to increase the number of physicians.
    d. Both (a) and (c).

12. The median income of physicians increased approximately 8 percent between 1975 and 1987 because:
    a. foreign-trained physicians were not allowed to practice medicine in the United States.
    b. supply increased too rapidly to prevent rapidly rising prices for physicians' services.
    c. of the restrictions on entry into the field of medicine.
    d. the supply of physicians in the short run is elastic.

13. The short-run supply curve of hospital services slopes to the right because:
    a. each additional worker adds the same amount to cost and a decreasing amount to output, thus cost per unit of output rises.
    b. each additional worker adds an increasing amount to cost and an increasing amount to output, thus cost per unit of output rises.
    c. the firm would be willing to sell additional units only at higher prices when the cost per unit of output increases.
    d. Both (a) and (c).

14. The efficiency of the present health-care system could be improved by:
    a. the development of group practices and health centers.
    b. the shortening of the period and cost of medical training.
    c. reducing entry barriers.
    d. the use of paramedical personnel.
    e. All of the above.

15. The cost of an immunization program to prevent the spread of a communicable disease:
    a. should be paid for entirely by the government.
    b. should be paid for entirely by the individuals receiving immunizations.
    c. should be divided between private individuals and taxpayers so that the ratio of marginal private benefits to marginal spillover benefits equals the ratio of private costs to taxpayer costs.
    d. is always less than the benefits.

16. Most national health insurance proposals are intended to:
    a. ensure everyone access to "adequate" health-care.
    b. eliminate the financial burden connected with the acquisition of health services.
    c. to control and limit rising health-care costs.
    d. All of the above.

17. Pro-competition health insurance proposals would:
    a. provide an incentive in the form of a cash rebate to employees selecting a low-cost health insurance plan.
    b. decrease the price of health-care services to users.
    c. cause consumers to be less efficient in the purchase of health-care services.
    d. discourage private health insurance companies from offering consumers a wide range of health insurance plans.

18. To restrain the rise in Medicare expenditures the government:
    a. placed limits on inpatient hospital cost per admission.
    b. required Medicare patients to enroll in prospective payment health-care organizations.
    c. replaced a prospective payment system with a retrospective payment system.
    d. All of the above.

19. Even a very competitive health-care industry may not perform satisfactorily because:
    a. externalities are created in the consumption of health-care services.
    b. the resulting distribution of health-care services may be inequitable.
    c. of third party payments.
    d. of the high price inelasticities of demand and supply.
    e. All of the above.

20. The economic performance of the health-care industry could be improved by implementing:
    a. a fee-for-service payment plan.
    b. a repayment plan based on a negotiated schedule of fixed fees.
    c. a third-parties payment system.
    d. None of the above.

21. Which of the following has been the leading contributor to the continuing growth in health care expenditures?
    a. population growth.
    b. price inflation.
    c. competition between health care providers.
    d. all other factors.

22. Which of the following programs provide health care for the poor and is administered by state governments?
    a. Medicare.
    b. Medicaid.
    c. Social Security.
    d. Workers Compensation.

23. It is estimated that approximately _____ million Americans do not have health insurance.
    a. 1 million.
    b. 15 million.
    c. 20 million.
    d. 40 million.

24. Since 1980, the average growth rate in the number of doctors in the U.S. has
    a. increased faster than the rate of population growth.
    b. lagged behind the rate of population growth.
    c. continued to decline at a rapid rate.
    d. remained virtually unchanged.

25. Which of the following is a primary goal of the proposed Health Security Act?
    a. to ensure everyone access to adequate health care.
    b. to eliminate the financial burden connected to the acquisition of health services.
    c. to control and limit the rise in health care costs.
    d. All of the above.

PROBLEMS

1. Suppose that the demand for health-care services is price inelastic and that the AMA is successful in using its monopoly power to restrict the supply of health-care services.

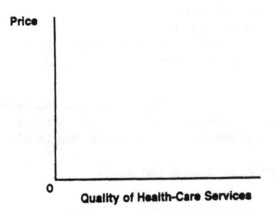

    a. Using supply and demand curves, show on the following graph the situation described above.
    b. The price of health-care services will _____
    c. The quantity of health-care services consumed will _____
    d. Total expenditures for health-care services will _____

2. In Chapter 4, the use of the equimarginal principle to allocate resources among alternative crime prevention activities was discussed. Review the equimarginal principle and then consider the following hypothetical data concerning the benefits from a county heath program consisting of ambulance services, an immunization program, and cafe inspection.

Benefits Received for County Health Program

Units of Each Activity*	Total Benefits of Ambulance Service	Marginal Benefits of Ambulance Service	Total Benefts of Immunization	Marginal Benefits of Immunization	Total Benefits of Cafe Inspection	Marginal Benefits of Cafe Inspection
1	$ 50,000	$ 50,000	$ 55,000	$ 55,000	$ 40,000	$ 40,000
2	98,000	_____	100,000	_____	75,000	_____
3	142,000	_____	135,000	_____	105,000	_____
4	180,000	_____	160,000	_____	133,000	_____
5	210,000	_____	180,000	_____	159,000	_____
6	230,000	_____	195,000	_____	183,000	_____
7	240,000	_____	205,000	_____	203,000	_____
8	242,000	_____	210,000	_____	213,000	_____

*Each additional unit of each activity costs $1,000.

a. Complete the above table by computing the marginal benefits of ambulance services, the immunization program, and the cafe inspection program.

b. Suppose you are the Director of the County Health Program and you have a budget of $18,000. How many units of each activity should be produced?
   _____ units of ambulance service at a cost of $_____
   _____ units of immunization services at a cost of $_____
   _____ units of cafe inspection services at a cost of $_____

c. If you were now to decrease expenditures on immunization by $1,000 and increase expenditures on cafe inspection by $1,000, would society be better or worse off? why?

3. The director of the University Hospital has the following information concerning the benefits from employing various numbers of nurses, paramedical personnel, and physicians to provide health services on campus.

Marginal Benefits form Health Care Services Provided by

Units	Employing One More Nurse	Employing One More Physician	Employing one More Paramedic
1	$ 81,000 _____	$ 300,000 _____	$ 48,000 _____
2	63,000 _____	240,000 _____	40,000 _____
3	45,000 _____	180,000 _____	32,000 _____
4	27,000 _____	120,000 _____	24,000 _____
5	18,000 _____	90,000 _____	16,000 _____
6	9,000 _____	60,000 _____	8,000 _____

The cost of each nurse is $9,000; the cost of each physician is $30,000; and the cost of each paramedic is $8,000.

a. Complete the above table by computing the marginal benefit per dollar spent in the blanks to the right of each column.

b. If the director of the University Hospital has $218,000 to spend on the labor services of nurses, physicians, and paramedical personnel, he should allocate his budget to employ:

_____ nurses at a total cost of $_____.

_____ physicians at a total cost of $_____.

_____ paramedics at a total cost of $_____.

4. Suppose you are scheduled to take a vocabulary exam in six hours. The table below indicates how fast you can memorize new vocabulary.

Output Hours of Study	(Words Memorized)	Additions to Output
0	0	0
1	30	30
2	65	—
3	90	—
4	110	—
5	122	—
6	127	—

a. Complete the third column of the table.

b. Name one input which is being held constant in this illustration.

c. What happens to output as study time increases by equal amounts? What is this relationship called?

ANSWERS TO SELF-TEST

PUZZLE

Across		Down	
1.	Hospital	2.	Per Capita
3.	Prospective	4.	Substitution
9.	Elasticity	5.	Diminishing
11.	Catastrophic	6.	Tastes
13.	Inflation	7.	Preferences
14.	Technology	8.	Medicaid
15.	Service	10.	Medicare
		12.	Investment

TRUE-FALSE QUESTIONS

1.	F	6.	T	11.	T	16.	F	21.	T
2.	F	7.	F	12.	F	17.	F	22.	F
3.	F	8.	T	13.	T	18.	T	23.	F
4.	T	9.	F	14.	F	19.	F	24.	T
5.	T	10.	F	15.	T	20.	T	25.	F

MULTIPLE-CHOICE QUESTIONS

1.	b	6.	a	11.	d	16.	d	21.	b
2.	b	7.	c	12.	c	17.	a	22.	b
3.	e	8.	c	13.	d	18.	a	23.	d
4.	d	9.	d	14.	e	19.	e	24.	a
5.	c	10.	d	15.	c	20.	b	25.	d

PROBLEMS

1. a.

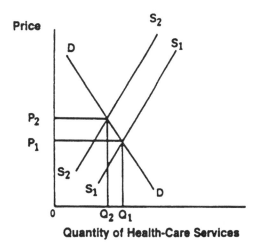

Quantity of Health-Care Services

b. rise
c. decrease
d. increase, since the demand for health-care services is price inelastic.

2. a.

Marginal Benefits of Ambulance Service	Marginal Benefits of Immunization	Marginal Benefits of Cafe Inspection
$ 50,000	$ 55,000	$ 40,000
48,000	45,000	35,000
44,000	35,000	30,000
38,000	25,000	28,000
30,000	20,000	26,000
20,000	15,000	24,000
10,000	10,000	20,000
2,000	5,000	10,000

b.
6 units of ambulance service at a cost of	$ 6,000
5 units of immunization services at a cost of	5,000
7 units of cafe inspection services at a cost of	7,000
	$18,000

c. Society would be worse off. By decreasing expenditures on immunization by $1,000 society would lose $20,000 worth of benefits and gain only $10,000 worth of benefits by spending the additional $1,000 on cafe inspection.

3. a.

Marginal Benefit per Dollar Spent from Employing One More

Units	Nurse	Physician	Paramedic
1	$9	$10	$6
2	7	8	5
3	5	6	4
4	3	4	3
5	2	3	2
6	1	2	1

b.
4 nurses at a total cost of	$ 36,000
5 physicians at a total cost of	150,000
4 paramedics at a total cost of	32,000
	$218,000

4. a. 0, 30, 35, 25, 20, 12, 5
    b. Aptitude
    c. Output increases, initially at an increasing rate and then after the second hour of study at a decreasing rate. Marginal output first increases (30 to 35) and then decreases (35 to 25, etc.). Principle of diminishing marginal returns.

Chapter 7
●Poverty Problems

Is Poverty Necessary?

LEARNING OBJECTIVES

After studying this issue, you should be able to:

1. Define poverty in both relative and absolute terms.

2. Determine what progress has been made in the reduction of poverty in the United States during the past 30 years.

3. Identify the poor by social and economic characteristics.

4. Argue whether or not poverty in the United States is mainly an income distribution problem.

5. Explain, using a Lorenz curve, what is meant by income inequality; discuss the nature of U.S. income distribution and the changes in it over time.

6. Explain, using a competitive resource market graph, what is meant by the phrase, "workers are paid about what they are worth to employers."

7. Explain how the pattern of resource ownership, the prices paid to resources, and the levels of employment contribute to the incidence of poverty.

8. Explain how programs to increase the productivity of the employable poor, and income-support programs, help to alleviate poverty.

9. Describe current government low-income programs and evaluate them in terms of the goals for low-income programs.

10. Distinguish between price floors and price ceilings and illustrate the consequences of each in terms of quantity supplied and quantity demanded.

11. Evaluate the effectiveness of government control of prices in a market economy as a method of helping the poor.

12. Explain how a negative income tax plan works and compare it with current low-income programs.

CHAPTER ORIENTATION

Some people argue that poverty is an absolute income-level problem, while others contend that it is a relative income-level problem. The approach taken in this chapter is that poverty is both. Thus, to "fight" poverty, persons and families have to be brought up to or above an arbitrary absolute level of income, and the "gap" between the poor and the rich must be narrowed. You should examine the chapter's data or evidence in regard to both poverty problems.

The poverty problem in the United States is essentially an income distribution problem. With our level of income and an operational definition of poverty, a redistribution of income could eliminate or, at the very least, greatly reduce the incidence of poverty. The method of redistribution is critical to both the relative reduction of poverty and to the efficient allocation of resources. Policies designed to alter the distribution of income should interfere as little as possible with the market allocation of productive resources. Such a redistribution is not easily accomplished.

Being poor is not being able to purchase what you want. What determines the amount of money a family has to spend? A family's income is determined mainly by the quantity and quality of the resources it can exchange in the market times the price per unit. To this earned income, public and private transfers are added and taxes, loan repayments, and interest are subtracted. In a pure market economy without private or public transfer payments, all income is derived from the sale of resources. Thus, poverty is caused by few or no resources available for sale, no demand for services actually available and/or very low prices for the resources available. How, then, is it possible to work and still be poor? A worker with a low-paying job will probably be poor.

In competitive markets, labor is paid what it is worth to the employer. In economic terminology, the wage rate is determined by the worker's marginal revenue productivity. That is, what the worker contributes to the receipts of the employer. A person's income, then, is closely connected to the productivity of the person. A person who can contribute very little to the receipts of the employer will be paid a low wage, and likely live in poverty. Differences in inherited real property or claims on real property also contribute to low income and differences in income.

The economic analysis of the causes of poverty should suggest to you two governmental approaches to eliminate or alleviate poverty. The first involves programs to increase the productivity of the poor, and the second involves a plan, such as the negative income tax plan, that will guarantee a minimum level of income for all persons.

CONSIDER THIS:

Drawing the Poverty Line[1]

At first glance, creating a "poverty line" may seem like something anybody could understand: Figure out how much money people need to live decently. But what exactly do we mean by "decently"? Enough food, certainly. A clean, dry place to live, probably. But what about a telephone? How about a television set... color? A bank account? A hot lunch? A car? A separate bedroom for the children? What about health insurance, day care, immunization?

The annual poverty line income—still computed according to a 30-year-old formula as three times the cost of the Agriculture Department's "economy diet"—was $13,924 for a family of four to 1991, the latest year for which full statistics are available. There were 35.7 million people in the United States, or 14.2 percent, living below it.

Last year a 13-member National Academy of Sciences panel began a congressionally mandated examination of the poverty line, seeking possible ways of changing the calculation so that it will more accurately describe who in the nation is poor. Its findings are due by July 1994, and will be eagerly awaited. This is because the poverty line is as important as any number in the United States, what NAS project director Connie Citro called a "leading indicator of our self-image." It is a bureaucratic necessity, the starting point in calculating eligibility for billions of dollars worth of social programs. Food stamps, Medicaid and some types of federal housing are just a few of the items pegged to the poverty line. But it is also a political bludgeon. The fact that 1.2 percent more people were living below the poverty line in 1991 than in 1980 gives Democrats a reason to damn 12 years of "Republican trickle-down economics" as a fraud. For many Republicans it is the poverty line itself that is the fraud.

The poverty line can be a way to measure society's progress, or it can be a way to document society's failures. Many experts think it is too low. Others think it is too high or, worse, meaningless. Everyone agrees, however, that there is nothing simple about it, and there never was.

---

[1]Guy Gugliotta, "Drawing the Poverty Line: A Calculation of Necessity and Self-Image," *The Washington Post*, May 10, 1993, p. A3. Copyright 1993 The Washington Post. Reprinted by permission.

The original poverty measure was conceived in the mid-1960s by Mollie Orshansky, an economist working in the Social Security Administration. It is based on the idea, deemed accurate at that time, that the average American family spent one-third of its cash income on food. Orshansky matched that concept with Agriculture Department studies describing an "economy" food plan that poor people could use for survival. She multiplied the plan's costs by three and produced the number that, with occasional fine-tuning and annual adjustments for inflation, has served as the "poverty line" ever since. In 1963, the base year for calculation, the annual poverty income for a family of four was $3,128, and 19.5 percent of all people nationwide lived below it.

One of the first tasks the academy panel will have is to decide whether to choose between an Orshansky-style "absolute standard," which sets a money hurdle and urges people to earn their way over it, and a "relative standard," which moves upward as a percentage of a national living standard. The most often discussed relative standard would simply place the poverty line at 50 percent of the median income of American families. This figure ($21,528 in 1991) would be useful in comparing U.S. poverty levels with those of other countries, because income figures for most nations could be derived from national accounts statistics.

The trouble with relative standards, however, is that they are "moving targets": No matter what the median income is, 50 percent of it will be the poverty line. "Americans like goals," said University of Wisconsin sociologist Robert Hauser, an NAS panel member. "How are you going to win a 'war on poverty' if the poverty line keeps climbing?" Hauser said he preferred an "updated" absolute standard that would include other components besides food. This would retain the Orshansky model's major strength—a fixed target one can shoot at. And it would attack the standard's major weakness—it is a "timebound" formula whose original flaws worsen as the years pass.

Urban Institute statistician Patricia Ruggles, for instance, argues that the Orshansky standard does not even have its own internal integrity. The portion of income spent on food has sunk below 20 percent during the past 30 years, she said, and "as we continue to use a multiplier of three, the discrepancy widens between the poverty line and the people we think of as 'poor'."

Updating, however, raises questions of its own. The NAS panel will need to examine the view held by many conservatives that periodic updating is simply a clever way for liberals to introduce a relative standard. "The fact is that the [proposed poverty] standards...are much higher than existed for most people [of whatever class] in 1960," said Robert Rector, a Heritage Foundation policy analyst for welfare issues. "Very few Americans realize that the standards of today are standards that their grandparents, or even their parents, couldn't have met."

Updating, Rector said, will likely lift the purchasing power of today's poor person above that of most middle-class people during the 1950s: "Basically what [reform advocates] are saying is that Ozzie and Harriet were poor." Not really, said Northwestern University sociologist Christopher Jencks. He said the Rector position is "half-right." Yes, poor people are bigger and better fed and more of them have indoor plumbing, cars, telephones, television sets and other assets than they did 30 or 40 years ago, but that is not the whole story.

Early in the century, he noted, Henry Ford designed his first assembly line so illiterates could do the work. Bosses expect workers to read and write now. In 1950, he added, "a substantial number of people didn't have telephones," and prospective bosses "wouldn't expect to be able to call you up to offer you a job." They do now.

"When you can't have or can't do something that 95 percent of the population has or does, you are in some sense a nonparticipant in society," Jencks said. "Yes, the goalposts are being moved, but in many cases it's not liberal academics who are doing it, it's circumstances and history."

If the NAS panel decides finally that the poverty criteria should be updated, then the fun really begins. Experts generally agree that food and housing will be included on the needs side, probably along with transportation (cars in the country and suburbs), energy (electricity and gas if needed), child care (if needed). "We're also going to have to do something with medical care," Hauser said. But what? Do you count how much medical care costs, or do you count only the cost of insurance? Do you count how much a poor person spends before he can apply for Medicaid, or do you just count the value of the Medicaid? "A real good way to become poor is to get sick," Ruggles said. "You can't work, your income goes down. You sell the TV, you sell the car, you sell the house and then, when you're broke, you get Medicaid."

And then there's the income side. The Orshansky measure is based on cash income before taxes. It does not add Medicaid, food stamps or other non-cash benefits (another big conservative complaint), nor does it subtract taxes (a big liberal complaint).

Finally, there is the unresolved question of how to treat assets. Do you need a television set, a telephone, air-conditioning, a car? If you count assets as potential income [if you sell them], then you should probably count their maintenance as a need: "In many cases it's maintenance of the asset that eats the money," Jencks said. "Everybody has a flush toilet, but poor people's toilets tend not to flush. What they need is...a plumber."

Ruggles said that any reassessment of the poverty line will lift the threshold by as much as 50 percent—substantially increasing the number of people regarded as poor. Rector said researchers should simply ask who's hungry, who lives in overcrowded or unheated housing, who is inadequately clothed or who needs a car and does not have one. "It would be a tiny percentage," he said.

Consider These Questions:

1. What are the inherent differences between absolute and relative measures of poverty as discussed above? Which do you feel is a more accurate measure of poverty in the United States? Why?

2. The portion of family income spent on food has declined since the original poverty line was first defined. To maintain internal consistency, how should the poverty multiplier be adjusted? Has this adjustment been made? Why or why not?

3. How does the concept of "poverty" relate to the concept of "standard of living?" Would someone who lives just below today's poverty line necessarily have been considered poor 50 years ago? Why or why not?

4. Does the current definition of poverty consider transfer payments received by the poor? Provide an economic argument for how family income should be measured.

STUDY QUESTIONS

1. Mary Nelson lives with her three children in Muncie, Indiana. Mary's annual income is $14,000. Are the Nelsons poor? Why is an operational definition of poverty needed in this case, and in the general sense?

2. Has the incidence of poverty changed since the 1960's? Explain.

3. Discuss the likelihood that a family with the following characteristic is poor—consider each separately.
   a. college graduate as family head
   b. working
   c. over 65 years of age
   d. black family

4. "We could, if we would, eliminate poverty in the U.S." Is this statement true? Does it tell us anything about the relevance of the scarcity concept to economic analysis?

5. Have the income shares in the United States changed during the last several decades? Explain using a Lorenz curve.

6. ''Workers are paid about what they are worth to employers.'' What is 0Q person-hours of labor (see graph) worth to the employer? At that wage, how many person-hours will be supplied? What is the relationship between quantity demanded and quality supplied at the wage determined by 0Q's worth to the employer?

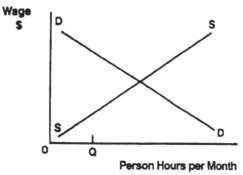

7. Can the ownership pattern of resources give rise to an unequal distribution of income? Explain. Is it possible to be employed and poor? Explain.

8. Using what you know about the determinants of income, explain how efforts to increase the productivity of the employable poor and income support programs, help to alleviate poverty.

9. To what extent have federal government outlays on low-income programs changed in nominal and real terms between 1980 and 1993? Have these programs produced the desired results of an effective welfare program? Explain.

10. Would a guaranteed annual income plan in the form of a negative income tax scheme tend to be more efficient than the current United States public assistance program? Explain.

PUZZLE Complete the following crossword puzzle.

Poverty Problems

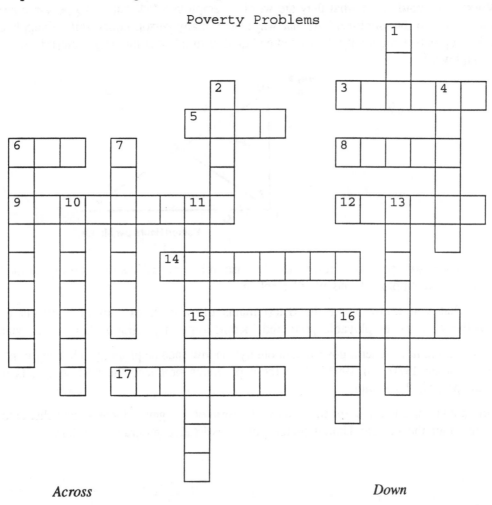

Across

3. Labor _____ is the quantity of labor offered to the market per unit of time by workers.
5. Job Training Partnership Act. (Initials)
6. Cash payment program for the blind and disabled. (Initials)
8. The minimum wage is a price _____.
9. The _____ pattern of resources may depend upon factors such as inheritance, luck, and propensities to accumulate.
12. The _____ for labor is dependent upon the marginal revenue product of labor.
14. A _____ income tax program would provide payments to households with incomes below an established guaranteed level.
15. The ratio of actual earnings to earning capacity is called the capacity _____ rate.
17. A rent control law is an example of a price _____.

Down

1. The change in revenue experienced by a firm when hiring one additional worker. (Initials)
2. The Food _____ program provides about 75% of government outlays for food and nutrition assistance for the poor.
4. The _____ Curve shows the cumulative percentage of total family income going to the lowest percentiles of families.
6. Any price ceiling will result in a _____.
7. A price floor in a market economy will always result in this.
10. City which has experienced the effects of rent control laws since World War II. (2 words)
11. Income _____ is graphically shown with a Lorenz Curve.
13. About 7.2 _____ families lived in poverty during 1992.
16. Cash payment program to poor households with children. (Initials)

TRUE-FALSE QUESTIONS Circle T (true) or F (false)

T F 1. The United States government defines the "minimum need" component of poverty's definition by determining a minimum food budget and multiplying its dollar cost by three.

T F 2. Since 1970, the poverty rate has remained about the same varying between 11 and 13 percent.

T F 3. The percentage of the population that is poor in the mid-1990's is greater than the percentage in the early 1960's.

T F 4. Incidence of poverty among blacks is higher than the average incidence of poverty.

T F 5. A job guarantees that a person or family will not be poor.

T F 6. A majority of persons that live in poverty remain in poverty over a long period of time.

T F 7. There is not enough income in the United States to go around; therefore, some people have to live in poverty.

T F 8. Middle-income groups receive about the same percent of income today as the did two decades ago.

T F 9. In competitive markets, a worker is not paid what he is worth.

T F 10. When a worker is paid less than what he is worth to his employer, he is also paid less than what he is worth to other employers.

T F 11. When a worker is paid less than what she is worth to her employer, wages tend to fall.

T F 12. Differences in capacity utilization rates explain most of the existing income inequality.

T F 13. Inheritance cannot explain any of the differences in capital resource ownership.

T F 14. People have the same tendencies in regard to the desire to save and accumulate capital resources.

T F 15. Income support programs are essential if no one is to live in poverty because some who are poor cannot produce at all and others who are poor cannot produce enough.

T F 16. The Job Training Partnership Act (JTPA) requires that a major portion of the block grant be used for training the economically disadvantaged.

T F 17. Medicaid accounts for about 85 percent of the federal outlays for health care services directed toward low-income groups.

T F 18. Approximately 70 percent of the federal government outlays on food and nutrition assistance is in support of the federal food stamp program.

T F 19. When adjusted for inflation low-income programs increase by 13 percent for the period of 1980-1993.

T F 20. Federal spending on employment and training programs for the poor were cut in half between 1980 and 1993.

T F 21. In 1993, spending on low-income programs accounted for a smaller percent of total federal budget than they did in 1980.

T F 22. Federal low-income programs provide a minimum standard of living for persons who otherwise would be poor and provide opportunities for persons currently living in poverty to move out of poverty.

T F 23. A guaranteed annual income plan in the form of a negative income tax scheme would tend to encourage recipients of government subsidies to earn income.

T F 24. There are three variables common to every negative tax scheme—guaranteed annual income (Y), the negative tax rate (r), and the break-even level of income (B). These variables are related by the equation y = rB. Thus, assuming the guaranteed level of income is $5,000 and the negative income tax rate is 50 percent, a family earning $12,000 a year would receive $5,000 from the government.

T F 25. If the guaranteed level of income is $5,000 and the negative income tax rate is 50 percent, then the break-even level of income would be $10,000.

T F 26. Rent controls contribute to the homeless problem in large cities.

T F 27. Price floors create market shortages.

T F 28. Price ceilings create market surpluses.

T F 29. Shortages and inefficiencies tend to result from rent controls in housing markets.

T F 30. Any government policy which does not allow the market to establish an equilibrium price will result in either a shortage or surplus.

MULTIPLE-CHOICE QUESTIONS Select the one best answer

1. Poverty:
   a. is not easily defined.
   b. is concerned with the relationship between minimum needs of people and their ability to satisfy these needs.
   c. is essentially an income distribution problem.
   d. All of the above.

2. The percentage of the United States population living in poverty:
   a. declined during the 1960s and most of the 1970s.
   b. increased in the 1980s.
   c. is lower today than in 1960.
   d. All of the above.

3. The incidence or burden of poverty falls most heavily on:
   a. families headed by persons 65 years and over.
   b. white families.
   c. nonfarm families.
   d. None of the above.

4. If the general economy is expanding, a person living in poverty today is:
   a. highly likely to live in poverty next year.
   b. less likely to live in poverty five years later.
   c. highly likely to live in poverty five years later.
   d. Both (a) and (b).

5. Within the next three years the elimination of poverty as it is currently defind by the U.S. Department of Labor is possible:
   a. in the United States but not in other countries of the world.
   b. in the United States and some other countries but not in all countries of the world.
   c. in any country that is determined to accomplish it.
   d. in all countries if the rich countries will help out the poor ones.

6. Income equality:
   a. is shown by a 45-degree line on the graph of a Lorenz curve.
   b. increased during the 1930s and the years of World War II.
   c. among families means that any given percent of families receive an equal percent of family income.
   d. All of the above.

Questions 7 through 9 are based on the following diagram:

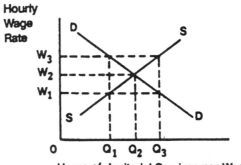

7. The demand curve for labor shows:
   a. that employers are willing to pay $0W_2$ for $0Q_2$ units.
   b. that $0Q_3$ units of labor is worth $0W_3$ to employers.
   c. the quantity of labor that will be placed on the market at different wage rates.
   d. Both (a) and (b).

8. What is $0Q_1$ hours of janitorial service worth to an employer?
   a. $0W_1$
   b. $0W_2$
   c. $0W_3$
   d. Insufficient information

9. At wage rate $0W_1$:
   a. the quantity of labor demanded is greater than the quantity supplied thus the wage rates will fall.
   b. labor is paid about what it is worth to any employer.
   c. $0Q_3$ units of labor want to work at this wage rate.
   d. a surplus exists.
   e. None of the above.

10. The poor, generally speaking, have:
    a. no economic resources.
    b. small quantities of resources that are often of low quality.
    c. plenty of resources but do not use them.
    d. plenty of resources that society values highly but the resources command very low prices (or wages).

11. A major cause of poverty in the United States is:
    a. inflation.
    b. exploitation of workers by capitalists.
    c. the low productivity of people's resources.
    d. the scarcity of labor and capital in existence.

12. Fundamentally, an unequal distribution of income among the population of the United States rests on:
    a. unsound monetary policies of the Federal Reserve system.
    b. laziness on the part of the poor.
    c. restrictive labor union policies.
    d. an unequal distribution of ownership of labor and capital resources.

13. Income inequality is due to differences in:
    a. capacity utilization rates among people.
    b. earnings capacity among people.
    c. actual earnings relative to capacity earnings among people.
    d. None of the above.

14. Capital resources are unequally distributed among the U.S. population because:
    a. most of the capital accumulated by a family can be inherited by its children.
    b. differences in luck or fortuitous events such as the discovery of oil or other minerals on some properties, but not others.
    c. None of the above.
    d. Both (a) and (b).

15. A comprehensive antipoverty program would include:
    a. price supports for farmers.
    b. minimum wage legislation.
    c. measures to increase the productivity of the poor.
    d. a guaranteed minimum annual income program.
    e. Both (c) and (d).

16. Income-support programs are required if no one is to live in poverty because some people:
    a. are unproductive due to old age, disability, and illness.
    b. have low productivity due to poor skills and limited knowledge.
    c. prefer not to work.
    d. Both (a) and (b).
    e. None of the above.

17. Federal outlays on low-income programs:
    a. grew 44 percent after adjusting for inflation between 1980 and 1993.
    b. grew approximately 13 percent after adjusting for inflation between 1980 and 1993.
    c. accounted for less of the total federal budget in 1993 that in 1980.
    d. Both (a) and (b).
    e. Both (b) and (c).

18. Successful federal programs for low-income persons would:
    a. provide a minimum living standard for persons who otherwise would live below the minimum.
    b. enable poor persons to move out of poverty.
    c. provide the opportunity for persons currently not living in poverty to remain above the poverty level.
    d. All of the above.
    e. None of the above.

Questions 19 and 20 are based on the following statement;

Suppose that nonfarm families of four are to be supported at a minimum level of $11,600 per year and that negative taxes are paid to people on the basis of $11,600 minus 50 percent of income earned.

19. The income level at which negative taxes become zero will be:
    a. $2,280
    b. $2,850
    c. $5,700
    d. $11,400
    e. $22,800

20. An increase to 60 percent in the percent of income earned used in computing the negative tax will:
    a. reduce the zero tax income level to $19,000.
    b. increase the spread between the minimum support income level and that at which negative taxes become zero.
    c. reduce incentives to work.
    d. increase incentives to work.
    e. Both (a) and (c).

21. Which of the following will result as a consequence of an increase in the minimum wage?
    a. all workers will remain employed at a higher wage.
    b. some workers will become unemployed.
    c. a few workers will leave the labor market.
    d. employers are given an incentive to increase worker training.

Questions below refer to the following graph for housing units

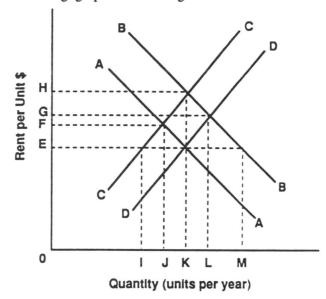

22. In the above diagram, the demand curve and the supply curve for housing units are AA and DD. As the result of an increase in incomes and an increase in the price of lumber:
    a. supply decreased to CC, demand decreased to BB, and the equilibrium price is unchanged at 0E.
    b. supply increased to CC, demand increased to BB, and the equilibrium price decreased to 0H.
    c. demand increased to BB, supply decreased to CC, and the equilibrium price increased to 0H.
    d. None of the above.

23. With price 0E as a price ceiling, the net effect on the housing industry of an increase in incomes and an increase in the price of lumber will be:
    a. an efficient reallocation of resources.
    b. a shortage, IM.
    c. a surplus, IM.
    d. an inefficient allocation of resources.
    e. Both (b) and (d).

24. If there is a change in demand only, what is the new equilibrium price?
    a. 0E
    b. 0F
    c. 0G
    d. 0H

25. If there is a change in supply only, what is the new equilibrium quantity of housing units?
   a. OJ
   b. OK
   c. OL
   d. OM

PROBLEMS

1. The curve of income inequality, called _____, shows what share of total family income is distributed among given proportions of the nation's families.

Percent of Income Received by Each Fifth

Family Income Rank	Year 1	Year 2
Lowest fifth	5%	10%
Second fifth	10%	15%
Middle fifth	15%	15%
Fourth fifth	20%	20%
Highest fifth	50%	40%

a. Based on the hypothetical data above concerning the distribution of family income in the economy in Years 1 and 2, complete the following table:

Cumulative Percent of Income Received

Cumulative Percent of Families*	Year 1	Year 2
_____%	_____%	_____%
_____%	_____%	_____%
_____%	_____%	_____%
_____%	_____%	_____%
_____%	_____%	_____%

*Ranked from lowest to highest income families.

b. Using the data calculated in 1(a), plot and label on the following graph:
   (1) The line of income equality. What does it depict?
   (2) The Lorenz curves for Years 1 and 2. What do they depict? What has happened to the distribution of income between Year 1 and Year 2?

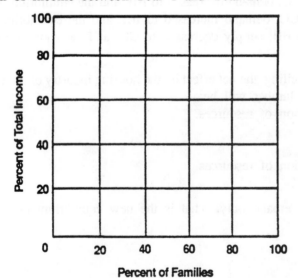

2. Suppose the government implements a negative income tax plan to deal with the poverty problem. The negative income tax rate is set at 50 percent and the break-even income level is set at $6,000.
   a. The guaranteed annual income level assured each family, regardless of the amount of income earned by the family, is $_____.
   b. Complete the following table by computing the negative tax subsidy and the disposable income.

Earned Income	Negative Tax Subsidy	Disposable Income
$ 0	_____	_____
$1,000	_____	_____
$2,000	_____	_____
$3,000	_____	_____
$4,000	_____	_____
$5,000	_____	_____
$6,000	_____	_____

   c. If the negative income tax rate were reduced from 50 percent to 40 percent, while the guaranteed annual income level is held constant, the cost of the negative income tax plan would _____.
   d. Given the guaranteed annual income level, reduction of the negative income tax rate from 50 percent to 40 percent, the incentives to work would be _____.
   e. Given the negative income tax rate of 50 percent, an increase in the guaranteed annual income level to $5,000 _____ the cost of the negative income tax plan.

3. Suppose DD represents employers' demand for secretarial services and SS represents the supply.

Hourly Wage Rate

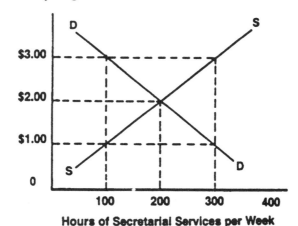

Hours of Secretarial Services per Week

   a. The demand curve for secretarial services, DD, shows _____, or, alternatively, how much an hour of secretarial services is worth at different possible employment levels.
   b. The supply curve of secretarial services, SS, shows _____.
   c. Under competitive conditions in the market for secretarial services, the equilibrium price paid per hour will be $_____ and the level of employment will be _____ hours per week.
   d. If secretaries are offered $1.00 per hour, the quantity supplied will be _____ hours per week, the quantity demanded will be _____ hours per week, and the resulting (shortage, surplus) will induce employers to _____.
   e. Alternatively, only 100 hours per week will be supplied at a wage rate of $1.00 per hour. But employers would be willing to pay as much as $_____ per hour for 100 hours of secretarial services per week. Since an hour of secretarial services contributes $_____ to employers' receipts and can be employed for only $_____, employers will be induced to increase the level of employment until _____.

ANSWERS TO SELF-TEST

PUZZLE

Across		Down	
3.	Supply	1.	MRP
5.	JTPA	2.	Stamp
6.	SSI	6.	Shortage
8.	Floor	7.	Surplus
9.	Ownership	10.	New York
12.	Demand	11.	Inequality
14.	Negative	13.	Million
15.	Utilization	16.	AFDC
17.	Ceiling		

TRUE-FALSE QUESTIONS

1.	T	7.	F	13.	F	19.	T	25.	T
2.	F	8.	T	14.	F	20.	T	26.	T
3.	F	9.	F	15.	T	21.	F	27.	F
4.	T	10.	T	16.	T	22.	F	28.	F
5.	F	11.	F	17.	T	23.	T	29.	T
6.	F	12.	F	18.	T	24.	F	30.	T

MULTIPLE-CHOICE QUESTIONS

1.	d	6.	d	11.	c	16.	d	21.	b
2.	d	7.	a	12.	d	17.	b	22.	c
3.	d	8.	c	13.	b	18.	d	23.	e
4.	b	9.	e	14.	d	19.	e	24.	c
5.	b	10.	b	15.	e	20.	e	25.	a

PROBLEMS

1. Lorenz Curve
    a.

Cumulative Percent of Families	Cumulative Percent of Income Received	
	Year 1	Year 2
20%	5%	10%
40%	15%	25%
60%	30%	40%
80%	50%	60%
100%	100%	100%

    b. (i)   The line of income equality depicts an equal distribution of income.
        (ii) The Lorenz curves show the actual distribution of income in years 1 and 2, respectively. The
              distribution of income between the two years has become more equal.

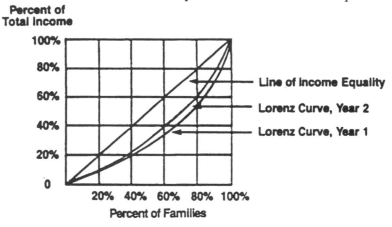

2. a. $3,000
    b.

Earned Income	Negative Tax Subsidy	Disposable Income
$ 0	$3,000	$3,000
$1,000	$2,500	$3,500
$2,000	$2,000	$4,000
$3,000	$1,500	$4,500
$4,000	$1,000	$5,000
$5,000	$ 500	$5,500
$6,000	$ 0	$6,000

    c. increase.
    d. increased.
    e. increase.

3. a. what employers are willing to pay at different quantities of secretarial services per week.
    b. the quantities of secretarial services that will be placed on the market at different wage rates.
    c. $2.00, 200.
    d. 100; 300; shortage; bid the wage rate back up to the equilibrium level, thus eliminating the shortage.
    e. $3.00, $3.00, $1.00, the wage rate is bid up to a level equal to the marginal revenue productivity.

Chapter 8
●Discrimination

The High Cost of Prejudice

LEARNING OBJECTIVES

After studying this issue, you should be able to:
After studying this issue, you should be able to:

1. Define market discrimination, identify its sources, and explain how it differs from exploitation.

2. Identify the major kinds of market discrimination and explain how each affects the allocation of resources.

3. Determine when wage and price differences are due to discrimination.

4. *Explain in what sense the market demand for labor is a derived demand and use marginal revenue product and the law of diminishing returns to explain the demand for labor curve's slope.

5. *Explain the slope of the labor supply curve using the substitutions effect, the income effect, and results of empirical studies.

6. Identify the individual's economic cost of discrimination and explain how some individuals may benefit from discrimination.

7. Identify, using a production possibilities curve, society's economic cost of market discrimination.

8. Identify the major kinds of nonmarket discrimination and distinguish market from nonmarket discrimination.

9. Identify and explain the major characteristics of effective policies to reduce market discrimination.

10. Evaluate the arguments for and against proposals to replace market determination of wages with comparable worth pay systems.

CHAPTER ORIENTATION

This chapter does not deal with all aspects of discrimination. It emphasizes the kinds of discrimination that might be found in the marketplace. Economists are concerned with discrimination because its presence indicates that the market is not working as it should. Discrimination reduces real output.

Market discrimination may be found in both produce and resource markets. In the product market, discrimination takes place when consumers are not treated equally, that is, when consumers pay different prices for the same product. Discrimination exists in the labor market, when persons are paid different wages, although they have the same productivity.

With few exceptions, the sources of market discrimination can be traced to monopoly power and to the tastes that some people have for discrimination. You should distinguish discrimination from exploitation which also originates from monopoly power.

The kinds of discrimination discussed in this chapter are age, employment, occupational, and race discrimination. In the presentation, examples of each kind of discrimination are given. You should study these examples carefully. Discrimination is not easy to detect. Differences in wages, job opportunities, etc.,

---

between two workers do not necessarily prove the case for discrimination since such differences may reflect differences in training and education.

There are both individual and social losses resulting from discrimination. It is clear that individual workers and consumers lose when they are discriminated against. Since discrimination means that resources are allocated on some other basis than productivity, it is also clear that this results in a loss of goods and services to society. You can illustrate this loss of goods and services to society, the dead-weight welfare loss, with the use of a production possibility curve.

Market discrimination is minimized under conditions of competition. With monopoly power obtained through legal and institutional barriers to competition, the ability to discriminate is enhanced. Without the ability to discriminate, the willingness to discriminate is essentially ineffectual. Thus, a comprehensive antidiscrimination policy would include, in addition to efforts to alter willingness to discriminate, measures to assure competitive product and resource markets.

Comparable worth legislation would extend the "equal pay for equal work" principal of the Equal Pay Act of 1963 to require "equal pay for similar or comparable work." The proposed legislation is controversial and a definitive conclusion of its merits is unlikely.

CONSIDER THIS:

Treading Water in the Secretarial Pool[1]

In many ways, Renee Jenkins exemplifies today's typical secretary.

She works in Denver for the federal government for $19,000 a year. She pays 100% of her health insurance and raises two children on her own. She answers to at least two bosses. She handles many standard clerical tasks—typing, filing, running mail between departments—but also must maneuver through four computer software programs: WordPerfect, Lotus, Paradox and dBASE. She takes a nursing class on her lunch hour, a night class and three correspondence courses with the hope of leaving secretarial work someday.

Jenkins, 27, says her salary reflects the 40 hours she puts in each week. And she offers, carefully, "I think I'm treated pretty good."

But when asked about National Secretary's Day on April 27, Jenkins turns resentful.

"It's a bunch of bull," she says about the holiday. "They give you a couple of flowers and a lunch but I just don't believe in it. It's not real. It's just a tradition. I stay (at this job) because it's a paycheck."

Certainly not all secretaries feel unappreciated. Many like their jobs. Some have sensitive bosses. And with the rapid rise of technology, most secretaries now undertake increasingly sophisticated duties that make them more valuable around the office.

But even among those who enjoy secretarial work, most concede they feel there's little chance of being promoted out of clerical work, even after being promised during job interviews that opportunities would arise.

Secretaries get pigeonholed as lifelong helpers, they complain. Their ability to solve problems is taken for granted, and their stress isn't recognized. Worst of all, salaries too often aren't a liveable wage, especially for the growing number of single mothers.

"If I'm doing such a great job, then they should rate me on my ability and performance and not just the job duties alone," says Jennifer Barela, a 21-year-old secretary at a Denver finance company and mother of two toddlers.

---

[1]Cathleen Ferraro, "Treading Water in the Secretarial Pool," *Rocky Mountain News*, April 17, 1994. Reprinted with permission.

Such conditions are almost exclusively the experience of women. Of the roughly 3.6 million secretaries nationwide, 98.9% are female. According to the U.S. Bureau of Labor Statistics, more working women still are employed as clerical workers than any other job. That's in spite of more women holding four-year college degrees or higher than any other time in history.

"Almost one out of three women work as secretaries or administrative assistants," says Karen Nussbaum, director of the Labor Department's Women's Bureau in Washington.

A few have risen to the "executive secretary" status where pay is decent, benefits reasonable and promotions more likely.

"But that's a very, very small part of the secretarial profession," adds Nussbaum. "It appears the same as women's work does on the whole. Over the past 20 years, there are more women managers but the overwhelming number of working women have not had significant pay raises or promotions."

The reason?

"Men still control the business world. That's an important reason for all of this," says Roberta Spalter-Roth, director of research at the Institute for Women's Policy Research.

In recent history, several economic factors also have created an explosion of clerical work.

As Japan and Germany became economic giants starting in the 1970s, international competition sped up. In the next decade, computers and other technology became commonplace, often increasing companies' output. Most profound of all, America quickly changed from a manufacturing economy to a service economy—something widely characterized by paper shuffling.

But it wasn't always like this. In a simpler time, business was neighborhood-based. And secretaries were men.

Before the Civil War, young, literate, white males performed all clerical work. They filed, took memos, tried to learn the business and sometimes married the boss's daughter. It was a period in U.S. history when male-dominated office work was literally marked by a spittoon next to every desk.

Then between 1860 and 1880 an economic revolution took shape, giving birth to the nation's first big department stores, giant railroads, powerful banks and a bloating bureaucracy in the federal government.

For the few men with office skills, the paperwork quickly became overwhelming. New factories, meanwhile, lured away others with somewhat better pay. And all the while, an escalating war had killed off scores of yet more men.

Still, commerce marched on. And businesses and government turned to the most plentiful supply of workers: women.

"They saw these women, often educated, as a cheap labor force. In the 19th century it was just a given that women could be hired for less than men. It's still true today," explains Cindy Aron, a professor of women's history at the University of Virginia. "A flood of women wanted these clerical jobs because it was a good wage for a woman. If she was educated, she didn't have a lot of choices other than being a school teacher."

Even today, highly educated women often work as secretaries. In 1992, the most recent year for which there are statistics, 41,000 female secretaries held master's degrees. Just 4,000 men with equivalent education were employed as secretaries. About 6,000 secretaries in 1992 held either a Ph.D., law or medical degree. Approximately 4,000 were women and 2,000 were men.

"Women will take these jobs below their education level to get health benefits. There's a lot of that going on," explains Judy B. Rosener, author of America's Competitive Secret: Women and a professor at the Graduate School of Management at the University of California-Irvine. "Many want an 8-to-5 job, especially if they have kids. So often these women are marking time."

And as time goes by, the pay often remains the same. It's a recurring theme in American labor history that women's wages are consistently lower than that of men doing exactly the same work.

In 1861, for example, female secretaries working for the federal government—the first U.S. employer to hire women in great numbers—tediously cut Treasury bills with scissors for $600 a year. Their male counterparts, meanwhile, were earning twice that amount.

By the end of World War I, women dominated secretarial jobs, supplanting male clerical workers for good. But it didn't mean men were pushed out to pound the pavement. They continued to work in the office - as higher paid managers now supervising the growing female workforce.

Low wages persisted for women, and the notion of being stigmatized as "nothing more than a secretary" took hold.

"There was something called 'The Marriage Bar' in the 1920s that kept women office workers from getting promoted and (enabled) employers to pay women less," says Sharon Hartman Strom, author of the 1991 book Beyond The Typewriter. "The social norm then held that women office workers would eventually leave their jobs to get married and, often, they were fired once they got married. This cast a pall over all women in the workforce. There was no chance for raises or promotions. It all fed on itself."

Once again, war was responsible for changing the so-called marriage rule of this gender-driven game. During World Ware II men swiftly moved from corporate boardrooms to military barracks while women—married and single—marched out of kitchens and nurseries back into offices. And for the first time, African-American females started to secure jobs as secretaries, too.

Since then, swift technological changes have been the single biggest impetus for altering secretaries' daily responsibilities. Learning spreadsheet software programs and organizing seminars, for example, are now the norm. Even the most cliched task—fetching coffee—is less common.

The steadfast trademark of secretarial work, nonetheless, has remained low pay. According to the Bureau of Labor Statistics, full-time secretaries earned an average $386 a week in 1993. That was 20% lower than the average for all men and women working full time in the United States.

"Today's wages reflect the long legacy of discrimination," said Ellen Bravo, director of 9 to 5, the Milwaukee-based organization that started in 1973 out of concern for secretaries' working lives. The irony, Bravo adds, is that many bosses readily admit their secretaries are indispensable.

"I do a lot of public speaking, and men come up to me afterward and say 'You're right. My secretary is golden. I don't know what I'd do without her.' I tell them to go to the person who can adjust her salary to reflect her value in the workplace."

An exhaustive study by the Institute for Women's Policy Research in 1990 explored this discrepancy between words and wages. The conclusion was that learning high-tech skills was simply expected of secretaries and that "high-touch" skills were considered innately female traits, not to be compensated.

"We found that the personal skills are widely considered part of women's nature, that we are born knowing how to soothe bad tempers, how to prioritize 16 things on your desk, stall someone on the phone when the boss is really in the office and know where all the office supplies are," said Spalter-Roth, co-author of the 1990 study. "But of course these skills are not genetic or hormonal. They are learned."

In an irritating twist, Jenkins, the government secretary in Denver, says those personal attributes can benefit or blackball a clerical worker. "At one company I was told I needed to work on being friendly, to socialize more. It was nowhere in my job description," she recalled. "But in another company where I talked to co-workers, managers said, 'She talks too much.' It seems to be OK for managers to talk and ask John about his skiing trip at length, but for secretaries, they don't want us to talk about our personal lives. Bosses just want to hear what I'm doing back at my desk."

Dee Willis, a legal secretary for 42 years who works at one of Colorado's largest law firms, agrees. "Yes, there's still a caste system. Bosses generally don't understand secretaries because chances are they've never been one."

Willis says such office tensions heated up, and never cooled down, with the advent of the copier machine. "That was in the 1970s and now everyone wants to see copies of every document whether or not it's relevant."

Just as profound as technology have been the effects of the recent recession on secretaries' lives.

As big corporations cut thousands of middle managers, much of their clerical staff went with them, too. Ironically, secretarial positions were still some of the easier jobs to come by during the economic downturn, thanks to the burgeoning temporary agency industry. Consequently, a laid-off secretary has had an easier go than her out-of-work husband at finding a new job, though usually at a lower wage. And for the first time secretaries in great numbers became the primary breadwinner in formerly dual-income households.

9 to 5 also reports that older secretaries, more than younger and middle-aged secretaries, seemed to have borne the brunt of corporate downsizings.

"Our (phone) hotline has seen a huge increase over the last several years from older secretaries with age discrimination complaints," says Bravo. "They've been let go after several years and usually think it's because they cost the company more" in salary and benefits.

Secretaries still holding jobs in newly scaled down offices now are answering to several bosses with equal power.

"It's a no-win situation because she can't usually make four people happy. That's the biggest distinction between secretaries and other jobs affected in this recession," says Joyce Goulet, president of Coalition of Employed Women, a Denver consulting firm.

But a few positive changes have taken place. Bravo notes that issues particularly important to women in low-paying, low-power jobs, finally are being recognized.

"Twenty years ago we didn't have terms like pay equity, family leave and sexual harassment. They were problems just considered part of life. But now we've named them, and solutions are part of the new public policy."

The Division of Occupational Outlook in Washington, D.C., predicts that secretarial jobs will grow about 1% a year in the next decade. That's slower than most other professions, which are estimated to increase at a 2% annual rate during the same period.

But Strom, the author, believes secretarial jobs have a kind of bittersweet built-in security.

"As long as we have the same traditional gender roles, powerful men will always want a Girl Friday whom they can turn to buy presents, stay late with no overtime, fix their buttons and handle a complicated project that can't be mechanized."

Consider These Questions:

1. Based on the evidence presented in this article, do you feel secretaries may be victims of discrimination? Why or why not?

2. What factors have increased the demand for clerical workers? What does economic theory say should happen to wages as the demand for labor increases? Has this happened in the secretarial labor market?

3. Why do so many female secretaries hold advanced degrees? Are these workers "underemployed"? Why is the same not true for male secretaries?

4. What is forecast for the growth in secretarial positions in the future? Will this help or hinder the struggle of female secretaries for higher wages and more benefits? Explain.

STUDY QUESTIONS

1. Is the definition of discrimination as "unfair treatment" an operational definition? Explain.

2. Can market discrimination exist in competitive markets? Explain.

3. Classify each of the following as either exploitation, discrimination, or both:
   a. Equally productive blacks and whites are paid a wage below their productivity.
   b. Consumers pay more for a product than it costs per unit.
   c. Equally productive women and men are paid wages below their productivity; women more so than men.
   d. Black youths are often paid less than white youths even though both are equally qualified for the job.

4. Two disk jockeys work for KISS radio. They have nearly equivalent experience and educational backgrounds. The disk jockey working the day shift is paid 10 percent more than the one who works the grave yard shift. Is this a case of wage discrimination? Explain. Are there other forms of market discrimination? Is market discrimination undesirable? Explain.

5. Suppose a man and a woman complete their Doctor of Divinity degrees at the same time and place, have identical records and recommendations, and are hired by the same theological seminary to teach church management. The man is paid $24,000 a year and the woman is paid $20,000 a year to teach. Is this a case of wage discrimination? Explain.

6. Are women affected by wage, employment, and occupation discrimination? Explain and provide examples.

7. Do individuals discriminated against experience a lower standard of living? Explain. Do some individuals benefit from discrimination? Explain.

8. Using a production possibilities curve, illustrate society's economic cost of market discrimination. How does market discrimination affect relative scarcity?

9. "I'll sell to minorities but I will not dine with them." Using this quote, explore the difference between market and nonmarket discrimination. Can the self-interest motive in the market overcome and reduce the effectiveness of social discrimination in the marketplace? Explain.

10. Would comparable worth pay systems reduce occupational segregation and increase the pay of women? Explain.

PUZZLE Complete the following crossword puzzle.

Discrimination

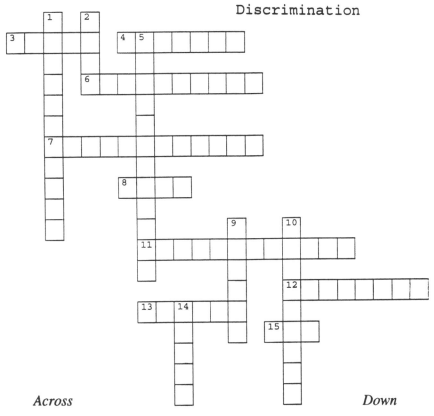

Across

3. _____ discrimination occurs when consumers are charged different amounts for identical products.

4. The demand for labor is _____ from the demand for the products which labor produces.

6. "Equal pay for similar work" is the idea behind _____ worth proposals.

7. The _____ effect measures the change in hours of work that occurs in response to a wage change, all else equal.

8. Discrimination in the price of labor is called _____ discrimination.

11. The segregation by gender of workers into traditional "male" and "female" jobs is called _____ discrimination.

12. _____ power is the degree to which sellers can control the supply and hence the price of what they sell.

13. The income effect measures the change in hours of work that occurs when there is a change in _____, all else equal.

15. Represent the firm's demand for labor curve. (Initials)

Down

1. The law of _____ returns indicates that the marginal product of labor declines as additional workers are hired.

2. The federal agency which administers the anti-discrimination laws. (Initials)

5. Occurs when resource owners receive a lower price for a resource than the value of marginal product of the resource.

9. _____ discrimination occurs when the terms of transactions are not based on economic factors.

10. Discrimination in access to education is a form of _____ discrimination.

14. The _____ Rights Act of 1964 made it illegal to engage in labor market discrimination.

TRUE-FALSE QUESTIONS Circle T (true) or F (false)

T F 1. A person is discriminated against when that person is treated differently on grounds other than individual merit.

T F 2. Discrimination exists in a labor market when persons with equal productivity are paid the same wages.

T F 3. Consumers are exploited when the price of a product is above the cost per unit of producing it, and workers are exploited when the wage rates paid are below their marginal revenue product.

T F 4. If blacks and whites with the same productivity are paid equal wages that are below their productivity then both groups are exploited but not discriminated against.

T F 5. Workers experience discrimination when the wage rates paid are below their marginal revenue product.

T F 6. Two persons with the same training and education apply for a job. One is black and one is white. If both have the same chance for the job, then employment discrimination exists.

T F 7. Difference in unemployment rates among whites and blacks prove that employment discrimination exists.

T F 8. Less than four percent of all full professors of economics are females. This is evidence of occupational segregation.

T F 9. An earnings gap between the earnings of women and men has persisted for a long period of time.

T F 10. The slogan ''equal pay for equal work'' suggests that workers with the same productivity should be paid equal wages.

T F 11. Price discrimination may prevent a person from having access to a market.

T F 12. Individuals discriminated against experience a reduced standard of living because they tend to be paid less for what they sell and to pay higher prices for what they buy.

T F 13. Discriminators may gain or lose income as they satisfy their taste for discrimination.

T F 14. Discrimination causes losses of goods and services to society because it results in unnecessarily low levels of economic efficiency.

T F 15. The elimination of discrimination would cause movement along a production possibilities curve.

T F 16. Social discrimination is difficult to root out, since it is based on deep-seated beliefs and customs often supported by law.

T F 17. Making certain acts of discrimination illegal has little effect on the amount of discrimination because the taste for discrimination is so strong.

T F 18. Policy directed to increase competition and reduce barriers to entry would help lessen discriminatory market behavior.

T F 19. Market discrimination could be reduced if investment in human capital (education, training, etc.) were equally distributed.

T F 20. Opponents of comparable worth pay systems argue that the appropriate remedy for the low pay and occupational segregation of women is more strict enforcement of existing laws rather than comparable worth legislation.

T F 21. The decline in the marginal revenue product of labor occurs when an additional unit of labor contributes less to output than previously employed units of labor.

T F 22. The marginal revenue product of labor is the firm's demand for labor.

T F 23. The substitution effect causes the hours of work offered to increase as the wage rate increases.

T F 24. Since research shows the substitution effect of a wage change to be greater than the income effect, a wage increase will decrease the supply of labor.

T F 25. A rational employer will hire an additional hour of work if the wage rate is greater than the marginal revenue product.

MULTIPLE CHOICE QUESTIONS Select the one best answer

1. Market discrimination exists because some buyers and sellers:
   a. with monopoly power have the ability and desire to discriminate.
   b. without monopoly power have the desire to discriminate.
   c. with monopoly power practice exploitation.
   d. Both (a) and (c).

2. Exploitation occurs:
   a. to all women.
   b. when people are paid less for their resources than those resources are worth.
   c. wherever wage rates are low.
   d. to all blacks.

3. Three workers—a white female worker, a white male worker, and a black male worker—are paid "equal pay for equal work." All three workers are paid wages below their marginal revenue productivity. This indicates:
   a. discrimination.
   b. exploitation.
   c. the white male worker is probably the most underpaid of the three workers.
   d. the white female worker is probably overpaid in relation to the other two workers.

4. Discrimination is indicated when:
   a. whites are paid more than blacks.
   b. equals are treated unequally.
   c. incomes differ between males and females.
   d. people are treated differently according to their individual merits.

5. Market discrimination exists in the form of:
   a. wage discrimination.
   b. employment discrimination.
   c. occupational discrimination.
   d. price discrimination.
   e. All of the above.

6. Market discrimination usually results in:
   a. misallocation of resources among alternative uses.
   b. lower productivity.
   c. more output of final goods and services.
   d. All of the above.
   e. Both (a) and (b) of the above.

Question 7 is based on the diagram below:

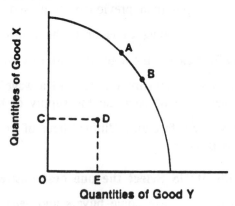

7. The impact on the economy of discrimination is:
   a. equal to the difference between OC and OE.
   b. best illustrated by point D.
   c. represented by a movement along the production possibilities curve from point A to point B.
   d. Insufficient information.

8. Discrimination occurs when:
   a. different prices are charged for essentially the same service to different persons.
   b. the supply of services by a perfectly competitive market are rationed.
   c. different prices are charged for different services.
   d. all people are charged the same price for equivalent services.

9. Suppose on average white females, black males and females pay more for a product than white males. One my conclude from this information that the price difference is due to:
   a. price discrimination.
   b. wage discrimination.
   c. employment discrimination.
   d. occupational discrimination.

10. Suppose a male and a female mechanic have the same education and experience but the male is paid more per hour. This would tend to indicate:
    a. the male is more productive.
    b. the male works harder.
    c. the employer is a male.
    d. discrimination.

11. People who experience discrimination tend to:
    a. be paid less for what they sell.
    b. pay higher prices for what they buy.
    c. have fewer employment opportunities.
    d. All of the above.
    e. None of the above.

12. Discriminators may:
    a. gain from discrimination if they can hire one of two equally productive workers for less money.
    b. pay a higher price for a resource with the same productivity.
    c. forfeit income in order to satisfy their taste for discrimination.
    d. All of the above.

13. Discrimination usually results in:
    a. a level of GDP lower than would occur in the absence of discrimination.
    b. a level of GDP not substantially different from potential GDP provided resources are fully employed.
    c. incentives for minority groups to increase their work efforts.
    d. a more stable social situation since there will be less mingling of people with different economic and social background.
    e. Both (a) and (d).

14. Ending discrimination against minority groups in educational processes and in employment situations would cause GDP:
    a. to fall because of the increased costs of training and living.
    b. to fall since training minority workers would knock some of the present workers out of their jobs.
    c. to rise because of an increase in the quality and productivity of the labor force.
    d. to rise because minority groups consume more goods and services.

15. Social discrimination is:
    a. difficult to root out.
    b. based on social tastes and attitudes, customs, and laws.
    c. the source of much market discrimination.
    d. All of the above.

16. A neighborhood swimming pool that excludes minorities from membership provides an illustration of:
    a. market discrimination.
    b. market exploitation.
    c. social discrimination.
    d. educational discrimination.
    e. All of the above.

17. An effective policy to reduce market discrimination might include efforts to:
    a. reduce tastes for discrimination.
    b. reduce market imperfections.
    c. increase access for all to education, training, and health care.
    d. reduce occupational segregation.
    e. All of the above.

18. The government can control discrimination due to the use of monopoly power through the:
    a. vigorous enforcement of antimonopoly laws.
    b. reduction of government-legislated monopoly power.
    c. payment of subsidies to business that do not discriminate.
    d. Both (a) and (b).

19. People's tastes for discrimination can be reduced by:
    a. educating people to understand one another.
    b. making certain acts of discrimination illegal.
    c. paying subsidies to employers who refrain from discriminating.
    d. All of the above.

20. Comparable worth pay systems:
    a. are used extensively by businesses.
    b. if successful, may reduce the employment of women.
    c. if successful, may reinforce occupational segregation rather than reduce it.
    d. All of the above.
    e. Both (b) and (c).

21. The market demand for labor is:
    a. dependent on the demand for the product produced.
    b. negatively sloped because of the law of diminishing returns.
    c. the summation of each firm's marginal revenue product.
    d. All of the above.

22. The supply of labor is positively sloped because:
    a. a wage increase increases the price of leisure and the amount of time a worker chooses to work.
    b. a wage increase and the resulting income increase decreases the demand for leisure and increases the amount of time a worker chooses to work.
    c. research studies show that the substitution effect dominates the income effect.
    d. Both (b) and (c).
    e. Both (a) and (c).

23. What should an non-discriminating employer do if workers' marginal revenue product was greater than the prevailing wage rate?
    a. hire additional workers.
    b. layoff workers.
    c. raise the wage rate.
    d. lower the wage rate.

24. What should an non-discriminating employer do if workers' marginal revenue product was less than the prevailing wage rate?
    a. hire additional workers.
    b. layoff workers.
    c. raise the wage rate.
    d. lower the wage rate.

25. Which of the following federal agencies is responsible for enforcing the Civil Rights Act and the Age Discrimination in Employment Act?
    a. Federal Anti-Discrimination Agency (FAA).
    b. Civil Rights Commission (CRC).
    c. Equal Employment Opportunity Commission (EEOC).
    d. Federal Labor Relations Board (FLRB).

PROBLEMS

1. Production possibilities

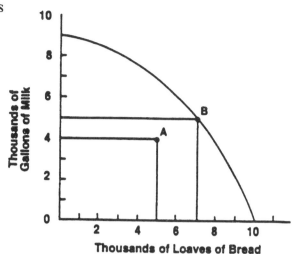

a. Point _____ represents one possible combination of bread and milk the economy could produce with all resources employed where they are more productive—no discrimination.

b. Point _____ represents one possible combination of bread and milk the economy could produce when some resources are unemployed or are not employed where they are most productive because of discrimination.

c. The social cost of discrimination in real terms is _____ thousand loaves of bread and _____ thousand gallons of milk.

d. If the price of bread is $.50 per loaf and the price of milk is $1.50 per gallon, the social cost of discrimination in monetary terms is $_____.

2. For each of the following identify if the situation is discrimination (D), exploitation (E), both (B) or neither one (N).

_____ a. At a recent meeting the price of a hotel room was more for those who advanced registered than for those who did not do so.

_____ b. The marginal revenue product of a worker who is an illegal alien is $3.10 per hour and she is paid $1.50 per hour.

_____ c. Very few men work as registered nurses.

_____ d. Three people with the same training and experience apply for a job. The minority applicant is not hired. The two new employees are paid a wage less than their marginal revenue product.

_____ e. Bob and Tom do the same work and receive the same pay from Green Thumb Lawn Care.

_____ f. The Last Chance Service Station charges local customers less for gasoline than out-of-town customers but both pay more than the cost per unit of producing and providing gasoline.

_____ g. The local theater charges less for afternoon shows.

3. Suppose that the demand schedule for unskilled labor force is as follows:

Hourly Wage Rate	Person-Hours per Day
$20	1,000
18	2,000
16	3,000
14	4,000
12	5,000
10	6,000
8	7,000
6	8,000
4	9,000
2	10,000
0	11,000

a. Plot the demand schedule.

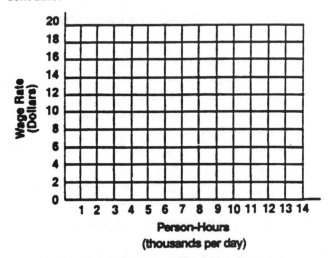

b. Suppose that the supply of unskilled labor is absolutely fixed at 8,000 person-hours per day regardless of the wage rate. Plot the supply curve.
c. What is the equilibrium wage rate?
d. What will be the effect of a law establishing a minimum wage rate of $8 per hour? Six dollars per hour?
e. What is the elasticity of demand for the change in the wage rate from the equilibrium level to the $8 per hour minimum level?
f. What happens to the total wage bill for the change to the $8 per hour minimum level?

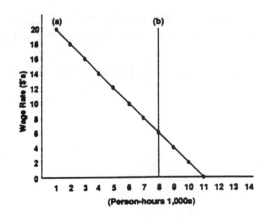

ANSWERS TO SELF-TEST

PUZZLE

Across	Down
3. Price	1. Diminishing
4. Derived	2. EEOC
6. Comparable	5. Exploitation
7. Substitution	9. Market
8. Wage	10. Nonmarket
11. Occupational	14. Civil
12. Monopoly	
13. Income	
15. MRP	

TRUE-FALSE QUESTIONS

1. T	6. F	11. T	16. T	21. T
2. F	7. F	12. T	17. F	22. T
3. T	8. T	13. T	18. T	23. T
4. T	9. T	14. T	19. T	24. F
5. F	10. T	15. F	20. T	25. F

MULTIPLE-CHOICE QUESTIONS

1. a	6. e	11. d	16. c	21. d
2. b	7. b	12. d	17. e	22. e
3. b	8. a	13. a	18. d	23. a
4. b	9. a	14. c	19. d	24. b
5. e	10. d	15. d	20. e	25. c

PROBLEMS

1. a. B
   b. A
   c. 2,1
   d. $2,500

2. a. D, price discrimination
   b. E, worker exploitation
   c. D, occupational discrimination
   d. B, employment discrimination and worker exploitation
   e. N, since both workers have the same productivity and are paid identical wages.
   f. B, price discrimination and consumer exploitation
   g. N, if the price difference reflects cost difference

3. a. See diagram.
   b. See (b) on the diagram.
   c. $Q_d = Q_s$ at $6.
   d. Unemployment = 1,000. No effect.
   e. 3/8 or .375.
   f. Increases from $48,000 or to $56,000.

Chapter 9
● **THE ECONOMICS OF BIG BUSINESS**

Who Does What To Whom?

LEARNING OBJECTIVES

After studying this issue, you should be able to:

1. Explain the general public's view of big business enterprises.

2. Define monopoly power and explain the effects on monopoly power of the size of the firm's output relative to that of the industry.

3. Explain the profit maximization principles.

4. *Explain the product price and output decisions of a firm in a competitive market and show that a firm maximizes profits by producing the output level at which MR=MC.

5. Explain the competitive firm's supply curve and the competitive market supply curve.

6. Explain graphically the effects of monopoly power on the price and output of a product and on society's welfare.

7. Identify barriers to entry into an industry and explain their effects on product price, output, profits, and resource allocation.

● 8. Explain the motivation for nonprice competition and evaluate the impact of nonprice competition on the allocation of the economy's scarce resources.

9. Explain the differences between bigness and monopoly power.

10. Evaluate the effects of bigness and monopoly power on product outputs, product prices, resource allocation, and income distribution.

CHAPTER ORIENTATION

The general public consumes goods produced by big business enterprises. But the public is suspicious of big business behavior. It feels exploited because it believes big businesses restrict product outputs, charge exorbitant prices, make unjustifiable monopoly profits, and control the economy.

A firm that produces a significant part of an industry's output may have some degree of monopoly power. Concentration ratios are used to determine the degree of monopoly power in imperfectly competitive markets. Firms with monopoly power tend to restrict product output and charge a higher produce price than would prevail if the firms were in a competitive industry. They impose a significant economic cost on society in the form of reduced welfare.

Monopoly power may allow firms to restrict entry into their industries, thus limiting the reallocation of resources in the economy according to consumer preferences. When firms with monopoly power engage in nonprice competition some of the economy's resources may be wasted.

It is difficult to substantiate the general public's view that big business enterprises cause unsatisfactory performance of the U.S. economy. Business enterprises, big and small, may have and do exercise monopoly power. However, big businesses in general may not exercise monopoly power in significant degrees.

It is important to guard against the abuses of monopoly power, because it can reduce social welfare. The price mechanism tends to allocate resources among their many uses more effectively in an economy with competitive markets.

CONSIDER THIS:

Software Giant[1]

You don't get to be the world's second-largest software company without stepping on a few toes.

Founded as a one-product boutique in 1976, Computer Associates International Inc. has emerged as the expansionist superpower of its industry. Many software firms rely on homegrown technology for growth; Computer Associates has systematically bought up other people's in an acquisition spree that has swallowed close to 40 companies, pumping annual sales up to $1.4 billion and moving operations into 26 countries.

Along the way it has acquired more than a few enemies. The company is locked in a court battle with computer services giant Electronic Data Systems Corp. (EDS), which accuses it of having built a monopoly. And some of its customers are dissatisfied with its products, according to research studies.

But today many analysts say CA is thinking twice about its often hard-nosed style and is trying to call a truce. Last month, the Islandia, N.Y.-based firm announced new pricing policies that are intended to head off disputes over where and how customers may use the complex software programs that Computer Associates provides.

Repairing relations won't be easy, many analysts say. They've done an awful lot of damage in their customer case, said Timothy McCollum, a senior vice president at Dean Witter Reynolds Inc....This isn't going to magically turn things in their favor.

Given its size, anything Computer Associates does will have long-term repercussions on one of the seminal debates taking place in the computer industry: who shares in the financial rewards of making software.

As hardware prices plunge, the money is increasingly in the tediously devised instructions that run the hardware. Computer Associates, like all software firms, contends that software creators have important rights. Software makers, they note, can employ armies of programmers for years to develop a single program. Arnold S. Mazur, CA's executive vice president said the firm must be vigilant in controlling use of its products, lest trade secrets contained in them leak out. If you lose it once, you've lost it forever "big problem," he said.

Indeed, CA's fans call it a little company that has finally grown big enough to put its foot down against customer abuses. When you're $1 billion-size you can say, 'Wait a minute,' said David Tory, a former CA executive who is now chief executive of the Cambridge-based Open Software Foundation, an industry joint venture developing nonproprietary software.

CA's chairman and co-founder, Charles Wang, is a Shanghai-born immigrant who arrived in the United States at the age of 8. Trained in mathematics and computer science, he has earned a reputation as having a rare combination of ability in both business and technology. We're not guys who have gone to all the proper business schools, declared Wang, 47. We're computer software people first. We may not have all the elegant and polished ways.

---

[1]Software Giant Keeps Its Blunt Edge; Computer Associates' Hard-Nosed Tactics Generate Revenue and Ruffled Feathers," *The Washington Post*, May 10, 1992, p. H1. The Washington Post. Reprinted by permission.

In contrast to Microsoft Corp. of Redmond, Wash., the largest U.S. software company and a familiar corporate name, Computer Associates is all but unknown to Americans in general. That is because about 75 percent of its business is in the world of mainframe computers, which are stuck away in the back rooms of corporate and government offices.

Many of CA's products are in the arcane niche known as systems software. Such programs exist essentially to supercharge the operations of programs that run on mainframes. They might make a database containing electronic files on 5,000,000 life insurance policies run faster or schedule the sequence of thousands of computing jobs that a mainframe may handle in a day.

Although mainframes are used by big companies, they run software programs that often have been developed by small-scale start-up operations. These small companies usually sell their products to large businesses and tend to be accommodating to these customers, analysts say.

CA spent $177 million in fiscal 1991 developing new products and improving old ones. But it is known more for buying tried-and-true technology through a concerted effort to acquire many of the smaller software firms, usually through friendly takeovers. In this way, it has avoided some of the risk that comes with investing in software research that doesn't produce results.

Wang said the company's internal surveys show 90 percent satisfaction on the part of customers. Richard Roskelley, who oversees Brigham Young University's financial computers in Provo, Utah, puts himself in that group. I've been very satisfied with Computer Associates and the direction they're going, he said.

Yet several outside surveys and anecdotal evidence suggest another side of the story. In a February survey of 50 major CA customers by SoundView Financial Group of Stamford, Conn., few ranked CA software as below average in reliability or said they planned to cut back on purchases. Yet 43 percent ranked the technological innovation of CA's software as below average, 75 percent rated its service as below average and 71 percent called the attractiveness of its pricing below average.

The Yankee Group research firm of Boston, surveying 100 companies, has found that about 20 percent of CA's customers feel mutinous, said Susan McGarry, a Yankee Group vice president. Another 40 percent are pretty sullen.

Customers with problems must think long and hard about switching to another firm, however. Once software is installed on a mainframe, operators typically work long and hard to customize other programs to run with it. Dumping CA's product would mean changing those as well, a job that can take months or years.

Wang said his company does encounter some ill feelings. He recalls one company's chief computer executive telling him that the company avoids CA products. But Wang defends his company's pricing and service record strongly and said the number of unhappy customers is exaggerated. He attributes what bad feelings that do exist to grumbling by employees of acquired companies who were laid off.

Wang said mainframe operators are in fact much better off with CA than other software firms. In an industry whose members aren't always known for longevity, he said, CA has the financial wherewithal to remain on the scene.

Consider These Questions:

1. Define the market in which Computer Associates International sells its products. Is this a competitive market, imperfectly competitive market, or a monopolistic market? Defend your answer.

2. Based on what you know about Computer Associates International, do you believe that it is a monopoly as claimed by Electronic Data Systems? Why or why not?

3. What factors allowed Computer Associates International to charge relatively high prices and to limit its services to customers? Is customer satisfaction a function of market structure?

4. Discuss what would happen if Computer Associates International was sold and divided into several smaller corporations that competed against each other. What would happen to prices, output, and customer satisfaction?

STUDY QUESTIONS

1. Locate and evaluate a newspaper story that illustrates the general public's view of big business enterprises.

2. Industry A's four-firm concentration ratio is 30. For Industry B the concentration ratio is 85. Which firms are most likely to have monopoly power? Why?

3. Why do businesses sponsor little league baseball teams, contribute to community welfare organizations like the United Way, and provide nonfinancial assistance to nonprofit and government agencies? Are these activities consistent with profit maximization? Explain.

4. If the market price for a competitive firm's product is $5 and the marginal cost of producing 10 units of the product is $6, what will happen to the firm's output level? Why?

5. If one of 2,000 identical firms in an industry will place 10 units per day of a product on the market at a price of $15 how may units per day will all the firms together place on the market? Is this price and the quantity supplied the market supply curve? Explain.

6. If a market is monopolized, can the monopolist maintain price and output levels and earn a profit? Explain and illustrate your answer graphically.

7. Identify an industry you would wish to enter if you were an investor. Are there barriers to entry? What impact would you expect barriers to have on market price, industry output, firm profits and resource allocation?

8. "Don't leave home without it." What impact did American Express expect this advertising slogan to have on sales and market shares? Is the allocation of the economy's scarce resources affected by nonprice competition? Explain.

9. Can the Chug-A-Lug, a small pub located near a state university campus, have monopoly power? Explain and provide another example.

10. Does bigness and monopoly power tend to cause major problems in the performance of the economy in terms of industry outputs, product prices, resource allocation, and income distribution? Explain.

PUZZLE Complete the following crossword puzzle.

Big Business

Across

1. A _____ market has many sellers and many buyers. No one seller or buyer is large enough to affect the price of the product.
2. Advertising and changes in design and quality of products are forms of _____ competition.
4. The difference between a firm's total revenue and a firm's total costs.
5. Impediments to the entry of new firms into a market.
7. Marginal cost is equal to the change in _____ cost resulting from a one unit change in output produced.
10. Product _____ is a non-price form of competition which results in brand name products.
12. An _____ competitive market contains elements of both monopoly and competition.
13. In a competitive market, the marginal cost curve is the firm's _____ curve.

Down

1. The percent of an industry's sales controlled by the largest firms in the industry is called the _____ ratio.
3. _____ - _____ welfare loss is the reduction in social satisfaction due to monopolists' restrictions on output.
6. Occupational _____ laws are governmental barriers to entry in many labor markets including those for plumbers and doctors.
8. The change in a seller's total revenue resulting from a one unit change in quantity sold is called _____ revenue.
9. A market with a single seller of a good, service, or resource.
11. In setting their price, even monopoly firms cannot ignore the law of _____.

TRUE-FALSE QUESTIONS Circle T(true) or F(false)

T F 1. The general public tends to believe that big business can charge whatever prices they please for their production.

T F 2. A very large firm that produces an insignificant part of its industry's output usually exercises some degree of monopoly power.

T F 3. Profit maximization is a goal unique to firms that have monopoly power.

T F 4. If MR>MC, profits will increase as it increases output.

T F 5. An individually competitive firm can determine only the quantity per unit of time to sell at a market determined price.

T F 6. A competitive firm maximizes profits by producing and selling the output at which marginal revenue equals marginal cost.

T F 7. A competitive firm's MC curve is its supply curve for the product.

T F 8. The market supply curve of a product is the horizontal summation of individual firm supply curves of the firms in a competitive market.

T F 9. The demand and marginal revenue curves facing a monopolistic firm induce it to restrict output below what it would be if the industry were competitive.

T F 10. Monopolistic firms restrict outputs and charge higher prices than competitive firms because the management of monopolized firms have less social conscience.

T F 11. The monopolization of a competitive industry tends to reduce product price and increase product output.

T F 12. Firms with monopoly power may be able to restrict entry into their industries and thus limit the reallocation of resources from uses where they contribute less to consumer satisfaction to uses where they contribute more to consumer satisfaction.

T F 13. The use of nonprice competition by firms with monopoly power may result in an inefficient use of the economy's scarce resources.

T F 14. A relatively small firm as measured by its dollar sales may have substantial monopoly power.

T F 15. Monopolistic elements within the economy serve to reduce economic welfare, as measured by GDP, by about 1 per year.

T F 16. In some industries government regulations create entry barriers for new firms.

T F 17. Advertising is a major form of price competition often employed in highly competitive markets.

T F 18. The largest firm in an industry with a concentration ratio of 93 most likely experiences monopoly power.

T F 19. For a competitive firm, marginal revenue always equals price.

T F 20. Product differentiation in an industry makes it easier for new firms to enter the market.

T F 21. Because of their market power, monopoly firms do not obey the law of demand when setting the price for their product.

T F 22. For a monopoly, marginal revenue is always less than product price at any given level of output.

T F 23. Agencies of the government, such as the Federal Communication Commission, impose barriers to entry in regulated markets.

T F 24. Advertising and other forms of nonprice competition clearly reduce economic welfare.

T F 25. Compared to a competitive market, a monopoly will charge a higher price for its product and produce a lower level of output.

MULTIPLE CHOICE QUESTIONS Select the one best answer

1. Often the general public believes that big business enterprises:
   a. control the economy.
   b. deliberately withhold output and charge unfair prices.
   c. pay exploitative wages and salaries.
   d. earn exorbitant profits.
   e. All of the above.

2. Monopoly power refers to:
   a. the absolute size or bigness of a firm in terms of its assets or sales.
   b. the extent of a firm's control over the market supply of its product.
   c. the power of government to block entry into certain industries or occupations.
   d. All of the above.

3. Profit maximization:
   a. is a goal peculiar to firms with monopoly power.
   b. tends to be a major objective of firms in all types of market structures.
   c. is the only goal of business firms.
   d. None of the above.

4. Business firms tend to set prices and output levels primarily to:
   a. assure goodwill in the community.
   b. block entry of new firms into the industry.
   c. provide employment for people.
   d. maximize profits.

5. If MC>MR, a competitive firm would maximize profits by:
   a. reducing price.
   b. increasing price.
   c. increasing price and decreasing output.
   d. decreasing output.
   e. increasing output.

6. A competitive firm's supply curve:
   a. shows how much it will place on the market at alternative possible prices, other things being equal.
   b. is its marginal revenue curve.
   c. is its marginal cost curve.
   d. Both (a) and (c).

7. A monopolist maximizes profits by producing the output where:
   a. marginal cost is equal to price.
   b. average total costs are at a minimum.
   c. marginal cost equals marginal revenue.
   d. marginal revenue is equal to price.

Answer Questions 8-10 using the graph below.

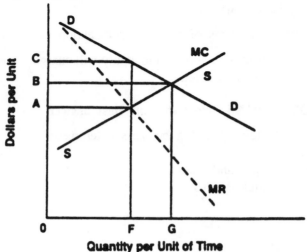

8. If the market is competitive, the market price will be:
   a. 0A.
   b. 0B.
   c. 0C.
   d. insufficient information to determine market price.

9. The monopolization of the market causes:
   a. the firm to see DD as the demand curve it faces.
   b. the price to increase to 0C.
   c. the profit-maximizing output to decrease to 0F.
   d. All of the above.

10. The manager of the monopolized firm:
    a. faces a demand and marginal revenue horizontal at price 0B.
    b. will produce output 0G at a marginal cost of 0B.
    c. will charge price 0C for output 0F.
    d. has a marginal cost of 0C for output 0F.
    e. None of the above.

11. A higher than average return on investment:
    a. induces investors to leave the industry.
    b. results in falling supplies and rising prices relative to costs in the industry.
    c. provides an incentive for new investment and new firms to enter the industry.
    d. can be sustained indefinitely in competitive industries.

12. To the extent that firms with monopoly power are able to restrict entry of new firms into an industry:
    a. outputs tend to be lower.
    b. prices tend to be higher.
    c. profits tend to be greater than they would be if entry were not restricted.
    d. resources tend to be misallocated.
    e. All of the above.

13. Nonprice competition:
    a. is a common practice in industries containing many firms.
    b. may increase a firm's monopoly power.
    c. is easier for other firms to duplicate than price cutting competition.
    d. may lead to substantial shifts in market shares when all firms in the industry have successful campaigns.

14. A business enterprise has monopoly power if:
    a. it is big in terms of the value of its output and assets.
    b. it is big in terms of the value of its assets and it supplies a large percent of the product.
    c. it is small in terms of the value of its output and it sells a large percentage of the units sold in the market.
    d. All of the above.
    e. Both (b) and (c).

15. Big business enterprises:
    a. usually cause severe problems in the performance of the economy.
    b. generally exercise monopoly power in significant degrees.
    c. cause the distribution of income in the United States to be more unequal than would be the case if all business firms were small.
    d. None of the above.

16. Which of the following domestic industries is most likely to contain firms with monopoly power?
    a. newspaper.
    b. automobile.
    c. retail grocery.
    d. higher education.

17. Entry barriers may be caused by:
    a. product differentiation.
    b. brand loyalty.
    c. occupational licensing.
    d. government regulation.
    e. All of the above.

18. A profit maximizing firm will increase its production of output when:
    a. marginal revenue is greater than marginal cost.
    b. total revenue is greater than marginal cost.
    c. marginal cost is greater than marginal revenue.
    d. total cost is greater than total revenue.
    e. marginal revenue is equal to marginal cost.

19. Dead-weight welfare loss occurs:
    a. in a competitive markets.
    b. when firms have monopoly power.
    c. when firms advertise.
    d. only in resource markets.

20. Compared to a competitive market, a monopolist will:
    a. charge a lower price and produce a larger output.
    b. charge a lower price and produce a smaller output.
    c. charge a higher price and produce a larger output.
    d. charge a higher price and produce a smaller output.

21. Which of the following is a barrier to entry imposed by the government?
    a. a chauffeur's license.
    b. a patent granted on a new invention.
    c. a construction zoning ordinance.
    d. All of the above.

22. Which of the following conditions must hold true for a competitive firm to maximize its profits?
    a. marginal revenue equals marginal cost.
    b. total revenue equals marginal cost.
    c. marginal revenue equals total cost.
    d. demand equals marginal revenue and total cost.

23. Which of the following do competitive firms and monopolies have in common?
    a. both will produce as much output as their technology will allow.
    b. both seek to maximize profit by producing a level of output such that marginal revenue equals marginal cost.
    c. both face barriers to entry which significantly effect the price of their product.
    d. both produce a dead-weight welfare loss for society due to profit maximizing behavior.

24. The difference between a firm's total revenue and total cost is
    a. a dead-weight welfare loss.
    b. known as the market concentration ratio.
    c. profit.
    d. called marginal revenue.

25. The dead-weight welfare loss due to monopoly, for the economy as a whole, is estimated to be about
    a. 1% of GDP.
    b. 10% of GDP.
    c. 20% of GDP.
    d. 35% of GDP.

PROBLEMS

1. Complete the following table for a competitive firm:

Output (X per Day)	Total Cost	Marginal Cost	Market Price	Total Revenue	Marginal Revenue
3	$ 47		$ 26	$78	
4	57	_____	26	_____	_____
5	70	_____	26	_____	_____
6	84	_____	26	_____	_____
7	110	_____	26	_____	_____
8	140	_____	26	_____	_____
9	175	_____	26	_____	_____
10	216	_____	26	_____	_____
11	264	_____	26	_____	_____
12	320	_____	26	_____	_____

   a. For a market price of $26, what output will the competitive firm produce?
   b. If the market price increases to $35, what is the profit maximizing or loss minimizing output? Calculate the profit or loss.
   c. If the competitive firm's current output is 7 units and market price is $30, should the firm change its output? Why?

2. Use the diagram below to answer the following questions:

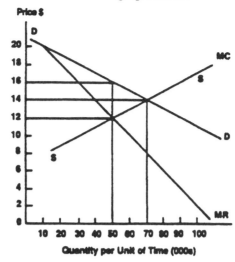

Price $

Quantity per Unit of Time (000s)

a. If the market is competitive, the market price will be _____ and the output will be _____ units.

b. Monopolization of the market results in a profit maximizing output for the monopolistic firm of _____ units which will be sold at a price of _____ per unit.

c. If the market is monopolized and the monopolist continues with 70,000 unit output level, the monopolist's MC is (equal to, greater than, less than) its MR. To maximize profits, the monopolist will need to (increase, decrease) output.

d. The new output will be sold at a (higher, lower) price.

ANSWERS TO SELF-TEST

PUZZLE

Across	*Down*
1. Competitive	1. Concentration
2. Nonprice	3. Dead-Weight
4. Profit	6. Licensing
5. Barriers	8. Marginal
7. Total	9. Monopoly
10. Differentiation	11. Demand
12. Imperfectly	
13. Supply	

TRUE-FALSE QUESTIONS

1.	T	6.	T	11.	F	16.	T	21.	F
2.	F	7.	T	12.	T	17.	F	22.	T
3.	F	8.	T	13.	T	18.	T	23.	T
4.	T	9.	T	14.	T	19.	T	24.	F
5.	T	10.	F	15.	T	20.	F	25.	T

MULTIPLE-CHOICE QUESTIONS

1. e	6. d	11. c	16. b	21. d
2. b	7. c	12. e	17. e	22. a
3. b	8. b	13. b	18. a	23. b
4. d	9. d	14. e	19. b	24. c
5. d	10. c	15. c	20. d	25. a

PROBLEMS

1.

Output (X per Day)	Total Cost	Marginal Cost	Market Price	Total Revenue	Marginal Revenue
4	$ 57	$ 10	$ 26	$ 104	$ 26
5	70	13	26	130	26
6	84	14	26	156	26
7	110	26	26	182	26
8	140	30	26	208	26
9	175	35	26	234	26
10	216	41	26	260	26
11	264	48	26	286	26
12	320	56	26	312	26

a. 7 units, MC = MR for 7 units of output.

b. 9 units, TC = $175.00, TR = $315.00, Profit = $140.00

c. Yes. For 7 units of output and a market price of $30, MC is less than MR. To maximize profits or minimize losses the competitive firm would increase output to 8 units where MC = MR.

2. a. $14; 70,000 units

b. 50,000 units; $16

c. greater than, decrease

d. higher

Chapter 10
Airline Regulation and Deregulation

Who Gains From Regulation?

LEARNING OBJECTIVES

After studying this issue, you should be able to:

1. State the economically justifiable circumstances for government regulation of business.

2. Evaluate the desirability of regulation when its primary justification is economic.

3. State and evaluate the case for government regulation of business because of natural monopoly, deficient information, and poorly defined property rights.

4. Evaluate the impact of airline deregulation on fares, services, and safety.

5. Determine whether airline regulation was economically justifiable.

6. Explain the capture theory of regulation and decide whether the airline industry was captured by its regulatory agency.

CHAPTER ORIENTATION

This chapter introduces the economic justifications for government regulation of business and uses them to evaluate the regulation and deregulation of the airline industry. Government regulation may be desirable when the market results in an inefficient allocation of resources or when market outcomes may be improved by some degree of government control over the production process. Thus government regulation may be appropriate in the presence of natural monopoly, deficient information, or poorly defined property rights. As in all economic decisions, the decision to regulate businesses must be based on the relative benefits and costs of regulation. If the expected benefits of regulation exceed the expected costs, the appropriate government policy is some form of regulation. However, if net costs are expected, the government should not regulate.

When an industry's average cost of production is minimized with only one firm, that industry is a natural monopoly. The natural monopolist has a U-shaped long run average cost curve and thus can experience economies and diseconomies of scale. Government regulation of a natural monopoly allows the benefits of a low long run average cost of production while promoting the competitive output and price.

Deficient information leads to a misallocation of resources. Too many or too few of the product or service may be produced. Appropriate government actions include safety testing, product labeling, health and safety codes, and product banning in extreme cases of deficient information.

Poorly defined property rights may also lead to a misallocation of resources. Appropriate government regulation including taxes, subsidies, and direct controls may improve the allocation of resources.

Many people thought deregulation of the airlines would harm consumers because of increased fares, reduced service availability, and reduced airline safety. However, these fears were unfounded. Consumers saved about $5.5 billion in 1988 and service availability increased—since deregulation small towns have seen weekly departure increase and passenger miles more than double. Deregulation appears to have had little or no impact on airline safety.

Is airline regulation justified economically? The airline industry is not a natural monopoly. Regulation for safety concerns is justified because of the information deficiencies that exist in the airline industry. Safety concerns, however, do not justify regulation of fares, routes, and entry and exist in the airline industry. Poorly defined property rights, for example, navigable air space, provide a legitimate role for government in the airline industry. That role is essentially limited to safety concerns.

When government regulation is economically justifiable, does it always work to the benefit of the consumer? What does the capture theory of regulation suggest?

What government actions are justified by the continuing concerns about airline safety and heighten concerns about increasing concentration in the airline industry?

CONSIDER THIS:

Making Rules for the Airline Game[1]

Since airline deregulation in 1978, the feds have had a hard time policing industry business practices. Not safety practices. There, federal oversight and airline self-interest have combined to cut the number of fatalities per mile flown by 90 percent since deregulation.

No, the problem has been in adopting regulations for competition. Mostly the feds have simply watched as airlines stumbled through one strategy after another—not surprising when you consider the same executives who ran things when the government didn't let them really compete are now trying to turn their thinking around 180 degrees.

After a wave of mergers that attracted no attention from the Reagan-era Justice Department's antitrust division, airlines were hit by a price-fixing suit during the Bush administration.

It was a strange kind of suit. Justice didn't accuse airline executives of talking to each other about prices. Instead, the department said they were sending each other signals via the prices posted in airline computerized reservation services.

Rather than fight the allegation, the airlines agreed to make the changes the feds wanted. If the airlines were guilty of price-fixing, they certainly were inept at it. During the period it allegedly occurred, the industry lost more money than it had earned in profits in its entire history.

Now the Justice Department is back again, in a little-noticed investigation into the airlines' so-called fortress hubs.

After deregulation almost all airlines—Southwest Airlines being the major exception—set up hub-and-spoke operations.

You don't fly Birmingham-New York City. Instead you fly to Atlanta and change to a New York-bound plane with passengers from the other smaller cities in the Southeast.

The system allows our Birmingham passenger more frequent flights to New York City than if an airline had to depend upon the number who wanted to go from that city alone.

Over the years, airlines have played the hub-and-spoke business so well many now dominate traffic out of a particular city. Here are some examples, assembled by Aviation Daily, a trade journal. USAir has 85.6 percent of the market in Charlotte, N.C., and 81.8 percent in Pittsburgh. Delta has 81.4 percent in Atlanta, 76.4 percent in Salt Lake City and 76.1 percent in Cincinnati. Northwest has 78.8 percent of the traffic in Minneapolis/St. Paul and 74.3 percent in Detroit. Continental has 78.5 percent of the traffic at Houston Intercontinental.

---

[1]Jim Barlow, Making Rules for the Airline Game,'' *The Houston Chronicle*, May 31, 1994, Reprinted with permission.

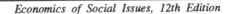

Often, fares on a per-mile basis are higher at these fortress hubs than at ones with more competition. But not always. Houston has reasonable air fares. One reason is that Southwest—king of the discount fliers—dominates flights at Hobby, the city's second airport.

The latest Justice Department investigation—started last year in Salt Lake City after a complaint by little Morris Air against Delta but now expanded to include American, Continental, Northwest, TWA and USAir—involves travel agents and commissions, according to reports in Travel Weekly and other trade publications.

The travel agent takes a percentage of what you pay the airline—or other travel provider—as a commission. If the agent gives a particular airline a bigger percentage of her business, she gets a higher percentage commission—called in the trade an override.

The investigation apparently is looking at whether airlines use that override—in the words of the Sherman Antitrust Act—to attempt to gain or maintain monopoly power.

Despite the investigation, please remember that the airline industry still is not making any kind of decent return on investment. And, on the other side of the equation, note that the only consistently profitable airline is Southwest, which has mostly eschewed this hub-and-spoke business.

There's no word on when, or even if, the investigation will officially surface.

Stay tuned.

Consider These Questions:

1. What has happened to airline safety since deregulation? Why? What does the author mean by "self-interest"?

2. Explain why the airline industry experienced a wave of mergers sine deregulation. What has this done to the concentration of the industry?

3. How does the "hub and spoke" system allow airlines to dominate air traffic into and out of specific cities? Is this a form of monopolization?

4. Why are the airlines earning lower rates of return today than in the past? Explain in terms of competition.

STUDY QUESTIONS

1. Under what circumstances is government regulation of business desirable?

2. "Regulation of business may be economically desirable but that does not insure the desirability of regulation." Evaluate.

3. Does an industry with an average cost of $1 per unit if one firm produces, and $4 per unit if five firms produce, provide an economically justifiable case for government regulation? Explain.

4. A recall has been issued by Ford Motor Co. for 1988-89 Ford Taurus and Mercury Sable. Power-seating wiring could short out and cause a fire. Use a market graph for the Mercury Sable to show the effect of deficient information on the allocation of resources.

5. Can the pollution of the White River by a municipal sewage treatment plant lead to an inefficient allocation of resources? Is there a role for government regulation? Why?

6. Have the fears that airline deregulation would increase fares, reduce service, and reduce safety been realized?

7. Can the government's regulation of the economic aspects of air transportation be supported on economic grounds? Explain.

8. Was the Civil Aeronautics Board captured by the airline industry? Explain.

PUZZLE   Complete the following crossword puzzle.

Regulation

Across

3. A firm experiences _____ of scale when the average cost of production rises as output is increased.

5. _____ theory suggests that regulatory agencies serve the interests of the regulated firms and not those of the general public.

8. A firm experiences _____ of scale when the average cost of production falls as output is increased.

10. The ratio of total costs to total output is called _____ costs.

11. Evidence concerning airline accidents does not indicate that _____ has declined since deregulation.

12. Federal Aviation Administration (Initials)

Down

1. Government control of business behavior designed to improve the general welfare of the public.

2. Poorly defined _____ rights can justify the need for governmental regulation of an industry.

4. Mergers of airlines after deregulation has increased the _____ of the industry.

6. The FAA is charged with safety regulation of the _____ industry.

7. Regulatory agency of the airline industry established in 1938 and now defunct. (Initials)

9. When average cost of production is minimized by having only one firm produce a product, the firm is known as a _____ monopoly.

TRUE-FALSE QUESTIONS Circle T (true) or F (false)

T F   1. When the market, operating on its own, fails to lead to an efficient allocation of resources, government regulation may increase social welfare.

T F   2. Government information in the marketplace may be desirable when market outcomes can be improved by the regulation.

T F   3. Government regulation is always appropriate for natural monopolies, and cases of deficient information or poorly defined property rights.

T F   4. If the expected benefits of a government regulation outweigh the expected cost, then the regulation should be eliminated.

T F   5. A government regulation that is economically desirable would be appropriate if the expected benefits exceed the expected cost.

T F   6. As normally drawn, the long run average cost of production for a typical firm is U-shaped.

T F   7. A firm experiencing increasing average cost as it expands outputs is incurring diseconomies of scale.

T F   8. Monopolists tend to impose costs on society in the form of reduced output and higher prices.

T F   9. The existence of a natural monopoly provides an economically justifiable case for government regulation.

T F   10. Deficient information may cause the production of a product to be extended to where marginal social benefits are less than marginal social costs.

T F   11. The misallocation of resources due to deficient information does not justify government regulation.

T F   12. Poorly defined property rights often lead to circumstances in which government regulation may be economically justifiable.

T F   13. The fears of increased airline fares as a result of deregulation were justified.

T F   14. Airline service availability actually increased in response to deregulation.

T F   15. Airline safety was the responsibility of the Civil Aeronautical Board.

T F   16. Safety fears associated with airline deregulation have proven to be unfounded.

T F   17. Consumers have incurred approximately $10 billion in net costs per year from airline deregulation.

T F   18. Government regulation of the economic aspects of air transportation can be supported on economic grounds.

T F   19. Because information deficiencies and poorly defined property rights exist in the airline industry, fares, routes, and entry and exit must be regulated.

T F   20. High fares and completely restricted fares in the airline industry before deregulation are consistent with the capture theory of regulation.

T F   21. The airline industry is a clear case of a natural monopoly.

T F   22. Firms producing on the downward sloping segment of their average cost curve are experiencing economies of scale.

T F   23. Due to mergers, the airline industry became more concentrated after deregulation.

T F   24. Regulation of business by the U.S. goverment is a very recent phenomena.

T F   25. After deregulation, both the CAB and FAA were disbanded.

MULTIPLE CHOICE QUESTIONS Select the one best answer

1. Government regulation is economically desirable when there is:
   a. market failure.
   b. an inefficient allocation of resources by the market.
   c. an opportunity to improve on market outcomes.
   d. None of the above.
   e. All of the above.

2. Government regulation is appropriate when:
   a. firms do not bear a compliance cost.
   b. the expected benefits of regulation exceed the expected costs.
   c. the expected benefits of regulation are less than the expected costs.
   d. None of the above.

3. If government regulation is successful:
   a. natural monopolies will be eliminated.
   b. consumers will have perfect information.
   c. property rights will be completely defined.
   d. social welfare will increase.
   e. All of the above.

4. When a firm is operating on the downward sloping portion of the long run average cost curve, the firm:
   a. can reduce long run average cost by increasing the firm's size and producing more output.
   b. is experiencing diseconomies of scale.
   c. can reduce long run average cost by decreasing the firm's size and producing less output.
   d. Both b and c.

Use the following graph to answer Questions 5 and 6.

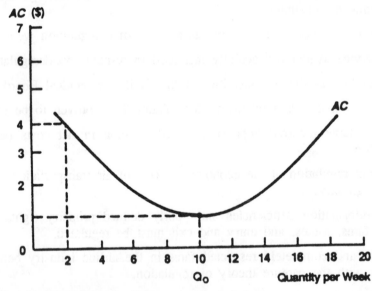

5. The long run average cost curve reaches a minimum at:
   a. two units at an average cost of $4.
   b. six units at an average cost of $2.
   c. ten units at an average cost of $1.
   d. fourteen units at an average cost of $2.

6. If only 10 units per week may be sold in the market:
   a. only one efficient firm, a natural monopolist, can be supported.
   b. the industry is a natural monopoly.
   c. government regulation requiring more than one firm to produce the product will increase average cost and decrease social welfare.
   d. government regulation is needed to force the monopolist to produce the competitive output and charge the competitive price.
   e. All of the above.

7. Deficient information:
   a. causes consumers to over-consume products.
   b. results in a misallocation of resources.
   c. and its economic effects may be corrected by government regulation.
   d. All of the above.

Use the following graph to answer Questions 8 & 9.

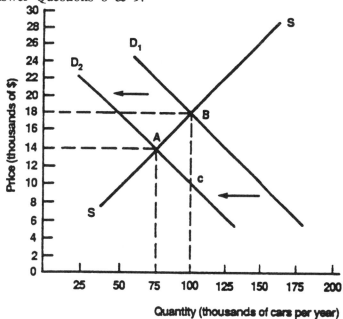

8. Lacking information concerning a safety defect, an equilibrium is reached with:
   a. 75,000 cars at $14,000 per car.
   b. 75,000 cars at $22,000 per car.
   c. 100,000 cars at $10,000 per car.
   d. 100,000 cars at $18,000 per car.

9. When a product safety defect is made known to consumers:
   a. demand increases (D_1 to D_2).
   b. fewer cars are sold at a higher price ($18).
   c. fewer cars are sold at a lower price ($14).
   d. None of the above.

10. Poorly defined property rights:
    a. may lead to circumstances in which government regulation is economically justifiable.
    b. assure an efficient allocation of resources.
    c. cause firms to pollute and under-produce.
    d. All of the above.

11. The available evidence supports the fears that airline deregulation:
    a. increased fares.
    b. reduced service availability.
    c. reduced airline safety.
    d. None of the above.

12. Following airline deregulation:
    a. the number of carriers serving the public more than tripled but have decreased in recent years.
    b. service availability increased.
    c. no small communities lost airline service.
    d. most small towns experienced increases in weekly departures.
    e. All of the above.

13. Continuing concerns about airline safety:
    a. suggest a failure of regulation, not deregulation.
    b. are the result of an increase in accident rates since deregulation.
    c. indicate that safety regulation of the airline industry should be restored.
    d. None of the above.

14. The government regulation of the economic aspects of air transportation:
    a. can be supported because the industry is a natural monopoly.
    b. can not be supported because the industry is not a natural monopoly.
    c. can be supported because of poorly defined property rights.
    d. can be supported because of deficient information.

15. The capture theory of regulation may apply to the airline industry because:
    a. the airlines supported the Airline Deregulation Act.
    b. fares were exceptionally high under regulation.
    c. the Civil Aeronautics Board rejected price competition between the carriers.
    d. the Civil Aeronautics Board rejected entry of new firms.
    e. All of the above except a.

16. Government regulation of business often results from circumstances where there is:
    a. a natural monopoly.
    b. poorly defined property rights.
    c. deficient information.
    d. all of the above.

17. The downward sloping portion of a long-run average cost curve reflects:
    a. monopoly power.
    b. the effect of regulation.
    c. economies of scale.
    d. market competition.
    e. diseconomies of scale.

18. When a firm becomes too large to be effectively managed, it is likely to experience:
    a. diseconomies of scale.
    b. monopoly power.
    c. non-price competition.
    d. economies of scale.

19. Which of the following is most likely to be a natural monopoly?
    a. General Motors, an automobile manufacturer.
    b. United Airlines, a passenger airline.
    c. Smallville Gas, a local natural gas distributor.
    d. McDonald's, a fast-food hamburger chain.
    e. All of the above.

20. In the years since airline deregulation:
    a. market concentration has risen.
    b. safety has deteriorated.
    c. fewer mergers between airlines have taken place.
    d. all airlines have become more profitable.

PROBLEMS

1. Suppose the long run average cost of an industry reaches a minimum of $1 when output is 100,000 units per week.
    a. If 10 million units can be sold per week, how many cost minimizing firms can the market support? Is the industry a natural monopoly? Explain.
    b. If sales are 100,000 units weekly, is the industry a natural monopoly?
    c. Is government regulation justified for "b" above?

2. Use the graph below to answer the following questions:

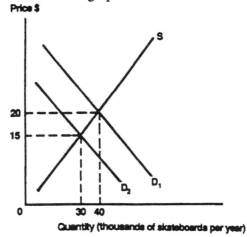

a. In the absence of deficient information, the market price will be _____ and the output will be _____.

b. If a product defect is called to the consumer's attention, the market price will increase/decrease by _____ and output will increase/decrease by _____ units.

c. Before the product defect information is available too few/many skateboards were produced and resources were _____.

ANSWERS TO SELF-TEST

PUZZLE

Across	Down
3. Diseconomies	1. Regulation
5. Capture	2. Property
8. Economies	4. Concentration
10. Average	6. Airline
11. Safety	7. CAB
12. FAA	9. Natural

TRUE-FALSE QUESTIONS

1.	T	6.	T	11.	F	16.	T	21.	F
2.	T	7.	T	12.	T	17.	F	22.	T
3.	F	8.	T	13.	F	18.	F	23.	T
4.	F	9.	T	14.	T	19.	F	24.	F
5.	T	10.	T	15.	F	20.	T	25.	F

MULTIPLE-CHOICE QUESTIONS

1.	e	6.	e	11.	d	16.	d
2.	b	7.	d	12.	e	17.	c
3.	d	8.	d	13.	a	18.	a
4.	a	9.	c	14.	b	19.	c
5.	c	10.	a	15.	e	20.	a

PROBLEMS

1. a. 10,000,000 units/100,000 units = 100 firms
   No. We would expect a high level of competition among a large number of firms each of which is small relative to the market.
   b. Yes. Only one efficient (cost minimizing) firm can be supported by the market.
   c. Yes. To maintain the low average cost of production and to force the monopolist to produce the competitive output and charge the competitive price.

2. a. $20, 40
   b. decrease, $5, decrease, 10
   c. many, misallocated

Chapter 11
The Economics of Professional Sports

What Is The Real Score?

LEARNING OBJECTIVES

After studying this issue, you should be able to:

1. Distinguish between product markets and resource markets.

2. Explain why professional sports leagues are cartels.

3. Identify the conditions necessary for successful formation and operation of a cartel.

4. Explain how a cartel maximizes joint profits for member firms.

5. Explain why firms in a cartel will produce less output and command a higher price for their output than purely competitive firms.

6. *Determine when a firm is a monopsony.

7. Identify the conditions that provide professional sports teams with monopsony power.

8. Explain and illustrate with a graph how a monopsony determines the optimum number of workers to hire and the wage rate to pay them.

9. Identify the sources of monopsony profits.

10. Explain how free agency has increased the average salaries of professional athletes.

11. Provide a sound economic argument to explain why professional athletes earn their lofty salaries.

CHAPTER ORIENTATION

Professional team sports has become a multi-billion dollar entertainment industry in the United States. Stories concerning player salaries, broadcast rights, ticket prices, and league expansion plans routinely capture newspaper headlines. Why does the business of professional sports capture so much public attention? In this chapter you will learn that many situations behind the headlines are the result of the economics that govern the imperfect markets faced by professional sports clubs.

The first section of this chapter introduces you to a few of the unique economic aspects of professional team sports. To fully understand the economics of the sports industry you must first understand the organizational structure of professional sports leagues and appreciate the relationship between teams and their players. Professional sports leagues, like the NFL in football, serve as the mechanism for cooperation in the marketplace between teams that compete against each other on the playing field. League rules strictly govern the employment agreements between teams and players. These rules are designed to prevent successful teams from hoarding quality players and promote competitive athletic parity between teams.

Next, you will learn that economists view cooperative agreements between firms, like those institutionalized by the professional sports leagues, as cartels. A cartel exists when a group of firms formally agree to coordinate economic decisions in a manner to maximize joint profits. A cartel is often characterized as a "shared monopoly" because the group of firms behave in the market as if it were one firm. Cartels are illegal in most American industries under antitrust law, but exemptions have been allowed for professional sports leagues given that cooperation between teams is necessary to promote fair athletic competition and therefore survival of the industry. As an illustration of the economic affects of cartel agreements in professional sports, the chapter presents an example of how a league determines the price and number of games sold to broadcasters. You will see that formation of a cartel has the same effects as monopolizing a competitive market (discussed in Chapter 9). Using marginal analysis you will find that a cartel will charge a higher price and produce a lower level output than would be observed in a competitive market. League rules determine how joint profits will be distributed between teams.

You will also learn that professional sports teams operate in imperfect resource markets for players. Player drafts and league rules designed to generate competitive balance between teams result in an imbalance of power between the employing teams and their employees — the players. In fact, professional sports teams are often characterized as monopsonies. A monopsony exists when there is only one buy in the market for a factor of production. Contractual arrangements that limit the mobility of players between teams and the limited alternative employment opportunities of athletes with highly specialized skills contribute to the monopsony power of sports teams.

The economic affects of monopsony power are illustrated with an example of the hiring decision faced by a baseball club. Once again, marginal analysis is used to determine the optimal wage and number of players to hire. You should pay close attention to the distinction between the market supply curve of labor and the marginal cost of labor (MCL) curve. Because a monopsony is the only employer in the market, it must increase its wage offer in order to attract additional workers. This results in a MCL curve that lies above the labor supply curve. Marginal analysis implies that a monopsony will hire players up to the point where the last player hired contributes just as much to the firm's total revenues as his employment contributes to total costs (MRP = MLC). You will learn that a profit maximizing monopsony will hire fewer workers and pay a lower wage than a firm in a competitive labor market. The recent dramatic increases in the salaries of professional athletes are in part due to the advent of "free agency" which reduces the monopsony power of teams. Free agents are players whose contracts allow them to sell their services to the highest bidder after a specific number of years played in the league.

The chapter concludes with a brief discussion of why professional athletes earn relatively high salaries. Recall from Chapter 8 that the demand for labor is based on the workers' marginal revenue product. Star players contribute large sums to a firm's receipts in the form of ticket sales and broadcast rights. If a player contributes more to total revenue than he contributes to total costs, it is profitable to hire the player. As long as fans are willing to pay millions to see their favorite athletes in action, athletes will earn millions in pay.

CONSIDER THIS:
Salaries in Professional Baseball[1]

One thing is different in recent sports decades: Athletes are getting richer a lot faster than the rest of us. Professional athletes have long made more money than the average worker. But since the 1970's, the disparity between the salaries of players and average wage earners has jumped dramatically, as the revenues of pro sports also soared.

In 1929, the average major league salary, $7,531, was nearly 5.3 times the $1,428 of the average U.S. wage earner. When Babe Ruth made a record $80,000 in 1930, it was $5,000 more than President Hoover and almost 58 times the $1,390 salary of the average wage earner. Asked about making more than the president, Ruth noted: I had a better year than he did.

In 1950, the average major league salary of $13,228 was 4.6 times the $2,876 salary of the average wage earner. From the 1970's on—as the growth of TV sports reached full bloom—the disparity between the pay of pro athletes and that of the average Joe and Jane became even greater. By 1991, the average baseball salary was 34 times the annual wages of men and 49 times the earnings of women in the USA.

---

[1]Taken from "Wage Gap Expanding Rapidly," *USA Today*, May 11, 1993, p. 8-C, Reprinted with permission.

Baseball salaries since 1980 have risen an average of 17.83% a year. But the increase from 1992 to '93 was the smallest since the collusion period of 1986-88. (That's when the Major League Baseball Players Association charged owners with colluding to restrict player movement by not bidding for free agents. In December 1990, owners agreed to pay players $280 million in damages.)

Yearly Average Salary and % Increase

1980	$ 143,756	—
1981	185,651	29.1
1982	241,497	35.5
1983	289,194	19.8
1984	329,408	13.9
1985	371,571	12.8
1986	412,520	11.0
1987	412,454	0.0
1988	438,729	6.4
1989	497,254	13.3
1990	597,537	20.2
1991	891,188	49.1
1992	1,012,424	13.6
1993	1,089,666	7.6*

Estimated. Report includes player not on final rosters.

How salaries compare:

Average Salaries	1982	1991
Male U.S. Worker	$ 21,077	$ 29,421
Baseball Player	241,497	1,012,000
NFL player	95,925	414,920
NBA player	235,000	1,041,667

Barry Bond's $7.3 million baseball salary might be mind-boggling. Yet it's hardly even close to the earnings of popular entertainers in 1992.   (in millions):

Oprah Winfrey	$46
Bill Cosby	40
Prince	35
Steven Spielberg	30
Arnold Schwarzenegger	28
Guns' n Roses	26
Michael Jackson	26
Garth Brooks	24
Madonna	24
Charles M. Schultz	24
Dustin Hoffman	23
Kevin Costner	21

Consider These Questions:

1. What did Babe Ruth's 1930 quote imply about President Hoover's marginal revenue product?

2. Explain why the growth of TV sports has contributed to the dramatic increases in the salaries of professional athletes.

3. Evaluate this statement: The average professional baseball player is 34 times more productive than the average American male worker.

4. Why was the average salary in the NFL during 1991 less than half that of the average NBA salary?

5. Explain why Oprah Winfrey (TV talk show host and actress) earns more than 40 times that of the average professional baseball player.

STUDY QUESTIONS

1. The business of professional sports often captures public attention. What factors distinguish professional sports teams from other business enterprises? Are these factors unique?

2. Discuss why the product markets faced by a professional sports league can be described as imperfectly competitive. Why is the resource market for professional athletes also imperfectly competitive?

3. Explain how competition between professional sports teams on the playing field is enhanced by cooperation in the marketplace.

4. What factors are necessary for firms to form a successful cartel? In what ways do these factors apply to professional sports leagues?

5. Why are cartels often described as "shared monopolies?" Discuss the process whereby firms in a cartel determine the price and level of production necessary to maximize joint profits.

6. Compare and contrast pricing and output in a cartel relative to a competitive market.

7. What is a monopsony? What factors give professional sports teams monopsony power? Provide examples.

8. Why does a monopsony's marginal cost of labor (MCL) curve lie above the market supply of labor curve?

9. How does a monopsony determine the optimum number of workers to employ and the wage to pay them? How does this compare to the decisions of a competitive employer?

10. In what way does a monopsony "exploit" its employees? Discuss the sources of this exploitation.

11. What is free agency in professional sports? What has free agency done to the salaries of professional athletes? How does free agency affect the monopsony power of a professional sports team?

12. Many people argue that professional athletes are overpaid and some professional athletes claim they are underpaid. What economic factors determine how much any employee will be paid in a market economy? Given this, under what circumstances can a professional athlete be overpaid?...underpaid?

PUZZLE   Complete the following crossword puzzle.

Professional Sports

Across

2. The change in total cost due to hiring one additional worker is called the marginal cost of _____.
4. The AL, NL, NBA, NHL, and NFL.
5. The professional basketball league in the U.S. and Canada.
6. The change in a firm's total cost resulting from a one unit change in quantity sold is called _____ cost.
9. The _____ and National Leagues together are known as Major League Baseball.
10. The difference between workers' contributions to a monopsony's receipts and the wage is known as _____ profit.
11. The change in a firm's revenue due to hiring one additional worker is called the marginal revenue _____ of labor.
12. Legislation that prohibits the formation of cartels in most U.S. industries.
14. The primary goal of all professional sports leagues.
15. The process whereby new players are allocated between teams in all four major professional team sports.

Down

1. A group of firms that formally agree to coordinate production and pricing to maximize joint profit.
3. The ''R'' in MRP.
5. The professional hockey league in the U.S. and Canada.
6. A market with only one buyer.
7. Buyers and sellers exchange factors of production in _____ markets.
8. The essential element of all sports.
13. Collusion between firms allows for the maximization of _____ profit.

TRUE-FALSE QUESTIONS Circle T (true) or F (false)

T F 1. A professional hockey team is a business owned and operated for profit.

T F 2. It is in the best interest of professional sports for teams to compete with each other in the marketplace as well as on the field.

T F 3. From an economic perspective, professional sports teams are interdependent with their rivals.

T F 4. Tickets to the World Series and the Superbowl are sold in resource markets.

T F 5. The NFL is a cartel of professional football teams.

T F 6. A cartel is a group of firms that compete against each other in both product and resource markets.

T F 7. Antitrust laws prohibit the formation of cartels in most American industries.

T F 8. The five largest firms in Industry A produce 93 percent of industry output. The five largest firms in Industry B produce 52 percent of industry output. Firms in Industry A are more likely to form a successful cartel than firms in Industry B.

T F 9. The commissioner of a professional sports league enforces league rules which prevent teams from cheating on their cartel agreement.

T F 10. Each team in a professional sports league is individually responsible for selling the television broadcast rights to the games in which it plays.

T F 11. Competitive firms maximize profits by producing a level of output such that marginal revenue equals total cost.

T F 12. Market output will rise and price will fall when firms in a competitive market form a cartel.

T F 13. Cartel agreements between professional sports teams determine how league revenues are distributed between teams.

T F 14. By restricting output and raising price, successful cartels can increase the joint profits of member firms.

T F 15. Teams which belong to the NBA share monopoly power.

T F 16. Player drafts tend to increase competition between professional sports teams in the resource market for athletes.

T F 17. A monopsony exists when there are many buyers in a market.

T F 18. Drafts and employment rules enforced by professional sports leagues create monopsony power for individual teams.

T F 19. Athletes who possess highly specialized skills are less likely to be "exploited" by professional sports teams.

T F 20. The marginal cost of labor (MCL) schedule reflects the additional cost incurred by a firm due to hiring an additional worker.

T F 21. For a monopsony employer, the marginal cost of labor (MCL) curve lies above and is steeper than the market supply of labor curve.

T F 22. The marginal revenue product (MRP) schedule represents the demand for workers.

T F 23. A monopsony will hire additional workers if MRP is less than MCL.

T F 24. As additional players are hired, a team's MCL fails.

T F 25. Free agents can sell their athletic talents to the highest bidder.

MULTIPLE CHOICE QUESTIONS Select the one best answer

1. Economists consider professional sports leagues like the National Football League (NFL) and the National Basketball Association (NBA) to be:
   a. organizations of purely competitive firms.
   b. not-for-profit organizations.
   c. cartels.
   d. non-essential for the survival of professional team sports in a market economy.

2. The primary reason team sports are played professionally in the United States is to:
   a. entertain the fans.
   b. earn profits for team owners.
   c. provide jobs for athletes.
   d. promote the competitive spirit.

3. Each professional sports league enforces rules which limit the ability of players to sell their talents to the highest bidder. These rules:
   a. enhance athletic competition by preventing successful teams from hoarding quality players.
   b. protect the players from exploitation in the resource market.
   c. insure that all players have an equal chance of finding employment with a member club.
   d. prevent players from earning less than their marginal revenue product.

4. A cartel is a group of firms that formally agrees to coordinate its production and pricing decisions in a manner that:
   a. ket share.
   b. eliminates competition from other firms.
   c. increases the profits of each member firm.
   d. maximizes joint profits.

5. Laws that prohibit the formation of cartels in most American industries are known as:
   a. antitrust laws.
   b. tariffs.
   c. usuary laws.
   d. common laws.

6. Each of the major sports leagues has eliminated competition from outside their cartel by:
   a. controlling the contracts of star players.
   b. holding exclusive rights to major stadiums and arenas.
   c. merging with the competition.
   d. All of the above.

7. A cartel can be described as a:
   a. competitively shared market.
   b. purely competitive monopoly.
   c. jointly shared monopoly.
   d. disorganized monopoly market.

8. Cartel rules are enforced in professional sports through:
   a. contractual obligations by the teams with the league.
   b. the good faith efforts of team owners.
   c. the judicial power of the league commissioners.
   d. legislative acts of Congress.

9. The primary source of revenue in professional sports are:
   a. ticket sales.
   b. the merchandising of souvenirs and novelties.
   c. concessions, vending, and parking.
   d. television and radio broadcast rights.

10. Relative to a competitive market, a cartel will cause:
    a. prices to fall and market output to increase.
    b. prices to fall and market output to decrease.
    c. prices to rise and market output to decrease.
    d. prices to rise and market output to increase.

11. Firms in a cartel will produce a level of output such that:
    a. marginal revenue equals marginal cost for each firm.
    b. joint marginal revenue equals joint marginal cost.
    c. joint marginal costs equals market demand.
    d. marginal revenue equals joint total costs.

12. A monopsony is a market with:
    a. many buyers and sellers.
    b. only one seller.
    c. only one buyer.
    d. only a few buyers.

13. The two major factors which generate monopsony power for professional sports teams are:
    a. the mobility of players and free agency.
    b. the immobility of new players and the highly specialized talents of athletes.
    c. the competition between athletes who are free agents and the numerous employment opportunities of athletes.
    d. the new player drafts and high ticket prices.

14. Because a monopsony is the sole buyer of labor in the market:
    a. it faces a positively sloped market supply of labor curve.
    b. it can hire all its workers at the competitive wage rate.
    c. the marginal cost of labor must be less than the wage rate.
    d. the demand for labor does not reflect the workers' marginal revenue product.

15. The marginal revenue product (MRP) of labor represents the:
    a. supply of workers.
    b. cost of hiring additional workers.
    c. demand for workers.
    d. revenue generated by selling additional output.

16. A monopsony will continue to hire workers up to the point where:
    a. S = D
    b. MRP > MCL
    c. MRP < MCL
    d. MRP = MCL

17. If a baseball player contributes more to his team's total revenues than he receives in wages, the team is experiencing:
    a. monopsony profit.
    b. monopoly profit.
    c. competitive profit.
    d. economic losses.

18. Relative to a competitive employer, a monopsony will employ:
   a. more workers at a higher wage.
   b. fewer workers at a higher wage.
   c. more workers at a lower age.
   d. fewer workers at a lower wage.

19. Free agency in professional sports has:
   a. reduced monopsony power and increased average salaries.
   b. increased monopsony power even though salaries have risen.
   c. led to the exploitation of athletes by professional sports leagues.
   d. had little effect on the economics of professional sports.

20. The salary of a professional hockey player is determined by:
   a. the league commissioner.
   b. the U.S. Department of Labor.
   c. his marginal revenue product (MRP).
   d. his contribution to society's welfare.

Use the following graph to answer questions 21 through 23.

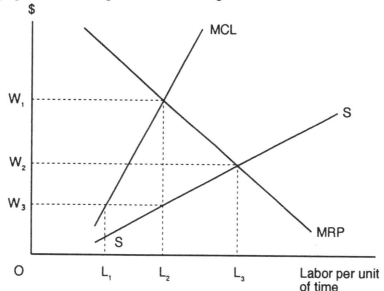

21. This monopsony will employ:
   a. 0 workers.
   b. L_1 workers.
   c. L_2 workers.
   d. L_3 workers.

22. This monopsony will pay its workers:
   a. 0
   b. W_1
   c. W_2
   d. W_3

23. This firm will receive monopsonistic profit equal to the difference between _____ and
   _____.
   a. W_1 0
   b. W_1 W_2
   c. W_1 W_3
   d. W_2 W_3
   e. 0 L_1

24. What is the term for a work stoppage initiated by the management of a firm?
   a. strike.
   b. walk out.
   c. lock out.
   d. boycott.

25. Which of the following provides the best economic description of salary caps in professional sports?
   a. Salary caps are mechanisms for owners to enforce the monopsonistic employment of players league-wide.
   b. Salary caps are essential for owners to earn a "fair profit" on their investment.
   c. Salary caps allow owners to fairly compete against each other in hiring professional athletes.
   d. Salary caps prevent players from exploiting team owners.

PROBLEMS

1. Assume the following data represent the demand for and cost of providing broadcast rights for professional hockey games during one month of the season.

Output	Total Costs ($000)	Marginal Costs ($000)	Price ($000)	Total Revenue ($000)	Marginal Revenue ($000)	Profit ($000)
1	50	50	140	140	140	90
2	110	60	130	260	120	150
3	180	70	120	360	100	180
4	260	80	110	440	80	180
5	350	90	100	500	60	150
6	450	100	90	540	40	90
7	560	110	80	560	20	0

   a. Complete the table by calculating the marginal cost, total revenue, marginal revenue, and profit for each level of output.
   b. To maximize profits the hockey league should sell broadcast rights up to the point where

   _____ = _____

   c. How many games should the hockey league sell to broadcasters in order to maximize profit?

   _____

   d. What happens if the hockey league sells 7 games to broadcasters each month of the season?

2. The hypothetical data below represent the cost and revenue situation faced by a professional baseball team trying to decide how many relief pitchers to hire.

Number of Players	Wage ($000)	Total Cost of Labor ($000)	Marginal Cost of Labor ($000)	Marginal Revenue Product ($000)
1	600	_____	_____	2,000
2	650	_____	_____	1,750
3	700	_____	_____	1,500
4	750	_____	_____	1,250
5	800	_____	_____	1,000
6	850	_____	_____	750
7	900	_____	_____	500

   a. Complete the table by calculating the total cost of labor and the marginal cost of labor for each number of relief pitchers kept on staff.

b. The baseball club should continue to employ relief pitchers up to the point where _____ = _____.

c. How many relief pitchers should the baseball club employ to maximize profit? _____

d. How much will each relief pitcher hired be paid? _____

e. Will this baseball club earn monopsonistic profit? _____ If yes, how much? _____

ANSWERS TO SELF-TEST

PUZZLE

Across		*Down*	
2.	Labor	1.	Cartel
4.	Leagues	3.	Revenue
5.	NBA	5.	NHL
6.	Marginal	6.	Monopsony
9.	American	7.	Resource
10.	Monopsonistic	8.	Competition
11.	Product	13.	Joint
12.	Antitrust		
14.	Profit		
15.	Draft		

TRUE-FALSE QUESTIONS

1.	T	7.	T	13.	T	19.	F	25.	T
2.	F	8.	T	14.	T	20.	T		
3.	T	9.	T	15.	T	21.	T		
4.	F	10.	F	16.	F	22.	T		
5.	T	11.	F	17.	F	23.	F		
6.	F	12.	F	18.	T	24.	F		

MULTIPLE-CHOICE QUESTIONS

1.	c	7.	c	13.	b	18.	d	23.	c
2.	b	8.	a	14.	a	19.	a	24.	c
3.	a	9.	d	15.	c	20.	c	25.	a
4.	d	10.	c	16.	d	21.	c		
5.	a	11.	b	17.	a	22.	d		
6.	d	12.	c						

PROBLEMS

1. a.

Output	Total Costs ($000)	Marginal Costs ($000)	Price ($000)	Total Revenue ($000)	Marginal Revenue ($000)	Profit ($000)
1	50	50	140	140	140	90
2	110	60	130	260	120	150
3	180	70	120	360	100	180
4	260	80	110	440	80	180
5	350	90	100	500	60	150
6	450	100	90	540	40	90
7	560	110	80	560	20	0

b. MR = MC

c. 4

d. No profit will be earned.

2. a.

Number of Players	Wage ($000)	Total Cost of Labor ($000)	Marginal Cost of Labor ($000)	Marginal Revenue Product ($000)
1	600	600	600	2,000
2	650	1300	700	1,750
3	700	2100	800	1,500
4	750	3000	900	1,250
5	800	4000	1000	1,000
6	850	5100	1100	750
7	900	6300	1200	500

b. MRP = MCL

c. 5

d. $800,000

e. Yes, $200,000

Chapter 12
Protectionism Versus Free Trade

Can We Restrict Ourselves Into Prosperity?

LEARNING OBJECTIVES

After studying this issue, you should be able to:

1. State the protectionist and free-trade viewpoints.

2. Explain why a country must import in order to export.

3. Use consumption possibilities curves and the principle of comparative advantage to explain why countries benefit from voluntary exchange.

4. Determine if a country has a comparative advantage or a comparative disadvantage in the production of a good.

5. Explain and illustrate with a graph how the forces of demand for and supply of a foreign currency determine the equilibrium exchange rate and the equilibrium quantity of currency exchanged.

6. Use the determinants of demand and supply for a foreign currency to explain changes in the equilibrium exchange rate.

7. Distinguish between current account and capital account transactions and evaluate the importance of any differences between the total demand for and the total supply of foreign exchanges.

8. Explain and evaluate the outcomes of limiting international voluntary exchange.

9. Explain and illustrate with a graph the effects of pegging an exchange rate below the equilibrium level.

10. State and evaluate the key industries component of the protectionist argument.

CHAPTER ORIENTATION

Advocates of free trade usually have more difficulty during recessions than during periods of economic expansion convincing others of the merits of voluntary free exchange among countries. Who benefits from international trade? Who loses? What are the net effects on living standards of international trade? Are the net effects substantially altered by recessions? To answer these questions, we use the now familiar tool of economic analysis—production possibilities curve and the consumption possibilities curve.

A country's population as a whole will lose from important restrictions because trade usually increases a country's consumption possibilities curve. With trade, a larger real per capita GDP is available for consumption and/or investment.

Another tool of economic analysis, market analytics, allows us to better understand international exchange markets and the balance of payments problems. When the forces that determine the demand and supply of foreign exchange are allowed to determine exchange rates, shortages or surpluses of foreign exchange will a short-term transitional phenomena. Pegging exchange rates provides incentives to restrict trade.

CONSIDER THIS:

The Importance of Trade[1]

With the nation's economic expansion still strong but aging, this year is likely to provide a crucial test of whether increased trade can visibly deliver on its promised benefits to Americans. For now the advance in domestic demand is expected to slow at least somewhat, trade specialists say.

"If the U.S. slows down in the next couple of years," said Jeffrey E. Garten, Under Secretary of Commerce for International Trade, "A lot of slack can be taken up by the resurgence in Europe, Japan and the emerging markets."

Trade, in fact, is becoming the new standard currency of American diplomacy, and not just because the cold war has ended. The nation's annual exports have more than doubled in the last decade, accounting for a sharply rising share of the nation's output.

Although economists see no recession soon, increasing interest rates could retard economic growth at home. But many of America's major trading partners are just getting their own recoveries under way, while much of Asia and Latin America is growing much faster than the United States.

Mexico caught up with Japan last year to become the nation's second-largest export market, behind Canada. Although the recent plunge of the peso and an austerity plan is likely to curb Mexican imports this year, most economists expect Mexican demand for American products to continue rising over the longer run.

For almost a decade now, exports have been one of America's secret economic weapons. United States corporations did so well in foreign markets last year — merchandise exports were up 9.5 percent through September — that they favored the General Agreement on Tariffs and Trade with near-unanimity. From 1985 to 1994, exports rose from 7.2 percent to 10.2 percent of the nation's gross domestic product as American firms vastly improved their competitiveness. With the new global trade agreement and a worldwide economic expansion, business leaders say, things should only get better.

"America has a huge potential for increased export opportunities," said Eckhard Pfeiffer, chief executive of the Compaq Computer Corporation, which gets half its sales from abroad. In an interview, he spoke of having penetrated the Japanese market in 1992, and now expanding in Europe as more companies learn to take advantage of technology. Among the recent visitors at Compaq's headquarters in Houston have been oil executives from the former Soviet republic of Kazakhstan and bankers from Poland.

Labor leaders point out, however, that the trade deficit also swelled last year, despite a weak dollar, which would normally favor exports over imports by making American goods less expensive in foreign markets. And they say the export of jobs, promoted by the year-old North American Free Trade Agreement, is only beginning. While the Administration says that each billion dollars in exports creates 20,000 jobs, the unions respond that each billion dollars in imports destroys 20,000 jobs. And the merchandise trade deficit for 1994 is expected to reach about $160 billion, which would nearly match the 1987 record.

"The trade deficit, the huge deficit, represents a net loss of employment to this nation," said Mark A. Anderson, director of the A.F.L.-C.I.O. Task Force on Trade. "We are losing the broad middle class that provided stability in this country."

Economists ascribe the imbalance to the economy's gathering strength. Import demand is stronger in the United States than abroad because growth is more robust here. They also say that trade promotes the most efficient allocation of resources, which helps lift living standards across the board for nations that participate in the global economy.

---

*[1]Allen R. Myerson, "Looking Outward to Keep U.S. Economy Chugging," *The New York Times*, January 8, 1995. Reprinted with permission.

That is little solace to many union officials. While champion exporting companies tend to pay higher wages, labor leaders contend that the surge in international trade has led to little more than stagnating incomes for many workers.

They point to Caterpillar Inc., a leading supporter of GATT, which has gotten the United Automobile Workers union to allow some new workers to receive $8 winning seats on the plane.

When Brazil wanted to build a $1.5 billion satellite and radar system in the spring to monitor the Amazon environment, Mr. Garten said, the chiefs of the United States space, environmental and interior agencies lobbied their Brazilian counterparts. Secretary Brown visited the country and the United States promised to match any financing that its chief rivals, the French, could offer. The United States won the contest.

As the Administration and many corporations are discovering, the most rapidly growing export markets are sure to be among such rapidly developing nations. For the first three quarters after the new trade pact took effect, exports to Mexico were up 21.7 percent, imports up 22.8 percent.

That's why when other goals conflict with the pursuit of foreign trade these days, those other goals usually give way. The Chinese Government hardly bothered to make even cosmetic improvements in its human rights record in 1993, but the Clinton Administration decided it had little choice but to grant China the most favorable trade status.

Consider These Questions:

1. What does this article's author mean by ''exports have been one of America's secret economic weapons''? Explain.

2. Discuss the debate regarding job losses vs. job gains due to international trade. What does economic theory tell us about this debate?

3. What are the benefits to freer trade for the American consumer? Provide some specific examples.

4. What nations represent the fastest growing segment of total U.S. exports? Why?

STUDY QUESTIONS

1. Identify the viewpoint about international trade that is best illustrated by each of the following quotes.
   a. "Buy a foreign car and put 10 Americans out of work."
   b. "Importing foreign steel reduces America's defense capability."
   c. "Grain exports benefit the American farmer."
   d. "Buy American goods and eliminate the balance of payments deficit."
   e. "As a consumer I want the highest quality product at the lowest possible price. I do not care who produced it."
   f. "If the price of putting Americans back to work is having fewer Nissans and Sonys in America, by all means let's erect the trade barriers."
   g. "My job depends upon a strong import market."
   h. "Save American jobs; buy American-made shoes."
   i. "Trade deficits cost U.S. jobs."

2. American farmers want to export more grain to Japan. How can the Japanese acquire the dollars to purchase American grain?

3. Country A has a comparative advantage in producing shoes and a comparative disadvantage in producing wheat, while country B has the opposite comparative advantage and disadvantage. Use production and consumption possibilities curves to show that both countries would benefit by specialization and trade.

4. The country of Upland uses 5 times the units of labor and capital to produce a million pairs of shoes than does neighboring Flatland. To produce a million pairs of shoes Upland must give up one-half million bolts of cloth. What must be the terms of trade with Flatland for Upland to have a comparative advantage in the production of shoes? Cloth? Explain.

5. Illustrate with graphs the impact on demand, supply, equilibrium exchange rate and quantity exchanged of the following events:
   a. United States reduces import barriers.
   b. Foreign purchases of United States manufactured pharmaceuticals increases 33% in one year.
   c. IBM decides to manufacture the IBM PC in Germany.
   d. An Arab buys a hotel chain in the United States.

6. What determines if an international transaction is a current account or a capital account transaction? Is this distinction an important factor in determining the significance of payments problems?

7. Do "free traders win the arguments" and "protectionists win the elections"? Explain.

8. Illustrate with a graph two ways to eliminate a shortage of foreign exchange resulting from a fixed exchange rate. Which method is preferred? Why?

9. In what sense is the key industries component of the protectionist viewpoint a political rather than an economic argument? Explain.

10. Using the ideas discussed in this chapter, analyze the effect of NAFTA on the American and Mexican economies.

PUZZLE   Complete the following crossword puzzle.

International Trade

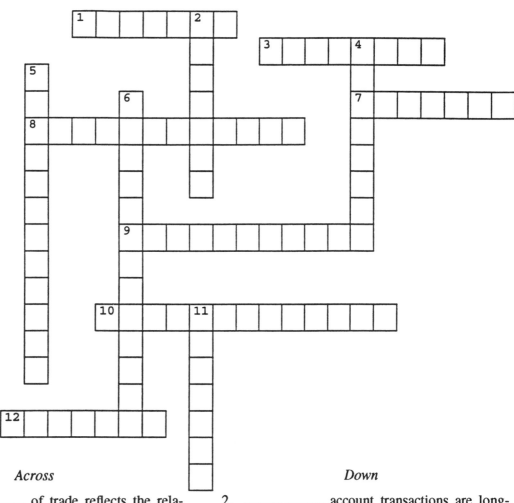

Across

1. The _____ of trade reflects the relationship of the value of a nation's imports to the value of its exports per unit of time.

3. Balance of _____ refers to the relationship between one nation's monetary obligations to other nations, and vice versa.

7. International trade transactions that are more or less immediate or short-term in character are _____ account transactions.

8. Import _____ increase the price of products for the domestic consumer.

9. _____ advantage is the ability of a nation to produce goods and services with a smaller opportunity cost than other nations.

10. The consumption _____ curve shows the maximum quantities of 2 goods or services that may be consumed in an economy.

12. Goods and services that economic units in one country sell to other countries.

Down

2. _____ account transactions are long-term in character and are usually investment types of exchanges.

4. Cost of another nation's currency in terms of units of the home nation's currency is called the _____ rate.

5. Cost of importing goods or services from other countries. (3 words)

6. The view that imports should be restrained to protect domestic industries and jobs.

11. Goods and services purchased and brought into a country from abroad.

TRUE-FALSE QUESTIONS Circle T (true) or F (false)

T F 1. Free traders argue that we are all made better off through specialization and voluntary exchange.

T F 2. Protectionists favor import restrictions as a remedy to the balance of trade and balance of payments problems.

T F 3. A country can export without also importing.

T F 4. In order to by American made IBM microcomputers, Germans must acquire dollars by exporting to the United States.

T F 5. The consumption possibilities curves of trading countries usually increases with trade.

T F 6. A country has a comparative advantage in the production of any good that it can produce with a greater sacrifice of some alternative good or goods than is required in the rest of the world.

T F 7. Different resource endowments and states of technology confer on countries or regions of countries certain comparative advantages and disadvantages that make specialization and exchange worthwhile.

T F 8. A country that must give up two dozen shirts to produce one dozen pairs of shoes domestically but gives up only one dozen shirts if it specializes in the production of shirts and imports shoes, has a comparative disadvantage in the production of shirts.

T F 9. The supply curve for a foreign currency slopes downward to the right.

T F 10. At the equilibrium exchange rate the quantity demanded of a foreign currency exceeds the quantity supplied.

T F 11. Import restrictions would decrease the demand for a foreign currency and reduce the equilibrium exchange rate.

T F 12. Increased exports of United States wheat would increase the supply of foreign currencies and decrease the equilibrium exchange rates.

T F 13. When Nissan decided to manufacture automobiles and trucks in the U.S., the demand for United States dollars and the equilibrium exchange rate of U.S. dollars in Japan both decreased.

T F 14. Capital account transactions have a short-term influence on the demand for and the supply of foreign exchange.

T F 15. A United States balance of payments deficit results from failure to restrict imports and foreign investments by United States firms.

T F 16. The costs of an import restriction usually exceed the benefits.

T F 17. Free trade may reduce domestic profits, wages, and employment levels in export industries.

T F 18. If a government sets its currency exchange rate above the market clearing rate, a shortage will occur.

T F 19. In freely flexible foreign exchange markets shortages or surpluses of foreign currencies usually are short-term phenomena.

T F 20. The key industries component of the protectionists' viewpoint is essentially a political rather than an economic argument.

T F 21. Every product exported from the United States, becomes an import somewhere else in the world.

T F 22. Economic analysis indicates that a nation's population as a whole gains as a result of import restrictions.

T F 23. Exchange rates are determined by the forces of demand and supply of currency.

T F 24. A balance of payments deficit is a foreign exchange surplus.

T F 25. World output for the global economy is larger due to international trade.

MULTIPLE CHOICE QUESTIONS Select the one best answer

1. Protectionists assert that the importation and sale of foreign goods result in:
    a. higher unemployment rates.
    b. balance of trade and balance of payments problems.
    c. weakened defense preparedness.
    d. All of the above.

2. According to the free-trade viewpoint specialization and voluntary exchange among nations:
    a. confer the same benefits on the exchanging parties as trade among individuals in any one country.
    b. benefits importers at the expense of exporters.
    c. inhibit domestic economic activity.
    d. threaten our national defense.
    e. All of the above.

3. A country can:
    a. import without exporting.
    b. export without importing.
    c. export only if it also imports goods.
    d. increase its standard of living by exporting but not by importing.

4. The U.S. must import in order to export because:
    a. foreigners must earn dollars to be able to buy United States exports.
    b. the U.S. has a comparative advantage in the products it imports and exports.
    c. foreign goods can displace a large part of the domestic production and sale of goods.
    d. None of the above.

Use the following diagram for Questions 5-7.

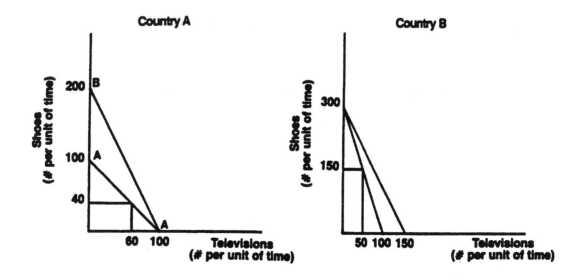

5. As a result of specialization and trade country A's consumption possibilities curve shifts from AA to AB; we can conclude that country A:
   a. has a comparative advantage in shoes and a comparative disadvantage in televisions.
   b. has a comparative advantage in television and should specialize in the production of shoes.
   c. has a comparative disadvantage in shoes and could increase welfare by specializing in the production of televisions.
   d. should produce 60 televisions and 40 shoes.
   e. None of the above.

6. If country B concentrates all of its resources on producing shoes and trades for televisions:
   a. it is 50 television sets better off than it was before trade.
   b. it can import one television for every two pairs of shoes it produces and exports.
   c. its consumption possibilities curve increases.
   d. All of the above.

7. After specialization and trade:
   a. country A could double its consumption of shoes.
   b. country B could consume fifty percent more televisions than before.
   c. the total production for the two countries combined can be 300 shoes and 100 televisions.
   d. All of the above.

8. Country X has a comparative disadvantage in the production of microcomputers if it:
   a. uses 6 times as many units of labor and capital to produce microcomputers than do other countries.
   b. produces microcomputers with a greater sacrifice of some alternative good than do other countries.
   c. produces microcomputers at a lower absolute cost than can other countries.
   d. produces microcomputers with a smaller sacrifice of some alternative good than can other countries.

9. Every country has comparative advantages in the production of some goods and comparative disadvantages in the production of others because countries have different:
   a. resource endowments.
   b. technology levels.
   c. currencies.
   d. All of the above.
   e. Both (a) and (b).

Use the following diagram to answer Question 10.

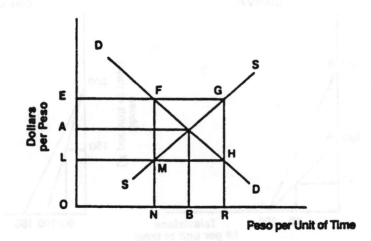

10. The equilibrium exchange rate is measured by distance:
    a. OE
    b. OL
    c. HG
    d. OA

11. The demand for foreign currencies in the United States occurs as a result of:
    a. exports.
    b. foreign investments in the United States.
    c. cash gifts sent by persons in the United States to relative and friends abroad.
    d. All of the above.

12. Import restrictions would:
    a. reduce the demand for foreign currencies and increase the exchange rate.
    b. reduce the demand for foreign currencies and decrease the exchange rate.
    c. increase the demand for foreign currencies and increase the exchange rate.
    d. increase the demand for foreign currencies and decrease the exchange rate.

13. Capital account items:
    a. are immediate and short-term in character.
    b. yield continuing influence on the demand for and supply of foreign exchange.
    c. persist into the future.
    d. Both (b) and (c).
    e. None of the above.

14. The balance of payments:
    a. is a cause for concern when it is negative.
    b. refers to the difference between total demand for and the total supply of foreign exchanges.
    c. is a statistical discrepancy of considerable importance whether it is positive or negative.
    d. All of the above.

15. International voluntary exchanges:
    a. increase the real per capita incomes and living standards in the trading countries.
    b. shift consumption possibilities curves outward.
    c. may injure certain segments of a country's economy.
    d. All of the above.

Use the following diagram to answer Questions 16-18.

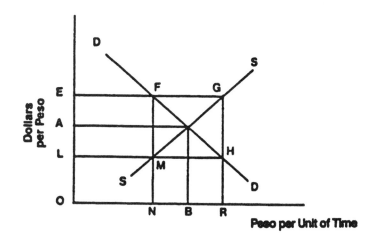

16. If the Mexican government establishes price OE as an exchange rate ceiling for the peso, there will be:
    a. a shortage equal to NR.
    b. a surplus equal to NR.
    c. a shortage equal to OB.
    d. None of the above.

17. Given exchange rate OL, if import restrictions are now imposed on goods produced in Mexico, then:
    a. the exchange rate will increase to OA.
    b. the DD curve would increase and the exchange rate would increase to OE.
    c. the DD curve would decrease and the new equilibrium exchange rate could be OL.
    d. None of the above.

18. If the government eliminates OL as the exchange rate ceiling, then:
    a. the price of the peso will move towards its equilibrium level of OA.
    b. the shortage of pesos at price OL will induce buyers of Mexican goods to bid up the exchange rate.
    c. the balance of payments deficit of NR will be eliminated.
    d. the United States will import less from Mexico.
    e. All of the above.

19. Economic analysis indicates that:
    a. a country's population as a whole usually loses as a result of import restrictions.
    b. balance of payments problems are essentially exchange rate problems caused by pegged exchange rates.
    c. the key industries component of the protectionist viewpoint is essentially political rather than economic.
    d. the benefits of import restrictions rarely outweigh the costs of such protection.
    e. All of the above.

20. To determine if an industry should be protected from foreign competition to assure our national defense, economists would:
    a. weigh the benefits of self-sufficiency in the industry against the costs of self-sufficiency.
    b. use the equimarginal principle.
    c. use the opportunity cost principle.
    d. All of the above.

PROBLEMS

1. Country A's resources will produce 100 Yo-Yos, or 200 Frisbees, or any combination containing less of both products. The resources available to country B will produce 100 Yo-Yos, or 50 frisbees, or any combination of the two products containing less of both products.

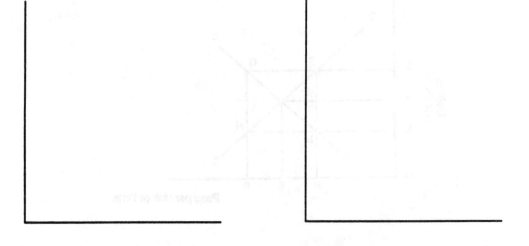

a. Graph the production possibilities information and label the graphs.
b. Which country has a comparative advantage in Yo-Yos? Explain.
c. Suppose the terms of trade are one for one; graph the consumption possibilities curves.
d. What are the gains for specialization and trade for country A? For country B?

2. Suppose the United States pegs its exchange rate for the Mexican peso below the equilibrium level.
a. Using supply and demand curves, illustrate with a graph the situation described above.

b. An effective price ceiling will _____.
c. Congress will have an incentive to _____.
d. If Congress acts, the (shortage/surplus) of the peso will (decrease/increase) and the standard of living will (decrease/increase).

ANSWERS TO SELF-TEST

PUZZLE

Across	Down
1. Balance	2. Capital
3. Payments	4. Exchange
7. Current	5. Terms of Trade
8. Restrictions	6. Protectionist
9. Comparative	11. Imports
10. Possibilities	
12. Exports	

TRUE-FALSE QUESTIONS

1. T	6. F	11. T	16. T	21. T
2. T	7. T	12. T	17. F	22. F
3. F	8. F	13. F	18. F	23. T
4. T	9. F	14. F	19. T	24. F
5. T	10. F	15. F	20. T	25. T

MULTIPLE-CHOICE QUESTIONS

1. d	6. d	11. c	16. b
2. a	7. d	12. b	17. c
3. c	8. e	13. d	18. e
4. a	9. e	14. b	19. e
5. c	10. d	15. d	20. a

PROBLEMS

1. a.

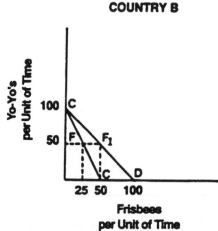

b. Country B has a comparative advantage in the production of Yo-Yos and would specialize in the production of Yo-Yos. Country B can concentrate on Yo-Yo production and trade for Frisbees at less than it would cost to produce them in country B.

c. The consumption possibilities curves are BA and CD.

d. Given country A's consumption possibilities curve, it could consume 200 Frisbees. By trading 100 Frisbees for 100 Yo-Yos, country A can move from combination E containing 50 Yo-Yos and 100 Frisbees to combination E_1 containing 100 Yo-Yos and 100 Frisbees. It is 50 million additional Yo-Yos better off than before specialization and trade. Country B has a net gain of 25 Frisbees. A movement from combination F to F_1.

2. a.

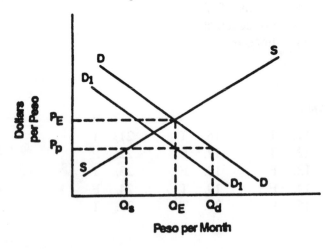

b. An effective price ceiling (P_p) will result in a shortage (Q Q_d).

c. Congress will have an incentive to restrict imports. The demand curve decreases to D_1D_1.

d. shortage, decrease, decrease.

Chapter 13
Unemployment Issues

Why Do We Waste Our Labor Resources?

LEARNING OBJECTIVES

After studying this issue, you should be able to:

1. Explain, using a production possibilities curve, the effect of unemployment on the current production of both consumer and producer goods and services.

2. Explain, using production possibilities curve, the effect of unemployment on economic growth.

3. Identify and discuss the social-psychological effects of unemployment.

4. Evaluate the importance of the economic effects of unemployment relative to the social-psychological effects.

5. Provide the official definition of the U.S. labor force and be able to identify the necessary characteristics to be included.

6. Define unemployment and explain how it is measured and in what sense the measurement procedure is satisfactory and unsatisfactory.

7. List and evaluate three types of unemployment in terms of the goals of economic stability, economic security, and economic freedom.

8. Identify the unemployed by demographic characteristics and discuss their unemployment rate differences.

9. *Explain, using the circular flow of economic activity, how the overall economy operates and identify the nature and extent of economic inter-dependency.

10. Define aggregate demand and explain its determinants.

11. Calculate multipliers and use them to determine the impact of changes in investment, government spending, and taxes on output demanded.

12. *Define aggregate supply and explain its determinants.

13. Explain diagrammatically, how an economy's output and employment are determined by aggregate demand and aggregate supply.

14. Explain why a portion of the aggregate supply curve is vertical (perfectly inelastic).

15. Explain what is meant by "deficient aggregate demand" and "weak aggregate supply" and relate them to unemployment equilibrium.

16. List the leakages from and the injections to the circular flow of economic activity and use them to explain why the level of economic activity fluctuates and why, under some circumstances, aggregate demand may fail to provide full employment.

17. List the reasons for a weak aggregate supply and explain how these factors may lead to cyclical unemployment.

18. Identify and evaluate the effectiveness of aggregate demand and aggregate supply policies for reducing cyclical unemployment.

CHAPTER ORIENTATION

You should move slowly through this chapter because the chapter covers a lot of new material. It introduces aggregate economic analysis. This analysis examines the economic forces that determine the level of production, income, and employment in the entire economy.

The social issue is economic instability. The goal is to reduce economic instability. As you will quickly discover, economic stability involves both prices and employment. As you deal with employment in this chapter, keep in mind that the two—price and employment stability—are not isolated concerns. Policies designed to stabilize one may lead to less stability of the other; i.e., price and employment stability are not necessarily complementary. Furthermore, the pursuit of either may adversely affect the attainment of other economic goals. As before, policy choices must be made and they are likely to be ambiguous.

Without an operational definition of unemployment, determining and evaluating employment policy would be difficult at best and at the worst unsuccessful. An operational definition of unemployment generates data that indicate the general unemployment rate, the unemployment rates among people of different age and socioeconomic backgrounds, the unemployment trends and the effects of policy on unemployment rates. You will want to attend carefully to the definition of unemployment and how unemployment is measured.

The circular flow of economic activity is presented in order to provide you with an insight into the operation of the overall economy. In addition, the circular flow of economic activity should be studied carefully as it will help you develop the concepts of aggregate demand and aggregate supply.

The price level and national output are determined when the total output demanded by consumers, investors, and government is equal to the output supplied by producers. Consumer spending is determined by many factors including income, wealth, and the interest rate. Investment spending is determined by the interest rate and the expected rate of return on investment. Government purchases are the final output of goods and services demanded by the government. Exports increase domestic output demanded and imports reduce domestic output demanded.

At the equilibrium level of prices and output, the economy may or may not be at full employment. You should be able to show diagrammatically an equilibrium level of prices and output at less than full employment and at full employment.

Aggregate economic analysis provides the framework for understanding why the economy has ups and downs. More specifically, it explains why people lose jobs and why jobs are created. People lose jobs when production in the economy contracts, say, because of a decrease in aggregate demand or a weak aggregate supply. In reference to the circular flow diagram and aggregate demand this means that leakages in the form of saving plus taxes plus imports are greater than injections. On the other hand, jobs are created when production in the economy expands, say, because of an increase in aggregate demand. In this instance, injections in the forms of investment plus exports plus government purchases are greater than leakages. Unemployment may also result from supply side forces including higher resource prices and inefficient techniques of production. Resource price increases unaccompanied by productivity increases cause aggregate supply to decrease and unemployment. In addition, a weak aggregate supply may be attributed to inappropriate incentives to save and work.

A successful employment stabilization policy acknowledges that unemployment may arise from the demand side and the supply side of the market. An aggregate demand approach to reducing unemployment involves increasing government expenditures related to taxes.

Policies designed to increase the productivity of resources and decrease the price of resources would reduce supply-side induced unemployment. A comprehensive policy would include both kinds of activities since jobs and employment opportunities depend upon both aggregate supply and aggregate demand.

CONSIDER THIS:

Joblessness and the Single Parent[1]

Single parents in developed nations are twice as likely to face unemployment as married workers, according to a study presented here last week.

To make matters worse, the crisis of unemployment stings single parents far more sharply, because they don't have another income in the household to support them until they find another job.

"Lone parents appear to be particularly vulnerable to above-average rates of unemployment," said John P. Martin, deputy director of education, employment, labor and social affairs with the Organization for Economic Cooperation and Development, a Paris-based group of advanced nations devoted to promoting economic growth.

Single parents "experience unemployment rates twice or more those of husbands and wives," Martin said.

Many single parents are trapped into unemployment by rules of public assistance programs and taxation, and a lack of affordable day care for their children, Martin said.

For example, in the United States, welfare recipients face curbs on employment earnings, and in many nations those on public assistance may find taxes take so much of their earnings if they find jobs that it isn't worthwhile to seek the low-paying jobs for which they are qualified.

Martin terms these conditions "unemployment/poverty traps."

While single parents in developed nations face a higher likelihood of becoming unemployed, they are still a minority among those without jobs, Martin said.

"Less than half of the unemployed live in households where no other family member is employed," Martin said. It's just that unemployment is far less of a problem if someone else in the household still brings home an income.

Female unemployment varies widely among developed nations, from a low of about 4 percent in Austria, Sweden and Switzerland to a high of almost 26 percent in Spain, Martin said. In most nations, the unemployment rate among women is higher than the rate among men.

Looking at the total unemployment problem throughout developed nations, Martin painted a dark picture, and nowhere is it bleaker than in Europe.

Unemployment in the European Community rose "sharply in the mid-1970s," and is currently "at record rates around 10-11 percent" Martin said.

In the EC, "more than 40 percent of the unemployed" have been out of work for more than a year, he said. "In the early 1990s, between 40 percent and 60 percent of the young unemployed in Belgium, Ireland, Italy and Spain had been out of work for over a year.

"Older workers tend to experience the greatest risk of long-term unemployment," Martin said. In 11 out of the 19 industrialized nations in the OECD for which figures are available," over 50 percent of unemployed males aged 55 and over had been out of work for a year or more in 1992."

In North America, unemployment rates that were relatively high in the 1950s and 1960s have risen only slowly since 1970, with the jobless rate for Canada, Mexico and the United States currently about 7 percent of the labor force, he said.

In Japan, things appear rosy on the surface, with unemployment rate less than 3 percent, he said. However, that may be misleading, concealing underemployment, he said.

---

[1]"Single Parents More Often Face Joblessness," *The Houston Chronicle*, August 28, 1994. Reprinted with permission.

"The rising tide of unemployment has been a major blot on the economic record of the OECD countries since the early 1970s," Martin said. Joblessness in developed nations "is close to a record high and, even though a cyclical recovery is now underway throughout the OECD area, this is not expected to make major or rapid inroads into the total of 35 million persons unemployed" in developed countries.

Solving the unemployment mess worldwide will require new government programs, and even then it won't be easy to reduce unemployment, Martin said. His comment supports proposals such as those by President Clinton to provide government jobs for some long-term unemployed people, worker retraining for those who lost their jobs when companies mod to foreign nations, and training for those on welfare so they can hold private-company jobs.

"The present problem has built up over several decades and will take time to unwind," he said.

Consider These Questions:

1. Why are single parents more vulnerable to unemployment? Explain with examples.

2. How can public assistance programs actually prolong the unemployment of parents? What should be the primary goal of public assistance programs - to receive property or to lower unemployment?

3. How does unemployment vary between the nations discussed in this article? Can you provide economic or sociologic explanations why unemployment rates vary across national boundaries?

4. How does the unemployment rate in the OECD nations compare today to decades of the recent past? Why has it changed over time?

STUDY QUESTIONS

1. How is the current production of consumer and producer goods and services affected by unemployment? Use a production possibilities curve to illustrate this effect of unemployment and the total cost of unemployment.

2. Using production possibilities curves, illustrate how the economic goals of economic growth and economic stability are interrelated.

3. From the following list identify those headlines which indicate either an economic or social-psychological effect of unemployment. Justify your classification.
   a. "Male Nurse Workers as Stripper"
   b. "Demand for Family Counseling Increases During Recession"
   c. "Unemployed Workers Meet to Discuss Problems"
   d. "Hundreds Lose Their Homes During Recession"
   e. "Suicides Increase During Recessions"
   In your opinion, which of the two effects of unemployment represents more of a problem to society? Why?

4. Amy Irwin is a full time study at Big State University. She does not have a job. Is Ms. Irwin unemployed? Explain. Identify and discuss situations in which an individual is not working and is not unemployed.

5. At any wage greater than the equilibrium wage, involuntary unemployment exists. What does involuntary unemployment mean? Why would some individuals (person-hours) voluntarily leave the market as the wage rates falls?

6. Jim Smith recently quit his job as a construction foreman for J.B. Tunnel Company. He is looking for a better job opportunity. What type of unemployment is Mr. Smith experiencing? Is this type of unemployment considered a significant economic problem? Explain.

7. Jill Peters does not expect to be called back to work on the auto assembly line. It has been modernized. Ms. Peters' work will be done by robots. What type of unemployment is created by the assembly line modernization? Is it considered a serious economic problem? Explain.

8. Linda Hall looked for work for eight months but has not attempted to find a job during the last five weeks. Ms. Hall says she is discouraged and cannot bear to be rejected again. Is Linda unemployed? Included in the labor force? What impact does her labor force status have on the unemployment rate? Explain.

9. What demographic groups have unemployment rates higher than the general unemployment rate?

10. The circular flow of economic activity, as a tool of analysis, helps explain how the overall economy operates. Use the circular flow to indicate how jobs and income are created in the economy, to describe how producers and households are related, and to identify the nature and extent of economic interdependency.

11. How is the output demanded of goods at any price level determined? Is this output aggregate demand? Explain

12. How much will output demanded increase as the result of an investment of $200 million if the marginal property to consume (MPC) is 4/5? Will output demanded increase or decrease if the MPC is 3/4?

13. What are the determinants of aggregate supply?

14. Construct an aggregate demand graph.
    a. Choose a price level at random and identify the aggregate quantity that will be demanded per unit of time at that price.
    b. What happens to aggregate quantity demanded if the price level increases?
    c. Show what happens to aggregate quantity demanded for the price level selected for (a) above if the output demanded by consumers decreases. Is this a change in aggregate demand or a change in aggregate quantity demanded? Explain.
    d. What happens to the aggregate demand curve if the outputs purchased by investors increases? Illustrate on the graph.

15. Graph an aggregate supply curve.
    a. For a price chosen at random identify the aggregate quantity supplied.
    b. Show what happens to aggregate quantity supplied if the price level decreases.
    c. What happens to the aggregate quantity supplied for the price level selected for (a) above if the aggregate supply increases? Resource prices increase? If the productivity of resources increases?

16. Use what you know about production possibilities curves to explain why a portion of the aggregate supply curve is perfectly inelastic.

17. When are aggregate demand and aggregate supply deficient? Can the deficiency exist at an equilibrium price and output? Use a graph to illustrate.

18. What are the three leakages from and the three injections to the circular flow of economic activity? When total leakages are greater than total injections, will aggregate demand be deficient? If yes, how will producers react and why? What will happen to the number of jobs?

19. Under what circumstances could aggregate supply decrease and cause unemployment?

20. Given cyclical unemployment, is it appropriate to use aggregate demand and aggregate supply policies? Explain.

PUZZLE   Complete the following crossword puzzle.

Unemployment Problems

Across

2. Unemployment above the full employment unemployment rate reduces _____. (Initials)
4. The change in consumption divided by the change in income. (Initials)
5. Aggregate _____ is the total quantity of goods and services offered for sale at various price levels, other things equal.
6. All noninstitutionalized persons 16 or older who are either working for pay, seeking a job or awaiting recall from a layoff. (2 words)
9. Withdrawals from spending in the circular flow.
11. New spending in the circular flow including new investment, new government expenditures, and new exports.
12. Expenditures for one group are the incomes for others, who in turn spend and provide income for still others. (2 words)
14. Brief periods of unemployment experienced by persons moving between jobs or into the labor market.
16. The level of national output that would be produced at full employment is called _____ GDP.

Down

1. The change in savings divided by the change in income.
3. Unemployment caused by economic fluctuations. It results from inadequate levels of aggregate demand.
4. The reciprocal of one minus the marginal propensity to consume.
7. Members of the labor force who are not currently working for pay.
8. Unemployed workers who stop actively seeking a job become _____ workers and are no longer part of the labor force.
10. Total quantity of output demanded per unit of time by the economy at various price levels, all else equal, is called _____ demand.
13. Unemployment caused by a mismatch between the skills of job seekers and the requirements of available jobs.
15. The difference between potential GDP and actual GDP is known as the GDP _____.

TRUE-FALSE QUESTIONS Circle T (true) or F (false)

T F 1. The social costs of unemployment is the economic value of the output lost due to unemployed resources.

T F 2. The ability of the economy to produce in the future is unaffected by the current level of unemployment.

T F 3. Potential GDP is the economic value of goods and services that would be produced if resources of the economy were fully utilized.

T F 4. Human relationships both inside and outside the family tend to be seriously affected by unemployment.

T F 5. The difference between what may be produced at full employment and what is produced at less than full employment measures both the economic and social costs of unemployment.

T F 6. The unemployment rate equals the ratio of the number of persons who are unemployed to the number of persons in the labor force.

T F 7. Persons who are not actively seeking employment are not included in the labor force and therefore are unemployed.

T F 8. A person who is seeking a job and willing to work only at a wage rate more than the market wage rate is called involuntarily unemployed.

T F 9. Work-study college students are members of the U.S. labor force.

T F 10. An increase in wages and/or a decrease in demand tends to reduce involuntary unemployment.

T F 11. Structural unemployment is a short-run phenomenon which is caused by the rational behavior of labor.

T F 12. Cyclical unemployment results from economic changes that cause the demand for specific kinds of labor to be low relative to the supply in particular markets and regions of the economy.

T F 13. If labor services are voluntarily not employed in the short run, we call it frictional unemployment.

T F 14. The unemployment rate among whites is usually about half of the unemployment rate among minority groups.

T F 15. The circular flow of economic activity shows in a simple way that the demand for resources depends on the demand for products.

T F 16. An aggregate demand curve relates the quantities demanded to the price level. This relation is a direct (positive) one.

T F 17. The determinants of aggregate demand are resource prices and the techniques of production.

T F 18. Exports increase domestic output demanded and imports reduce domestic output demanded.

T F 19. An increase in investment of $100 million will increase output demanded by $500 million if the marginal propensity to consume is 3/4.

T F 20. An increase in transfer payment financed by an equal increase in lump-sum taxes will increase the output demanded.

T F 21. The aggregate supply has a negative slope because as marginal output expands marginal costs increase.

T F 22. Starting from unemployment equilibrium, full employment output can be brought about if aggregate demand and/or aggregate supply can be increased sufficiently enough.

T F 23. Employment and job opportunities depend upon both aggregate demand and aggregate supply.

T F 24. A portion of the aggregate supply curve is vertical because supply increases as the price level increases.

T F 25. Aggregate demand is deficient when the equilibrium output is greater than the full employment output.

T F 26. Output and employment will increase when savings plus taxes plus imports are greater than investment plus exports plus government purchases.

T F 27. The weakness or strength of aggregate supply depends essentially upon the level of resources prices and the techniques of production.

T F 28. If government taxation and expenditure programs reduce incentives to work and people work less, then the supply of labor decreases, aggregate supply decreases, and unemployment increases.

T F 29. An increase in the price of labor, unless offset by an increase in the productivity of labor, would tend to increase aggregate supply, employment, and output.

T F 30. The recession which began in 1990 was relatively mild and of average duration.

MULTIPLE CHOICE QUESTIONS Select the one best answer

1. During the periods of unemployment:
   a. capital goods which become obsolete are not replaced.
   b. machines as well as persons are idle.
   c. the productivity of labor is reduced.
   d. the future production capacity of the economy increases less rapidly.
   e. All of the above.

Answer Questions 2 and 3 using the following diagram where AA is the country's initial production possibilities curve.

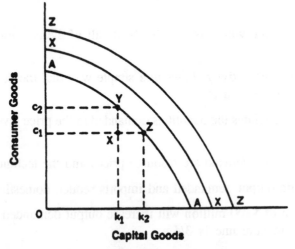

2. An economy with unemployed resources could produce:
   a. Oc_2 of consumer goods and Ok_1 of capital goods.
   b. Oc_1 of consumer goods and Ok_1 of capital goods.
   c. Oc_2 of capital goods and Oc_1 of consumer goods.
   d. None of the above.

3. Compared with point X, the full employment output of point Z results in:
   a. increased production of capital goods from Ok_1 to Ok_2.
   b. decreased output of consumer goods from Oc_2 to Oc_1.
   c. a larger shift in the production possibilities curve from AA to ZZ.
   d. Both (a) and (c).
   e. All of the above.

4. The effect of unemployment is that:
   a. the stability of the family as an economic and social unit is not threatened.
   b. without income or with a loss of income, the head of the family cannot play the role in which he/she was cast.
   c. family wants and needs are somehow always fulfilled, and family relationships do not suffer as a consequence.
   d. human relationships outside the family are not seriously affected.

5. Which of the following criteria are part of the official labor force definition?
   a. noninstitutionalized individuals 16 years of age and above
   b. working for pay
   c. actively seeking work or awaiting recall from a layoff
   d. All of the above.

6. The unemployment rate is defined by the number of persons:
   a. not working divided by number of persons in the labor force.
   b. in the labor force divided by number of persons unemployed.
   c. included in the labor force who are unemployed divided by number of persons in the labor force.
   d. included in the labor force who are unemployed multiplied by number of persons in the labor force.

7. Which of the following is true concerning discouraged workers?
   a. Discouraged workers are members of the labor force.
   b. Discouraged workers are unemployed members of the labor force.
   c. Discouraged workers cause the unemployment rate to be over-stated.
   d. Discouraged workers cause the unemployment rate to be under-stated.

Questions 8 and 9 are based on the following diagram:

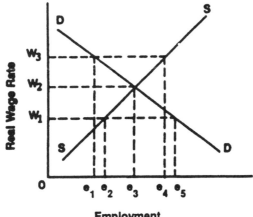

8. For real wage rate OW_3 the amount of labor:
   a. demanded is Oe_3.
   b. supplied is greater than the amount of labor demanded.
   c. supplied is Oe_1.
   d. None of the above.

9. Involuntary unemployment:
   a. is present at all levels of real wages rates above OW_2.
   b. at real wage rate OW_1, would disappear because purely competitive market forces would cause the real wage rate to increase.
   c. at real wage rate OW_3, is equal to the distance between Oe_1 and Oe_4.
   d. Both (a) and (c).
   e. None of the above.

10. Recently workers in the beef industry have lost their jobs largely due to a decrease in consumer preference for beef. The unemployment is best classified as:
   a. structural unemployment.
   b. frictional unemployment.
   c. cyclical unemployment.
   d. Both (b) and (c).

11. Frictional unemployment is:
   a. caused by economic fluctuations.
   b. usually originated on the demand side of labor.
   c. caused by economic changes that cause the demand for specific kinds of labor to be low relative to its supply.
   d. transitional or short run in nature and is caused by labor services not being voluntarily employed.

12. Cyclical unemployment is caused by:
   a. technological change.
   b. reductions in aggregate demand for goods and services in the overall economy.
   c. voluntary unemployment on the part of the labor force.
   d. increases in aggregate supply.

13. The lowest unemployment rates are for:
   a. the young between the ages of 16 and 19.
   b. ethnic groups.
   c. women 20 years and over.
   d. men 20 years and over.
   e. None of the above.

14. Which of the following statements is correct?
   a. Females normally have a lower unemployment rate than males.
   b. The unemployment rate among whites is approximately the same as the unemployment rate among minority groups.
   c. The youth unemployment rate is usually about three times higher than the overall unemployment rate.
   d. All of the above.

15. The circular flow of economic activity:
   a. shows that income is created in the process of production.
   b. has breaks called leakages and injections.
   c. indicates that if leakages do not equal injections people will lose their jobs.
   d. shows that aggregate demand may be deficient for a number of reasons.
   e. All of the above.

16. The determinants of aggregate demand are:
   a. resource prices and the techniques of production.
   b. consumer spending, investment spending, government purchases and net exports.
   c. the marginal propensity to consume and the investment multiplier.
   d. exports and the government purchase multiplier.
   e. None of the above.

17. Assuming a marginal propensity to consume of 3/4 a decrease in investment of $200 million will:
   a. increase output demanded by $800 million.
   b. increase output demanded by $1,000 million.
   c. decrease output demanded by $800 million.
   d. decrease output demanded by $1,000 million.

18. An increase in government purchases financed by an equal increase in lump-sum tax will:
   a. increase output demanded.
   b. decrease output demanded.
   c. not change output demanded.
   d. decrease output demanded if the tax multiplier is one.

19. Aggregate supply increases when:
   a. resource prices decrease.
   b. consumer spending increases.
   c. government spending increases.
   d. the techniques of production improve.
   e. Both (a) and (d).

20. Aggregate supply curves:
   a. have a positive slope.
   b. graph the positive relationship between output supplied and the price level.
   c. show that it is profitable to produce higher levels of national output only at higher price levels.
   d. All of the above.

21. Employment and job opportunities depend upon:
   a. aggregate demand.
   b. aggregate supply.
   c. both aggregate demand and supply
   d. None of the above.

22. A portion of the aggregate supply curve is vertical because:
   a. the price level and output are inversely related.
   b. producers tend to produce more at higher prices and less at lower prices.
   c. output can be expanded beyond a given level.
   d. of scarcity.

23. A deficient aggregate demand means that at the equilibrium price level output demanded:
   a. equals the full-employment output.
   b. is less than the full-employment output.
   c. is greater than the full-employment output.
   d. increases to create maximum production and no cyclical unemployment.

Questions 24 through 26 refer to the following diagram:

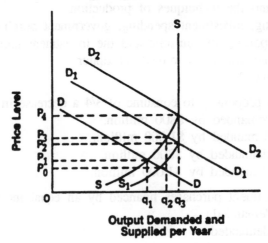

24. Given aggregate supply, SS, the increase in aggregate demand from DD to D_1D_1:
    a. increases the price level only.
    b. increases the level of prices and output.
    c. decreases the level of employment.
    d. increases the level of output only.
    e. None of the above.

25. Given aggregate supply, SS, the full-employment output is:
    a. Oq_1.
    b. obtained with aggregate demand D_1D_1.
    c. Oq_3.
    d. None of the above.

26. The full employment output can be obtained by an increase in aggregate demand:
    a. from DD to D_1D_1 given aggregate supply SS.
    b. from DD to D_2D_2 given aggregate supply SS.
    c. from DD to D_1D_1 if aggregate supply also increases from SS to S_1S_1.
    d. Both (b) and (c).

27. Aggregate demand may be deficient because:
    a. taxes are too low relative to government purchases.
    b. part of the income created by production does not return to producers in the form of spending.
    c. imports are less than exports.
    d. All of the above.

28. A deficient aggregate supply may be caused by:
    a. labor costs greater than productivity.
    b. government taxation and expenditure programs that reduce people's incentives to work.
    c. government taxation and expenditure programs that decrease incentives to save.
    d. All of the above.

29. The aggregate demand approach to unemployment:
    a. would increase aggregate demand directly by increasing government purchases and indirectly by reducing taxes.
    b. has been an unqualified success.
    c. provided a long period of growth and low unemployment rates in the 1970s.
    d. can reduce unemployment without increasing the price level.

30. The United States economy:
   a. has experienced foreign trade surplus since 1983.
   b. began the decade of the 1990's in a recession.
   c. has experienced eleven expansions during the past sixty years.
   d. Both (b) and (c).

PROBLEMS

1. Illustrate in the graph below the effect of a minimum wage law upon employment, assuming the legal minimum wage is above the competitive wage rate, w.

2. Circle the correct wording to complete the following statements.

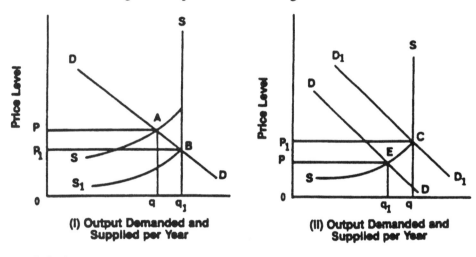

a. In graph I above, the movement from aggregate supply curve SS to aggregate supply curve S_1S represents (an increase, a decrease) in (aggregate supply, aggregate quantity supplied). The movement from point A to point B along aggregate demand curve DD represents (an increase, a decrease) in (aggregate demand, aggregate quantity demanded). Before the change from SS to S_1S the economy was at (full employment, less than full employment). After the change from SS to S_1S the economy was at (full employment, less than full employment) and the price level had (increased, decreased).

b. In graph II above, the movement from aggregate demand curve DD to aggregate demand curve D_1D_1 illustrates (an increase, a decrease) in (aggregate demand, aggregate quantity demanded). The movement from point E to point C along aggregate supply curve SS represents (an increase, a decrease) in (aggregate supply, aggregate quantity supplied). Before the change from DD to D_1D_1, the economy was at (full employment, less than full employment). After the change from DD to D_1D_1, the economy was at (full employment, less than full employment) and the price level had (increased, decreased).

3. Using aggregate demand and aggregate supply curves, illustrate an unemployment equilibrium and a full employment equilibrium.

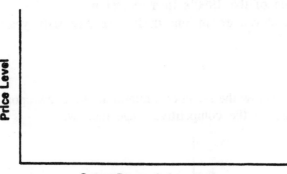

4. Show what happens to aggregate demand if:
   a. the money supply decreases.
   b. tax rates decrease.
   c. government expenditures decrease.

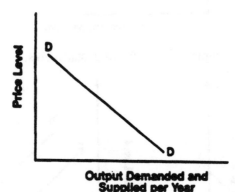

ANSWERS TO SELF-TEST

PUZZLE

Across		Down	
2.	GDP	1.	MPS
4.	MPC	3.	Cyclical
5.	Supply	4.	Multiplier
6.	Labor Force	7.	Unemployed
9.	Leakages	8.	Discouraged
11.	Injections	10.	Aggregate
12.	Circular Flow	13.	Structural
14.	Frictional	15.	Gap
16.	Potential		

TRUE-FALSE QUESTIONS

1.	F	9.	T	17.	F	24.	F
2.	F	10.	F	18.	T	25.	F
3.	T	11.	F	19.	F	26.	F
4.	T	12.	F	20.	F	27.	T
5.	F	13.	T	21.	F	28.	T
6.	F	14.	T	22.	T	29.	F
7.	F	15.	T	23.	T	30.	T
8.	T	16.	F				

MULTIPLE-CHOICE QUESTIONS

1.	e	9.	d	17.	c	24.	b
2.	b	10.	a	18.	a	25.	c
3.	d	11.	d	19.	e	26.	d
4.	b	12.	b	20.	d	27.	b
5.	d	13.	d	21.	c	28.	d
6.	c	14.	c	22.	d	29.	a
7.	d	15.	e	23.	b	30.	d
8.	b	16.	b				

PROBLEMS

1.

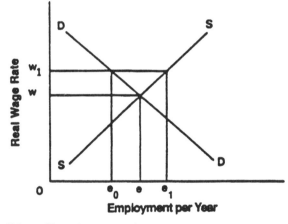

The effect is unemployment equal to $e_0 e_1$.

2. a. an increase, aggregate supply.
        an increase, aggregate quantity demanded.
        less than full employment.
        full employment, decreased.
    b. an increase, aggregate demand.
        an increase, aggregate quantity supplied.
        less than full employment.
        full employment, increased.

3.

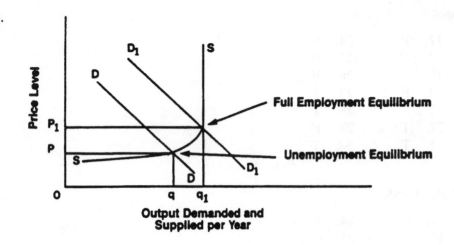

4. a. aggregate demand curve shifts to the left.
    b. aggregate demand curve shifts to the right.
    c. aggregate demand curve shifts to the left.

Chapter **14**
Inflation

How to Gain and Lose at the Same Time

LEARNING OBJECTIVES

After studying this issue, you should be able to:

1. Define inflation and explain how consumer and producer price expectations contribute to inflation.

2. Define and explain suppressed inflation.

3. Explain how inflation is measured; identify, compare, and contrast the indexes generally used.

4. Use index numbers to determine the rate of inflation.

5. List and discuss the major economic effects of inflation.

6. *Explain how some people may benefit from inflation.

7. Define money, list the components of the money supply, and explain the three functions of money.

8. Explain how the lending and investing activities of commercial banks and other depository institutions create money.

9. Calculate the money multiplier and use it to determine the maximum expansion of the money supply.

10. List the major monetary policy tools of the Federal Reserve System and explain how they affect the money supply and economic stability.

11. Explain, using quantity theory of money, the causes of inflation.

12. Explain, using aggregate demand-aggregate supply theory, demand-pull inflation.

13. Explain how fiscal policy and monetary policy can help control demand-pull inflation.

14. Explain, using aggregate demand-aggregate supply theory, the effect of cost-push inflation on prices and output.

15. Discuss and evaluate incomes policies designed to control cost-push inflation.

CHAPTER ORIENTATION

This chapter is compact and introduces new concepts and theories. Therefore, you should work through it with deliberation. The aggregate demand and aggregate supply tools developed in the previous chapter are used again in this chapter.

For consumers, inflation may result in falling real income. Unless income is increasing faster than prices, consumers' claims to real output must decline. Note that an increase in the price of a few products or services is not necessarily inflationary. While some prices may be increasing, others may be decreasing. Individuals whose earned incomes rise faster than prices benefit from inflation. Individuals whose earned incomes rise less rapidly than prices lose as a result of inflation. Thus, some people benefit while others lose from inflation. Why might even those who benefit in the above sense from inflation object to it? As you study the issue, be sure you understand under what circumstances inflation has undesirable equity, efficiency, and output effects.

The operation of a complex economy, one characterized by considerable specialization, is facilitated by money. When the money supply increases faster than real output, the price level increases. Failure to adequately control the money supply may lead to inflation. Thus, the money supply must be controlled. In the United States, the money supply depends mainly on the lending and investing activities of commercial banks and other depository institutions. It is controlled by the monetary policy tools of the Federal Reserve System, namely, the reserve ratio, open-market operations and the discount rate.

After you think you understand the meaning and the effects of inflation, study carefully the role of money in the inflationary process. Using the equation of exchange and the quantity theory of money, you should be able to determine the significance of the money supply in determining the price level and national output.

An aggregate demand and aggregate supply approach to the causes of inflation and the cures for inflation reveals that excess aggregate demand initiates and causes demand-pull inflation. In addition, the approach finds that cost-push inflation results from increases in resource prices that are not offset by productivity. Monetary and fiscal policies are appropriate for demand-pull inflation but not for cost-push inflation. An effective cost-push inflation policy might include measures designed to restore competitive markets, including an incomes policy and measures to control the money supply.

CONSIDER THIS:

Zero Inflation Not Always A Good Deal[1]

The Federal Reserve Board in its wisdom - whether infinite or infantile - is moving steadfastly forward in its goal to eliminate inflation. While it seems like an excellent idea whose time has finally come, this might be a good time to give it some more thought.

In a speech last week, San Francisco Federal Reserve Bank President Robert Parry said he thinks the Fed will eventually succeed in eliminating inflation through its control of the nation's money supply.

One's first thought might be that zero inflation would be helpful to those planning their retirement years. The only thing tougher on a fixed-income budget than inflation is runaway inflation. About the only way retirees on a fixed income can deal with inflation they didn't count on is to go back to work or reduce spending, even if it means canned goods instead of T-bone. Right? Not necessarily. Inflation is not the only thing that drives prices up. Supply and demand will always cause the price of some things to go up, others to fall.

Zero inflation also seems to suggest that the cost of the weekly grocery basket would remain the same for years to come, that a $20,000 car in 1994 would be about the same in 1998, and that homebuyers wouldn't have to rush to purchase a home when the price and interest rates are right. Unfortunately, it isn't as simply as that, even to economists. Few, in fact, can agree that inflation is an enemy or a foe - or on how much of it is a good thing and how much is a bad thing.

One thing to remember, however, is that the Federal Reserve Board makes the decisions about interest rates offered by the Federal Reserve Bank, which is - for better or worse - a banker's bank. It is highly likely then, that goals of the central bank are established more to please lenders (banks) than borrowers (consumers). Alan Greenspan, current chairman of the Federal Reserve Board if the coiner of the term "zero inflation," and remains its chief promoter.

Martin Kessler, a Central Florida economist who teaches at Rollins College and is president of Econometrics Corp., is among those who think that a little bit of inflation is not all bad. "A little inflation is a good thing," Kessler said, "too much is not good - but zero inflation is probably not good either."

---

[1]Dick Marlowe, "Zero Inflation Not Always Good Deal for Consumers," *Orlando Sentinel Tribune*, January 9, 1994. Reprinted with permission.

With zero inflation, he explains, pay raises may be harder to come by, our homes would not gain nearly as much resale value over the years, and business owners would have less incentive to invest in plant and equipment. "A businessman," Kessler said, "is not so much interested in protecting his principal. He want to sell at a price greater than his cost." Inflation, of course, helps him to do that, and that makes the economy tick.

Zero inflation, Kessler contends, does not provide "a solid basis for stimulating the national economy." In fact, he adds, it could have the potential of putting a damper on the economy - and prevent a satisfactory rate of economic growth. Given the choice, Kessler said he would rather have full employment than zero inflation.

Kessler feels that if the Federal Reserve Board attains zero inflation, it would be more beneficial to banks than to consumers. Zero inflation, he adds, "is for the protection of the creditor class - not the debtor class." While inflation enables borrowers to pay off debt with cheaper dollars, he explains, banks prefer to have loans repaid with money that is at least equal to the amount borrowed. That seems fair enough, but credit card loans at 18 percent should more than offset the difference.

At any rate, it is hard to imagine a world without inflation. Personally, I have always done very well during inflationary times. One reason for that is that I have always had a job, and - in most years - I have been fortunate enough to get a pay raise. The raises nearly always covered or exceeded cost-of-living increases. Interest rates are usually high during periods of high inflation, a situation that is not exactly undesirable to those who have been frugal enough to save money.

Anyone who retired when CDs were paying 12 percent will probably agree that both high interest rates or high inflation can be either a good thing or a bad thing - depending on which side of the borrow-lender counter you happen to be on. It may be a moot point, anyhow. The economies of many industrialized nations of the world already are experiencing disinflation, a condition in which prices are not only failing to go up - they are going down.

Maybe the best thing for the Fed to do is to stop manipulating things artificially. As Kessler puts it, "In some cases, attempts to manage the economy are actually creating the fluctuations we are attempting to avoid."

Consider These Questions:

1. Has the Federal Reserve actually eliminated inflation in the U.S. economy? What evidence supports your answer?

2. How can inflation be both "a good thing" or a "bad thing" as suggested in this article. Explain with examples.

3. What does this quote mean, "Zero inflation is for the protection of the creditor class - not the debtor class"?

4. How can the Federal Reserve's attempts to manage the economy actually generate economic fluctuations? Explain.

STUDY QUESTIONS

1. If the price of newspapers increased annually by approximately 9 percent, 4 percent, and 4 percent, are these price increases necessarily inflationary? Why or why not?

2. "Consumers expect the price of beef to increase in the next 60 days." Will the price expectation affect the current market for beef? Explain, using a market diagram. Is this process necessarily inflationary? Why or why not? Can consumer price expectations contribute to inflation? Explain.

3. "Despite their imperfections, price index numbers still provide useful indicators of trends in the level of prices." What are the imperfections? How is a price index constructed?

4. Does inflation alter the distribution of income and wealth? E explain. Do you object to the manner in which inflation redistributes income? Do some people benefit from inflation? Explain.

5. "A fully anticipated inflation may not alter the distribution of income and wealth." But even if inflation is fully anticipated, it is likely to reduce efficiency. Explain.

6. Under what circumstances does inflation stimulate production and employment in an economy?

7. What is money? What is the composition of the M2 money supply? What money supply definition does the Federal Reserve System use for policy purposes? Why?

8. How do commercial banks and other depository institutions create money? What is their motive?

9. Suppose that the reserved ratio is 10 percent and that excess reserves amount to $30,000. Calculate the money multiplier and the maximum expansion of the money supply.

10. What are the major monetary tools of the Federal Reserve System (Fed)? To combat inflation, the Fed should (buy,sell) government securities through the open-market operation, (raise,lower) the discount rate, and/or(increase,decrease) the minimum required reserve ratio. Explain how each action may reduce the money supply and, thus, help control inflation.

11. The Federal Reserve has three major policy tools. Which one is most powerful? Most often Used? Indicates the direction of Federal Reserve policy?

12. What causes demand-pull inflation? Using the aggregate demand-aggregate supply theory, show that demand-pull inflation is characterized by rising prices and rising production until full employment is reached. What happens at the above full employment? What is this outcome called?

13. To combat demand-pull inflation, the government, give the level of its expenditures, should (increase,decrease) its tax collections and/or given the level of tax collection, the government should (increase,decrease) its expenditures. Using the aggregate demand-aggregate supply model, illustrate the price and output effects of the fiscal policy.

14. What causes the decreases in aggregate supply that brings on cost-push inflation? Illustrate, using the aggregate demand- aggregate supply model, the price level and output effects of decreases in aggregate supply.

15. Can an income policy control cost-push inflation? Explain.

PUZZLE Complete the following crossword puzzle.

Inflation

Across

6. A rising average price level for goods and services.
7. Government restraints placed on wages and prices intended to reduce cost-push inflation is called _____ policy.
9. The rate of interest the Federal Reserve charges commercial banks for loans.
10. The central banking system in the U.S. which oversees commercial banks and regulates the money supply.
11. A price _____ is used to measure the rate of inflation relative to a base year.
13. The reciprocal of the legal reserve ration is called the money _____.
14. Demand-_____ inflation results from increases in the average level of aggregate demand.
15. M1 and M2 are part of the money _____.

Down

1. Subjective notion as to what constitutes fairness in the distribution of income and the output of the economy.
2. MV = PQ This is known as the equation of _____.
3. When the Federal Reserve buys and sells government securities for the purpose of changing commercial bank reserves.
4. Bank Reserves/Total Deposits. (2 words)
5. The extraction of the greatest possible value of product from given inputs of resources.
8. A bank _____ new demand deposits when it expands its loans.
12. The _____ theory of money states that changes in the money supply will lead to direct changes in total output and prices.
14. Cost-_____ inflation results from increases in the costs of production.

TRUE-FALSE QUESTIONS Circle T (true) or F (false)

T F 1. During inflations, the price of some goods and services rise while others fall but on the average, prices in general are rising.

T F 2. Individuals may react to increases in the price level such that they cause further increases in prices.

T F 3. Given government price controls, if the government does nothing to alter the relationship between aggregate demand and aggregate supply the rate of inflation will be reduced.

T F 4. The Consumer Price Index was 149 in 1994. This means that prices rose 49 percent between 1989 and 1990.

T F 5. Higher prices for some goods and services reflect higher costs for a better commodity rather than higher cost for the same commodity.

T F 6. Inflation affects the distribution of income, the allocation of resources and the national output.

T F 7. The arbitrary manner in which inflation may change the pattern of income distribution gives support to the claim that inflation reduces economic efficiency.

T F 8. During inflation real profit income tends to increase. Thus, producers tend to expand production and employ more people.

T F 9. The equity effects of inflation refer to the effects of inflation on the distribution of income.

T F 10. People who hold assets in the form of money and who have fixed claims on money may be made worse off by inflation.

T F 11. Without money, economic transactions would have to take place on a barter basis.

T F 12. The money supply is composed of assets that are completely liquid.

T F 13. Given a required reserve ratio of 25 percent, a new demand deposit of $20,000 can lead to a $60,000 expansion in the money supply.

T F 14. Decreases in the minimum required reserve ratio by the Federal Reserve System will permit demand deposit expansion.

T F 15. Economists tend to agree that monetary stability can best be accomplished by a Federal Reserve policy that strives to maintain a stable and reasonable money growth rate.

T F 16. When MV is increasing faster than Q, the price level will increase.

T F 17. The quantity theory of money stresses the importance of changes in the velocity or turnover of money.

T F 18. In a demand-pull inflation, production and employment rise until the economy reaches full employment.

T F 19. Once full employment is reached, further increases in aggregate demand increase prices and output.

T F 20. When an economy is experiencing a period of essentially demand-pull inflation, the government can combat it by raising taxes, reducing expenditures, or both without the risk of increased unemployment.

T F 21. A major problem in controlling inflation once it has gotten underway is that effective control measures almost inevitably cause unemployment.

T F 22. In the aggregate demand approach to inflation, the money supply is viewed primarily as an accommodating variable rather than an initiating variable.

T F 23. Increases in the costs of production cause aggregate supply to increase, which reduces the quantity of goods produced and increases prices.

T F 24. An economy can experience simultaneous inflation and recession if the inflation is initiated by an increase in aggregate demand.

T F 25. Cost-push inflation is caused by resource price increases or productivity decreases.

MULTIPLE CHOICE QUESTIONS Select the one best answer

1. Inflation occurs when:
   a. wages and salaries increase.
   b. the price of some commodities increase.
   c. prices in general are rising.
   d. a sack full of groceries costs too much.
   e. None of the above.

2. Expectations that future prices may be higher tend to:
   a. increase current consumer spending, causing current market prices to rise.
   b. decrease current consumer spending, causing current market prices to fall.
   c. increase current consumer spending, causing current market prices to decrease.
   d. decrease current consumer spending, causing current market prices to increase.
   e. None of the above because price expectations do not influence current consumer spending.

3. Inflation is measured by
   a. a very complex economic formula.
   b. dollars that are not worthless.
   c. alternative goods and services that were not produced due to unemployment.
   d. price index numbers.

4. Inflation affects the:
   a. distribution of income.
   b. allocation of resources.
   c. national output of goods and services.
   d. All of the above.

5. Which of the following statements is correct?
   a. Inflation benefits debtors as the expense of creditors.
   b. Inflation decreases the purchase power of the dollar.
   c. Inflation decreases the real value of savings.
   d. Inflation arbitrarily "taxes" fixed income groups.
   e. All of the above.

6. Inflation benefits people:
   a. who have a fixed income.
   b. whose income rises faster than prices.
   c. who hold assets in the form of money.
   d. who have fixed claims on money.

7. Money as a measure of value:
   a. allows barter to take place.
   b. makes possible value comparisons of goods and services.
   c. permits the summations of quantities of goods and services on a value basis.
   d. encourages the accumulation of wealth in noninterest-bearing assets.
   e. Both (b) and (c).

8. The nation's money supply (M2) is composed of:
   a. savings deposits, demand deposits, and currency and coins in circulation.
   b. currency and coins in circulation, nonbank traveler's checks, demand deposits and other checkable deposits.
   c. savings deposits, currency and coins in circulation, and traveler's checks.
   d. savings and time deposits less than $100,000 and money market mutual funds.
   e. Both (b) and (c).

9. Commercial banks increase the money supply when:
   a. the amount of new loans exceed old loans paid off.
   b. the amount of new loans is less than old loans paid off.
   c. currency is exchanged for demand deposits.
   d. None of the above.

10. Suppose a new demand deposit of $10,000 and a required reserve ratio of 10 percent, then:
    a. excess reserves are $9,000, the money multiplier is 10, and the money supply can be expanded by $90,000.
    b. excess reserves are $1,000, the multiplier is 10, and the money supply can be expanded by $10,000.
    c. excess reserves are $10,000, the multiplier is 10, and the money supply can be expanded by $100,000.
    d. Insufficient information to calculate excess reserves, the multiplier, and money supply expansion.

11. If the Open-Market Committee of the Federal Reserve sells securities, this action tends to:
    a. decrease the money supply.
    b. increase the money supply.
    c. reduce the reserve requirement.
    d. decrease the discount rate.

12. The equation of exchange states that:
    a. the supply of money times the velocity of money equals the price times the quantity of goods traded.
    b. the amount of money spent equals the value of the goods sold.
    c. the monetary value of purchases must equal the monetary value of sales.
    d. All of the above.

13. According to the quantity theory of money, a change in the money supply:
    a. will cause a change in the opposite direction in the volume of trade.
    b. in an upward direction is always a good thing.
    c. will tend to cause a change in the price level in the same direction.
    d. will usually be offset by velocity changes.
    e. will usually not affect the level of economic activity.

14. Demand-pull inflation is associated with:
    a. increases in production and employment until the economy reaches full employment.
    b. increases in cost of labor and higher business profit margins.
    c. unemployment in the economy.
    d. rising prices because of over production of goods and services.

15. Demand-pull inflation can be controlled by:
    a. reducing the ability of banks to expand loans and create money.
    b. reducing government purchases.
    c. reducing government transfer payments.
    d. increasing taxes.
    e. All of the above.

Questions 16 through 18 are based on the following diagram.

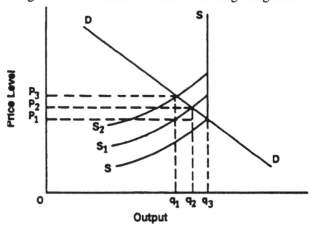

16. The above graph illustrates:
    a. cost-push inflation.
    b. rising prices and rising production.
    c. that increases in costs of production cause aggregate supply to decrease.
    d. Both (a) and (c).

17. Given price level OP_1 and output Oq_3, if aggregate supply decreases to S_1S then:
    a. all of the aggregate output demanded cannot be satisfied at OP_1.
    b. the price level will increase to OP_3.
    c. the equilibrium output decreases to Oq_1.
    d. None of the above.

18. Given S_1S and DD, cost-push inflation will result in:
    a. a price level of OP_1 and an output of Oq_3.
    b. a price level of OP_2 and an output of Oq_2.
    a. a price level of OP_3 and an output of Oq_1.
    d. None of the above.

19. If the price level rises due to the market power possessed by unions and producers in certain industries, it is:
    a. demand-pull inflation.
    b. cost-push inflation.
    c. structural inflation.
    d. cyclical inflation.

20. Cost-push inflationary pressures may be reduced by:
    a. promoting competitive markets.
    b. controlling the money supply.
    c. using a tax-based incomes policy.
    d. All of the above.
    e. None of the above.

21. If the aggregate demand curve shifts to the right, what will happen to prices and national output?
    a. both will rise.
    b. both will fall.
    c. prices will rise, but output will fall.
    d. prices will fall, but output will rise.

22. If the aggregate supply curve shifts to the left, what will happen to prices and national output?
    a. both will rise.
    b. both will fall.
    c. prices will rise, but output will fall.
    d. prices will fall, but output will rise.

23. A current price index number of 109 indicates which of the following?
    a. prices are 9% higher in the current year than last year.
    b. prices are 9% higher in the current year than in the base year.
    c. prices are 10% higher in the current year than in the base year.
    d. prices are 109% higher in the current yea than last year.

24. Which of the following actions of the Federal Reserve would slow the growth of the money supply?
    a. lowering of the legal reserve requirement.
    b. lowering of the discount rate.
    c. buying government securities on the open market.
    d. selling government securities on the open market.

25. Commercial bank reserves would increase if the Federal Reserve did which of the following?
    a. raised the legal reserve requirement.
    b. lowered the discount rate.
    c. raised the discount rate.
    d. sold government securities on the open market.

PROBLEMS

1. Using the hypothetical set of data below, construct a price index with 1984 as the base year.

Year	Cost of Market Basket	Price Index Numbers
1984	$ 700	_____
1985	950	_____
1986	1,000	_____
1987	1,300	_____
1988	1,500	_____

What was the rate of inflation between 1987 and 1988? _____

2. Use the equation of exchange to determine by how much the price level increases if the economy is at full employment, velocity is constant, and the money supply increases by 7.6 percent.

3. Using aggregate-supply and aggregate-demand curves, illustrate a demand-pull inflation.

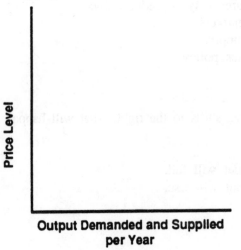

Output Demanded and Supplied
per Year

4. Using aggregate-supply and aggregate-demand curves, illustrate a cost-push inflation.

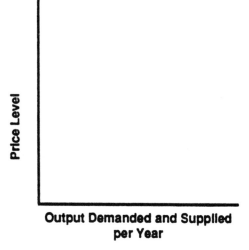

Output Demanded and Supplied per Year

5. If the Federal Reserve sets a 15 percent required reserve ratio and the total demand deposits of member banks are $220 billion:
   a. How much must the banks hold in reserve?
   b. Calculate the money multiplier.

   If banks presently hold $55 billion in reserves:
   c. What is the banks' excess reserve?
   d. Calculate the potential money supply increase.

ANSWERS TO SELF-TEST

PUZZLE

Across		Down	
6.	Inflation	1.	Equity
7.	Incomes	2.	Exchange
9.	Discount	3.	OMO
10.	Federal Reserve	4.	Reserve Ratio
11.	Index	5.	Efficiency
13.	Multiplier	8.	Creates
14.	Pull	12.	Quantity
15.	Supply	14.	Push

TRUE-FALSE QUESTIONS

1.	T	8.	T	14.	T	20.	F
2.	T	9.	T	15.	T	21.	T
3.	F	10.	T	16.	T	22.	T
4.	F	11.	T	17.	F	23.	F
5.	T	12.	T	18.	T	24.	F
6.	T	13.	T	19.	F	25.	T
7.	F						

MULTIPLE-CHOICE QUESTIONS

1.	c	6.	b	11.	a	16.	d	21.	a
2.	a	7.	e	12.	d	17.	a	22.	c
3.	d	8.	e	13.	c	18.	c	23.	b
4.	d	9.	a	14.	a	19.	b	24.	d
5.	e	10.	a	15.	e	20.	d	25.	b

PROBLEMS

1.

Year	Price Index Number
1984	100
1985	135.7
1986	142.8
1987	185.7
1988	214.3

Rate of inflation between 1987 and 1988 $= \dfrac{214.3 - 185.7}{185.7} = 15.4\%$

2. The price level increases by 7.6 percent.

3.

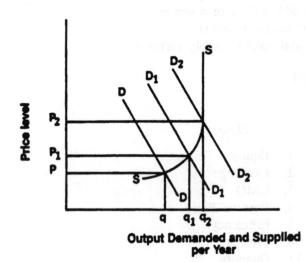

Demand-pull inflation results from increases in aggregate demand from DD to D_1D_1 to D_2D_2.

4.

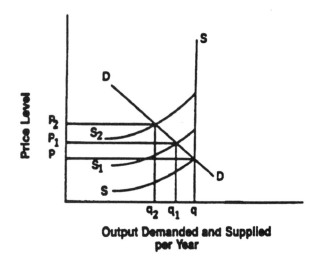

Output Demanded and Supplied per Year

Cost-push inflation results from decreases in aggregate supply from SS to SS_1 to SS_2.

5. a. $33 billion in reserves ($220 B x .15 = $33 B).
   b. 6.67 is the money multiplier (1 /.15 = 6.67).
   c. $22 billion in excess reserves ($55 B - $33 B = $22 B).
   d. $146.7 billion increase in the money supply ($22 B x 6.67 = $146.7 B).

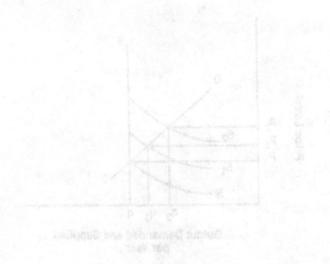

Output Demanded and Supplied
per Year

Cost-push inflation results from decreases in aggregate supply from S_0 to S_1 to ...

Chapter 15
Government Expenditures and Tax Issues

Who Wins and Who Loses?

LEARNING OBJECTIVES

After studying this issue, you should be able to:

1. Describe and evaluate the concern people have for the size of government and the distribution of tax burden.

2. Explain the changes over time of government expenditures and receipts as a percent of GDP.

3. Explain, using marginal benefits-marginal costs (MB,MC) analysis, what is meant by an efficient level of government expenditures.

4. Explain and evaluate, using the economic concept of efficiency, the role of government in the production of collective goods and services and of goods and services characterized by production and consumption externalities.

5. Use the concept of equity to explain and evaluate the role of government in the redistribution of income.

6. Explain the characteristics of an efficient tax, an equitable tax, and an equitable tax system.

7. Define and explain tax incidence.

8. Explain and evaluate proposals to limit the size of government.

9. Explain the 1986 Income Tax Reform Act using efficient, equitable, and neutral income tax criteria.

10. Explain the relationship between a comprehensive tax base and the distribution of income taxes among income groups.

CHAPTER ORIENTATION

When the American people discuss the role of government in the economy, they often express concern about the size of government and tax inequities. These concerns are not new, and while some of them are well founded others are unfounded. In this chapter, we use economic concepts—efficiency and equity—and economic analysis to sort out the relevant concerns and evaluate policy alternatives and the 1986 Tax Reform Act.

Both efficiency and equity considerations are involved in an analysis of the size of government. In part, the size of government is determined by government expenditures for goods and services that would not be provided at all or in efficient quantities in the market. The existence of collective goods and services and of externalities in the production and/or consumption of some other goods and services require government expenditures if society's scarce resources are to be used efficiently. In addition, the size of government is determined by expenditure programs aimed at altering the distribution of income. The nature and extent of government efforts to redistribute income are determined by people's values.

Proposals to balance the budget and limit the relative size of government are frequently suggested as ways to control the size of government. Our analysis suggests that they are not panaceas. Such restrictions may severely limit the flexibility needed to meet the changing economic and social problems of society. The income tax reform that was passed by Congress in 1986 appears to make the federal income tax system more equitable and efficient. These outcomes are due to lower tax rates and a much broader tax base.

CONSIDER THIS:

Taxes and Spending in Southern California[1]

There's likely to be a pitched political battle over a proposed half-cent increase in Orange County's retail sales tax, but if it is approved, there probably won't be much impact on retail spending in the financially strapped county.

County supervisors, seeking to increase revenue by as much as $150 million a year, voted early Wednesday morning to let voters decide on the increase in June — to the dismay of anti-tax groups and retailers who say their businesses will suffer if they have to raise prices.

But a review of sales tax increases in Orange County since the uniform local sales tax law took effect in 1962 with a 4% rate shows that sales tax hikes don't have nearly the impact on spending as do other economic factors.

Economists — and even some business owners — say it takes more than sales tax hikes to clamp down on family spending habits.

"A basic principal of economics is that as prices go up, consumption goes down," said Anil Puri, head of the economics department at Cal State Fullerton. "But there's a real question about how much impact at 0.5% increase would have. There might be some on big-ticket items, but I don't believe it has much direct bearing on retail sales."

Indeed, while sales taxes have risen six times in Orange County since 1962, taxable sales in the county continued to rise much faster than the statewide average through the first three increases, slowing only since the local economy hit the skids in 1989.

In 1967, when sales taxes rose to 5 cents on the dollar, taxable sales statewide increased only 0.1% when adjusted for inflation. In booming Orange County, however, the extra penny per dollar did nothing to cool a scorching business climate and retail sales jumped at a real, or inflation-adjusted, rate of 7.1%.

Just six years later, in the midst of one of California's greatest growth periods, the rate rose again, to 6%, and cash registers elsewhere in the state were ringing as retailers enjoyed an 8.5% taxable sales hike after adjusting for a 6% inflation rate. In Orange County, the registers didn't just ring — they roared. Taxable sales were up 13.3% as the population grew and consumers ignored the slightly higher cost of goods.

It has only been in the recent inflation years — things started souring in Orange County when the housing boom collapsed in 1989 — that the county's retail sales record has been worse than the statewide average.

There have been three sales tax hikes since 1989, pushing the rate in Orange County to its present 7.75%, but recession-caused layoffs and reductions in families' incomes have had far more impact on taxable sales, said Bruce DeVine, economist for the Southern California Assn. of Governments.

In 1991, when county voters approved a half-cent transportation tax and then were hit with a 1.25-cent state sales tax increase just three months later, retail spending in the county declined by 8.4%, slightly more than the 7.7% drop recorded statewide.

But how much of the drop was caused by the tax situation "is really difficult to determine," said economist Puri.

---

[1]John O'Dell, "What Price Hike? Past Increases in O.C. Sales Tax Didn't Hurt Retailers," *The Los Angeles Times*, March 30, 1995. Reprinted with permission.

Aileen Lee, research manager for the State Board of Equalization, tracks taxable sales data throughout the state. She said spending "doesn't stop" when sales taxes go up. "We see some behavior changes, because if people know that the tax is going to go up next month and they are planning big purchases, like a car, they might buy now in order to pay less tax, but they are still making the purchase," Lee said.

Tom Takahashi, sales manager at Showcase Chevrolet/Geo in Westminster, agrees. He said he's been selling cars for 35 years and has never head of a sales tax increase affecting a sale.

"Car buyers balk when the price isn't right, or the dealer doesn't have their favorite color in stock. But sales tax hikes aren't typically deal-killers," he said. "Of course, eventually you get to the point where you say, 'Wait a minute.' But right now, (the proposed tax hike) is a necessary evil."

Karen Raab, manager of Chemers Gallery in Tustin, also sells thing people use discretionary income to buy. The average purchaser spends $1,500 in her fine art and custom framing store, she said, and in her 17 years in business, she ha never seen sales tax increases affect a sale.

The proposed half-cent tax increase in Orange County is particularly frightening to many because it comes at a time when the economy is still staggering from the impact of a recession that lasted longer and cut deeper than any other since World War II and has been followed by an anemic recovery that only the economists seem able to measure.

"It affects the psychology of customers, just like when the county declared bankruptcy," said David Neishabori, owner of Kismet Rug Gallery in Corona del Mar. "Psychologically, that put everyone in jeopardy. And (cuts in personal spending) start with the things that are not necessities of life."

Neishabori was hard-pressed to point to a sale he's lost because of a sales tax increase, but is adamant that business has suffered every time the state or county has raised the rate.

"When you're talking about a $10,000 item, and you add one-half percent, that's terrible news," he said.

Actually, it's $50, about the amount economists figure a half-cent sales tax increase would cost the average Orange County household each year.

DeVine, the government association economist, says that if past performance is any indication, "that money will come out of people's savings, but they won't stop spending."

Consider These Questions:

1. What do the observations of the retailers quoted in this article tell us about the incidence of sales taxes? Who bears the burden of increases in sales taxes?

2. What factors other than sales taxes may have larger impacts on the behavior of consumers? Relate these to the Law of Demand.

3. How can announced future increases in taxes effect consumer buying today? Why?

4. What are the long-term consequences of paying taxes out of savings instead of consumption?

STUDY QUESTIONS

1. Have government expenditures and receipts as a percent of GDP change over time? Explain.

2. Suppose the marginal benefits per dollar spent in the public sector of the economy is less than the marginal benefits per dollar spent in the private sector. How should government expenditures be changed in order to move to an efficient level of government expenditures?

3. "Efficiency considerations justify government expenditures." Evaluate the quote. Name several goods and/or services for which government expenditures may be justifiable on efficiency grounds and several which may not be justified on efficiency grounds. Explain why.

4. "Income inequality needs to be reduced." Suppose that we all agreed with the quote and that we even agreed on the size of the reduction. Does the government need to be involved in the redistribution process? Explain.

5. "People in identical economic positions should pay equal taxes." Evaluate the quote in terms of the best indicator or measure of economic circumstances. How should people in different economic circumstances be treated? Is the United States government tax system an equitable system?

6. Does a liquor tax meet the neutral effects criterion? Explain.

7. In recent years, the federal government and many state governments have increased the tax on gasoline. Most of the additional revenue from the tax is to be used to build and maintain highways. In that sense, the gasoline tax is often referred to as a uses' fee. Under what circumstances can legislatures be certain that highway users pay the tax on gasoline?

8. In what sense will the 1986 Income Tax Reform Act make the federal income tax system more efficient, equitable and neutral? Will the reforms alter the amount of investment and economic growth? Explain.

9. Will some income groups benefit more than others as a result of the 1986 income tax reforms? Explain.

10. What effect did the 1991 tax rate increase have on the distribution of taxes? Explain.

PUZZLE   Complete the following crossword puzzle.

Government Spending and Taxes

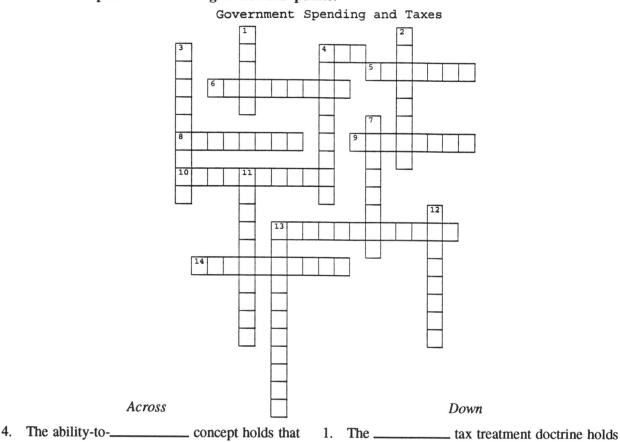

Across

4. The ability-to-_____ concept holds that taxpayers with higher incomes should pay more taxes than those with lower incomes.

5. Taxes shifted to consumers in the form of higher product prices is called _____ tax shifting.

6. Government _____ are payments made to persons or economic units which are not for services currently performed.

8. _____ benefits and costs do not accrue to the producing or consuming unit, but to the remainder of society.

9. The _____ tax treatment doctrine holds that taxpayers in different economic circumstances should pay different amounts of taxes.

10. _____ goods are consumed by a group and yield benefits to the group. No individual can single out his/her own specific benefit.

13. A _____ tax rate schedule results in a constant ratio of tax collection to income as income increases.

14. _____ equity is the notion that people in the same economic circumstances should receive the same economic treatment.

Down

1. The _____ tax treatment doctrine holds that taxpayers in equal economic circumstances should be treated equally.

2. _____ equity is the notion that persons in different economic circumstances should receive different rewards.

3. The final resting place or burden of any given tax — who actually pays it. This is known as the _____.

4. Government _____ are expenditures for currently produced goods and services.

7. The _____-received principle holds that taxpayers should pay in accordance with the benefits they receive from government.

11. The extent to which a tax has a neutral impact on resource allocation and is economical to enforce and collect is tax _____.

12. Shifting the burden of a tax to the owners of resources, usually in the form of lower resource prices is _____ tax shifting.

13. A _____ tax rate schedule results in an increase in the ratio of tax collection to income as income increases.

TRUE-FALSE QUESTIONS Circle T (true) or F (false)

T F 1. One of the arguments for controlling the size of government is that a large government can narrow individual choices and reduce individual rights.

T F 2. One of the major concerns people have about taxes is that they are "too low" for certain taxpayers and "too high" for certain other taxpayers.

T F 3. During the 1980s transfer payments as a percentage of GDP decreased.

T F 4. Over 30 percent of the GDP is diverted to government in the form of tax and nontax receipts.

T F 5. An efficient level of government expenditures is obtained when the marginal benefits per dollar spent in the public sector of the economy is less than the marginal benefits per dollar spent in the private sector.

T F 6. To obtain economic efficiency in the provision of collective goods and services, the government has to provide them at the lowest possible cost, and the output supplied has to equal the output demanded.

T F 7. The marketplace can, if not interfered with, assure the production of a good which is generally indivisible on an individual quantity basis.

T F 8. If the consumption and/or production of a good results in externalities then government intervention in the market may be required to achieve economic efficiency.

T F 9. The federal food stamp program can best be justified on efficiency grounds rather than equity grounds.

T F 10. Vertical equity is achieved when all taxpayers with the same income pay exactly the same amount in taxes.

T F 11. The equal treatment doctrine states that people in identical economic positions should pay equal taxes.

T F 12. Progressive and proportional income tax rates are consistent with the ability to pay principle because the amount paid in taxes falls as income rises.

T F 13. The ability to pay principle of taxation is concerned with an efficient allocation of taxes rather than to equitable allocation of taxes.

T F 14. An efficient tax is one that can be defended on the ability to pay principle rather than on the benefits received principle.

T F 15. Progressive and regressive income tax rates alter the price of work relative to the price of leisure; therefore, they are efficient taxes.

T F 16. An output tax will normally be shifted backward to resource owners if demand is inelastic.

T F 17. The United States tax system is moderately progressive.

T F 18. Legislation limiting the size of government to a constant percent of the GNP may not allow policy makers the flexibility needed to meet the changing economic and social problems of society.

T F 19. The income tax reform passed by Congress in 1986 made the federal tax system more equitable and efficient.

T F 20. The timing of the 1991 tax increase was appropriate because the economy was expanding rapidly.

T F 21. Because the incidence of most state and local taxes fall on capital instead of consumption, state and local taxes are less regressive than generally believed.

T F 22. The Tax Reform Act of 1986 moved the U.S. federal tax structure in the direction of greater equity and efficiency.

T F 23. Government spending as a percentage of GDP has actually been falling since the early 1960's.

T F 24. The highest marginal income tax rate has remained at 28% since passage of the Tax Reform Act of 1986.

T F 25. Using economic theory, all goods and services can be clearly identified as either private or collective goods and services.

MULTIPLE CHOICE QUESTIONS Select the one best answer

1. Proposals to limit federal expenditures to a certain percent of GDP express people's concern for:
   a. the efficient size of government.
   b. the equity of tax distribution.
   c. taxes that are too high generally.
   d. None of the above.

2. An efficient level of government expenditures is that level where:
   a. net benefits to society are maximized.
   b. the marginal benefits pre dollar spent in the public sector of the economy is less than the marginal benefits per dollar spent in the private sector.
   c. total benefits to society are maximized.
   d. Both (b) and (c).

3. Efficiency in the use of society's scarce resources requires:
   a. government expenditures for goods and services that would not be provided at all by the market.
   b. that government provide collective goods and services at the lowest possible cost, and output supplied has to equal output demanded.
   c. government subsidies to encourage more consumption when external benefits in consumption exist.
   d. All of the above.

4. A good is classified as a collective good if:
   a. one person's consumption excludes others from consuming the same good.
   b. one person's consumption does not exclude someone else from consuming the same good.
   c. a majority of the citizens want the particular good.
   d. the market can provide the good efficiently.
   e. the market prevents nonpayers from consuming the good.

5. Which of the following has the characteristics of a collective good?
   a. Video player
   b. Life insurance
   c. Crime prevention.
   d. None of the above.

6. It a steel mill were forced to pay the external cost of production, the equilibrium price:
   a. and equilibrium quantity would fall.
   b. would rise while equilibrium quantity would fall.
   c. and quantity would not change.
   d. and quantity would rise.
   e. would fall while equilibrium quantity would rise.

Questions 7 to 10 below refer to the following diagram:

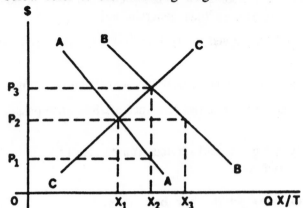

7. Curve CC:
   a. is the market supply curve for product X.
   b. indicates the marginal private costs of producing X.
   c. shows both the marginal private and external benefits of the consumption of X.
   d. shows that a divergence exists between private and social costs.
   e. Both (a) and (b).

8. Given curves AA and CC and assuming that there are no external benefits and costs, the efficient price and quantity of X would be:
   a. OP_1 OX_2.
   b. OP_2 OX_1.
   c. OP_3 OX_2.
   d. OP_2 OX_3.

9. Suppose external benefits appear in the consumption of good X. What would be the efficient price and quantity of X?
   a. OP_1 OX_2.
   b. OP_2 OX_1.
   c. OP_3 OX_2.
   d. OP_2 OX_3.

10. To assure the production of the efficient quantity of X, the government should pay a subsidy of:
    a. $(P_3 - P_1)$ x X_2.
    b. $(P_2 - P_1)$ x X_1.
    c. P_2 x X_2.
    d. None of the above.

11. Income distribution would not be improved by:
    a. the sales tax.
    b. the food stamp program.
    c. the social security program.
    d. rent subsidies.
    e. transfer payments.

12. Government income redistribution programs:
    a. can be rationalized on economic efficiency grounds.
    b. have been defended on the belief that income inequality needs to be reduced.
    c. shift income from those who are relatively productive to those who are relatively unproductive.
    d. Both (b) and (c).

13. On an income of $50,000, Ms. Peters pay $1,000 in taxes; however, if her income had been $10,000, her tax payment would have been $2,000. For this tax system the ratio of tax collection to income:
    a. rises as income rises.
    b. remains constant.
    c. falls as income rises.
    d. cannot be determined given the information provided.

14. The equal tax treatment doctrine:
    a. involves the benefits received principle.
    b. pertains to vertical equity.
    c. requires that people in identical economic conditions pay equal taxes.
    d. None of the above.

15. An efficient tax is one that:
    a. can be defended on the ability to pay or benefits received principles.
    b. adheres to the equal tax treatment doctrine.
    c. has neutral effects on the allocation of resources
    d. All of the above.

16. The incidence of a tax refers to:
    a. how frequent it is collected.
    b. how many taxpayers it covers.
    c. who actually bears the ultimate burden of paying it.
    d. how large a proportion of national income it collects.
    e. None of the above.

17. An output tax:
    a. increases the producer's cost of producing each unit of the commodity.
    b. decreases the supply of the commodity.
    c. tends to increase the price of the commodity enough to shift the burden of the tax forward.
    d. burden cannot be shifted.
    e. Both (a) and (b).

18. If the demand for cigarettes is inelastic, who will bear most of the burden of an increase in the cigarette tax?
    a. The sellers.
    b. The buyers.
    c. The buyers and sellers will bear the burden equally.
    d. Insufficient information to tell.

19. In general, the burden of the Federal Individual Income Tax is shifted:
    a. forward.
    b. backward.
    c. to the government.
    d. None of the above.

20. Individual income taxes are:
    a. progressive tax sources.
    b. not nearly as progressive tax sources as the statutory rates indicate.
    c. less progressive tax sources than the property tax.
    d. All of the above.
    e. Both (a) and (b).

21. There appears to be a growing feeling by people that government is too big. Which of the following indicates that this feeling is being acted upon?
    a. California's Proposition 13.
    b. Proposals to require balanced federal and state budgets.
    c. Proposals to set legal limits on the rate of increase in government expenditures.
    d. All of the above.

22. The 1986 Income Tax Reform Act:
    a. increased the individual income tax rates.
    b. decreased the income tax base.
    c. extended the investment tax credit.
    d. made the federal income tax system less equitable but more efficient.
    e. None of the above.

23. As a result of the 1986 income tax reforms:
    a. the average tax rate will be lower for all income groups.
    b. the distribution of income taxes among income groups is unchanged.
    c. federal income tax liabilities for the 30,000 to 50,000 dollar income groups will increase.
    d. All of the above.
    e. None of the above.

24. The estimated increase in tax collections from President Clinton's plan is:
    a. about 50 percent of his deficit reduction goal.
    b. more than enough to eliminate the federal deficit.
    c. not enough to reduce the deficit in the near future.
    d. about 20 percent above his deficit reduction goal.

25. The American tax system can be best described as:
    a. highly progressive.
    b. regressive.
    c. proportional or mildly progressive.
    d. proportional or mildly regressive.
    e. highly regressive.

PROBLEMS

1. Assume that an output tax is imposed on each of the commodities for which demand and supply curves are given below.

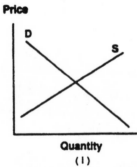  

    a. For what commodities is the full amount of the tax shifted forward?
    b. In which case is the price of the commodity unaffected by the tax?
    c. Is the price increase greater in Case (i) or Case (ii)? Why?

2. The graph below is for a good which has external benefits associated with its consumption. Label the graph and answer the questions.

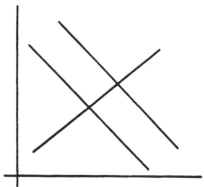

a. Given the supply curve, the optimum or efficient quantity is _____ where _____ equals _____.

b. The government could assume that the efficient quantity would be demanded by giving a subsidy payment to consumers equal to _____.

ANSWERS TO SELF-TEST

PUZZLE

Across	Down
4. Pay	1. Equal
5. Forward	2. Vertical
6. Transfers	3. Incidence
8. External	4. Purchases
9. Relative	7. Benefits
10. Collective	11. Efficiency
13. Proportional	12. Backward
14. Horizontal	13. Progressive

TRUE-FALSE QUESTIONS

1.	T	6.	T	11.	T	16.	F	21.	T
2.	T	7.	F	12.	F	17.	T	22.	T
3.	F	8.	T	13.	F	18.	T	23.	F
4.	T	9.	F	14.	F	19.	T	24.	F
5.	F	10.	F	15.	F	20.	F	25.	F

MULTIPLE-CHOICE QUESTIONS

1.	a	8.	d	14.	c	20.	e
2.	a	9.	c	15.	c	21.	d
3.	d	10.	a	16.	c	22.	e
4.	b	11.	a	17.	e	23.	a
5.	c	12.	d	18.	b	24.	a
6.	b	13.	c	19.	d	25.	c
7.	e						

PROBLEMS

1. a. ii.
   b. iii.
   c. ii, because the demand elasticity is less with the same supply.

2. a. OQ_E, MSB, MSC
   b. $(P_E - P_o) \times Q_E$

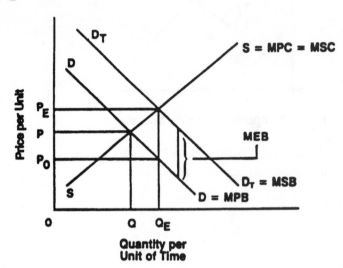

Chapter 16

● # The Big National Debt

Is It Bad?

LEARNING OBJECTIVES

After studying this issue, you should be able to:

1. Define the national debt and explain the major causes of its growth.

2. Discuss the types of government securities and identify the owners of the national debt.

3. List and explain the primary and secondary effects of the national debt and evaluate the public's concern regarding the national debt.

4. List and explain, using the aggregate demand-aggregate supply model where appropriate, the different ways the government can pay for goods and services.

5. Explain the different effects of tax financing, debt financing, and money creation.

6. Explain under what circumstances borrowing may be the most efficient method of government financing.

7. Define deficit and debt and explain how they differ.

8. List, explain, and evaluate the proposed three major federal budget accounts.

CHAPTER ORIENTATION

During political campaigns the national debt almost always surfaces as an issue. Most politicians oppose the national debt while campaigning for office, even though they press for measures that will increase it after they are elected. Opposition to a large national debt is as American as mom and apple pie. My neighbor, who readily admits to knowing little about the economy, talks at length and with conviction about the national debt. For many people, the national debt is the best example of government ineptness.

The national debt is a social issue but for reasons far removed from those identified by the general public. Conduct your own poll of friends and neighbors. Ask them to tell you about the national debt. No doubt they will mention bankruptcy and the burden on future generations.

People have misconceptions about the national debt because they fail to comprehend that what is true for the individual is not necessarily true for the collective—they commit the logical fallacy of composition. While you and I and even General Motors can go bankrupt, the federal government cannot do so in a legal sense. As a student of economics you should be able to explain why.

The national debt, although not likely to cause bankruptcy or to burden future generations, can and does affect income distribution, output, and prices. Thus, the national debt both affects and is affected by our economic goals. Under certain circumstances, the national debt and how it is financed may redistribute income away from low-income groups, reduce national output and the stock of capital, and increase prices. For these reasons, the national debt concerns us all and is a social issue.

The national debt grows when new debt created exceeds the repayment of old debt. New debt arises when the government spends in a given year more than it collects in tax revenues. Is government deficit spending over justified? You should search for the answer to this question. In some economic situations, deficit spending can be defended and in others it cannot be.

The economic effects of financing government goods and services from taxing, borrowing, and crating money are stressed in this chapter. Although the federal government could print money, it chooses to create money to finance budget deficits by selling its I.O.U.s (bonds) to banks. You should understand the three methods of government finance, and their differing effects on prices and output.

Federal debt management policy and principles are introduced in this chapter. Although less important than fiscal and monetary policy, debt management policy can be designed to complement economic stabilization.

By dividing the federal budget into three accounts—the current account, investment account, and the stabilization account—some of the misunderstandings about budget deficits and the national debt could be eliminated. They would provide a basis for evaluating government deficit spending and the resulting increase in the national debt.

CONSIDER THIS:

Questions and Answers about the Debt[1]

Q. What exactly is the federal deficit?

A. The deficit is the difference between the government's receipts from taxes, oil and gas royalties and other sources and its expenditures for all programs. These expenditures include Social Security, Medicare, defense, highways, foreign aid, farm programs and interest on the debt. In the fiscal year that ended Sept. 30, the government collected revenues of $1.09 trillion, spent $1.38 trillion, and borrowed $290 billion to make up the difference.

Q. To whom do we owe the debt?

A. The national debt—the accumulation of all of the deficits—is $4 trillion so far. The government has borrowed about $1 trillion from the Social Security trust fund, which is currently running a surplus because baby boomers are paying so much money into the fund and won't collect retirement benefits until later. Of the remaining debt, about 80 percent is owed to American individuals and institutions that have invested in government securities such as treasury bills and Savings Bonds. Less than 20 percent is owed to foreign investors, but that's still enough to make the United States the world's largest debtor nation.

Q. How did the deficit get so big? What do we spent the money on?

A. The debt has piled up over three eras. It took from th dawn of the republic until 1980 to accumulate the first $1 trillion in debt. Then, during the Reagan administration, $2 trillion was added to the debt because taxes were cut while government spending continued to grow to pay for defense buildup and for social programs. During President Bush's term, defense spending started declining and some government programs grew only slightly, but spending on Medicare and Medicaid mushroomed. The government also had to pump about $90 billion into the deposit insurance system to protect customers of failed savings and loans.

Q. Have we had big deficits before?

A. Yes. During the Depression, the government spent heavily to get the economy going again. Then the deficit increased dramatically to finance the World War II effort. By the end of the war, the government was borrowing $1 of every $2 if spent.

---

[1]Bill Mintz, "What You Should Know about the Deficit: Questions and Answers." *The Houston Chronicle,* January 17, 1993, p. Business 1. The Houston Chronicle. Reprinted by permission.

Q. What's wrong with running a deficit?

A. Money is like any other commodity in a market economy. If the demand increases, the price goes up. So, if the government is borrowing a lot of money, that drives up the cost of money—interest rates—for everyone else, including families buying homes and businesses that need to borrow money to expand and create more jobs. A growing deficit also makes the government reluctant to increase spending on programs such as education and highways that make the economy more efficient. Ultimately, an out-of-control deficit is likely to mean higher taxes for our children and grandchildren. That will mean less money to invest in the private sector of the economy, lowering the standard of living for everyone.

Q. If everybody's complaining about the deficit, why does it keep getting bigger?

A. The fastest-growing federal programs - Medicare and Medicaid - aren't limited by federal appropriations; everyone who qualifies for these "entitlements" gets to use the benefits.

Because health care costs are increasing much more rapidly than prices for other goods and services in the economy, the entitlement programs are grabbing a larger percentage of federal spending. So far, political leaders haven't been willing to limit the size of these extremely popular programs. Also, interest on the debt now consumes almost $200 billion per year.

Q. We've heard about the proposed balanced budget amendment to the Constitution. Is there any legal restriction now on how much the government borrows?

A. Congress is required to periodically set ceilings on the amount of money the government can borrow. The need to keep raising that debt limit has provided the impetus for many of the efforts to limit government spending.

However, because spending for the entitlement programs has increased so rapidly, recent efforts to limit government spending have not reduced the deficit.

Q. If we were to balance the budget tomorrow, what would we have to cut?

A. The government could eliminate spending for all discretionary programs - education, highways, housing, the space program and medical research - and still not balance the budget.

Even though the defense budget is shrinking, reducing the deficit would require significant cuts in entitlement programs, such as Medicare, Medicaid and Social Security.

Q. Is there anyone who says the deficit is not a problem?

A. No, but some economists and politicians on both the left and right say it can't be the only problem we try to solve. Some conservatives believe even lower taxes are needed to encourage spending by businesses and consumers. Although lower taxes would raise the deficit in the short term, these "supply siders" say, the nation would see economic growth and therefore greater revenues over time. Some liberals say the government needs to spend more on education, training and infrastructure to make the economy more productive, which would also raise revenues over the long term.

Q. Could the United States end up with the same economic problems that Mexico and other countries had in running up big national debts?

A. That's hard to say. The United States economy is so large—about a fourth of all world economic activity—that is it unlikely to become that weak. But just as we have become dependent on the Persian Gulf for oil, which has affected our foreign policy and resulted in our participation in the Persian Gulf War, there is a danger that we will become more dependent on foreign sources of capital.

Consider These Questions:

1. Separate the factual and subjective statements contained in this newspaper report. Do you believe the answers in this report are based on solid economic reasoning? Why or why not?

2. Evaluate the author's answer to the question, "What's wrong with running a deficit?" Will a deficit actually lead to higher rates of interest and a lower standard of living? Why or why not?

3. What would be the effect of a balanced government budget on the national economy? Explain how households and businesses would be affected.

STUDY QUESTIONS

1. "The growth in the national debt is generally associated with wars and economic slumps." Evaluate the statement. List the types of federal government securities and indicate who owns the national debt.

2. "The federal government, like individuals and businesses, cannot continue to incur debt without increasing the threat of bankruptcy." Evaluate the statement and discuss the fears of the public regarding the national debt.

3. Does a large national debt affect productivity and output? Explain. Are there other effects of the national debt? Are any of the identifiable effects of the national debt problems? Explain.

4. Can the federal government finance budget deficits by creating money? Explain. Are there alternatives? Using the aggregate demand-aggregate supply model, illustrate and discuss the impact on the price level and output of the different methods of government finance.

5. The economy is near full employment and the government needs to finance a budget deficit. In order to avoid demand-pull inflation, how should the government finance the deficit?

6. Should debt management policy play a positive role in stabilizing the economy? Explain. Should the maturity distribution of the national debt be increased? Explain.

7. Is it appropriate for the government to finance profitable investments and programs designed to stimulate employment by borrowing? Explain.

8. "Tax collections equal to government expenditures will eliminate the deficit but not the national debt." Explain.

9. Would dividing the federal budget into three major accounts improve government efficiency? Explain.

10. What are the pros ad cons of a balanced budget amendment? Explain.

PUZZLE Complete the following crossword puzzle.

National Debt

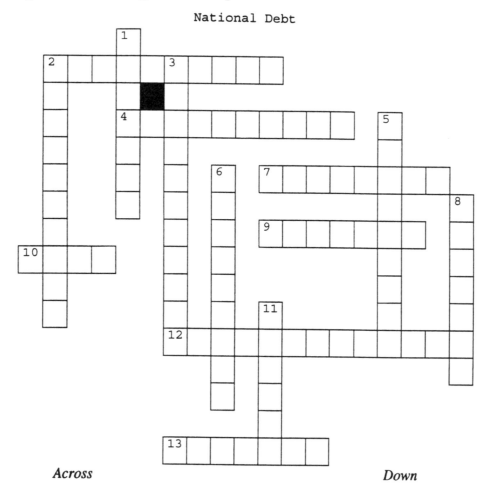

Across

2. Financing government deficits with newly created money is called _____ the debt.
4. The _____ account includes spending for capital goods and the debt used to finance such spending.
7. The government budget is _____ when total receipts are equal to total expenditures.
9. The present and future decrease in private production brought about by the national debt is the debt's _____ burden.
10. Total of all outstanding federal government securities is equal to the Gross Federal _____.
12. The _____ account would include all programs to stabilize the economy and methods used to finance them.
13. Occurs when government's receipts exceed government's expenditures.

Down

1. Occurs when government's current total receipts are less than government's current total expenditures.
2. A debt _____ policy determines the structural characteristics of the national debt, given the availability of money and credit.
3. Public _____ include all government spending on capital goods, such as roads, schools, and hospitals.
5. Expenditures the government must make on an ongoing basis.
6. The income distribution, output, and inflation effects of the national debt are the _____ repercussions of the debt.
8. The _____ account includes all present costs and revenues exclusive of government borrowing.
11. Government actions designed to stabilize the economy are called _____ policy tools.

TRUE-FALSE QUESTIONS Circle T (true) or F (false)

T F 1. The growth in the national debt is generally associated with wars and economic prosperity.

T F 2. The national debt as a percent of GDP was greater in 1994 than in 1980.

T F 3. Since 1975 the federal debt held by the public began to grow faster than the growth in state and local government debt and in private debt.

T F 4. Most of the marketable federal debt is concentrated in bonds.

T F 5. In 1994, foreign-held federal debt represented a lower percent of the non-bank owned public debt that in 1976.

T F 6. Economists conclude that a large national debt will bankrupt the economy.

T F 7. The primary burden of an internally held federal debt is the value of the private goods and services that could have been produced.

T F 8. The primary burden on an externally held national debt is shifted to the future.

T F 9. A large national debt may redistribute income away from low-income groups, reduce national output and the stock of capital, and increase prices.

T F 10. If the government pays $10 billion in interest on the national debt by increasing taxes by $10 billion, then the distribution of income tends to be shifted away from the rich to the poor.

T F 11. Servicing the national debt redistributes income and alters the distribution of the nation's output among people.

T F 12. The government can pay for goods and services from current tax collections, by borrowing, and by creating money.

T F 13. All methods of financing the national debt have a contractionary impact on the economy.

T F 14. Government borrowing decreases the demand for loanable funds.

T F 15. The money supply is increased when the federal government borrows from nonbank sources.

T F 16. When the government creates money to finance budget deficits, private saving and investment are reduced.

T F 17. Minimizing the interest cost of the national debt is an appropriate debt management policy if it can be done without worsening recessionary and/or inflationary forces.

T F 18. The creation of debt during war times can be defended on economic grounds.

T F 19. Government deficit spending increases the national debt.

T F 20. With the federal budget divided into three major accounts the current account would always be kept in balance.

T F 21. Government borrowing is an appropriate method to finance public investments.

T F 22. The federal government budget as not been balanced since the beginning of World War II.

T F 23. Many economists believe that the effects of the national debt could be minimized by issuing fewer short-term securities and more long-term securities.

T F 24. Government borrowing may increase interest rates and thereby reduce private investment.

T F 25. If the government budget had to be balanced each year, it would be harder for the government to stabilize the economy using fiscal policy.

MULTIPLE CHOICE QUESTIONS Select the one best answer

1. The recent increases in the national debt may be attributed to:
   a. the war on poverty.
   b. defense spending increases.
   c. major tax increase.
   d. reductions in government social welfare programs.

2. The federal debt as a percent of total credit market debt:
   a. increased significantly between 1945 and 1974.
   b. is expected to decrease in early 1990s.
   c. increased to 26.8 percent in 1993.
   d. All of the above.

3. A federal security:
   a. is a promissory note stating the federal government will pay the holder the principal plus interest over a specified period of time.
   b. may be marketable or unmarketable.
   c. is an obligation of the federal government to pay the holder principal plus interest.
   d. All of the above.

4. The price of marketable federal securities is determined by:
   a. market forces.
   b. the Treasury Department.
   c. the Federal Reserve bank.
   d. commercial banks.

5. Most of the national debt is held by:
   a. U.S. investors, but the percent of the privately held national debt owned by foreign investors has increased in recent years.
   b. U.S. investors, but the percent of the privately held national debt owned by foreign investors has been constant in recent years.
   c. foreign investors, but the percent of the privately held national debt owned by U.S. investors has increased in recent years.
   d. foreign investors, but the percent of the privately held national debt owned by U.S. investors has been constant in recent years.

6. The general public
   a. is concerned about the national debt.
   b. is concerned that a large national debt will bankrupt the government and the economy.
   c. is concerned about the national debt's burden on future generations.
   d. shares the same concerns as economists about the national debt.
   e. All of the above except (d).

7. The primary burden of an internally held national debt:
   a. is the value of the private goods and services that could have been produced.
   b. is shifted to the future.
   c. alters the distribution of the national output among people.
   d. reduces productivity and output.
   e. All of the above.

8. The secondary effects of the national debt include:
   a. income redistribution effects.
   b. output effects.
   c. inflationary effects.
   d. All of the above.

9. When tax collections are greater than government expenditures, aggregate demand:
   a. decreases.
   b. increases.
   c. remains the same.
   d. increases and inflation decreases.
   e. All of the above.

10. Government borrowing increases the demand for loanable funds and, consequently:
    a. increases the supply of loanable funds.
    b. exerts downward pressures on the rate of interest.
    c. makes it easier for private businesses to obtain loans.
    d. exerts upward pressure on the rate of interest.

11. Government borrowing from nonbanks:
    a. increases aggregate demand by decreasing saving available for private borrowing and investment and increasing the rate of interest.
    b. reduces aggregate demand by decreasing saving available for private borrowing and investment and increasing the rate of interest.
    c. increases aggregate demand by increasing the money supply.
    d. None of the above.

12. Debt financing:
    a. does not change the total assets of people.
    b. changes the composition of assets of people.
    c. is a way to pay for government goods and services over a period of time.
    d. All of the above.

13. Increases in the national debt increase the money supply:
    a. when the government borrows from nonbank sources.
    b. when banks buy government securities.
    c. whenever the government sells securities.
    d. when the Treasury prints more currency.

14. Debt management policy is essentially concerned with:
    a. the structural characteristics of the national debt.
    b. the size of the national debt.
    c. the availability of money and credit.
    d. All of the above.

15. There is general agreement among economists that:
    a. debt management policy should play a positive role in economic stabilization.
    b. debt management policy designed to minimize the interest costs on the national debt is not always a desirable policy.
    c. the national debt should be composed of more long-term securities.
    d. Both (a) and (c).
    e. Both (b) and (c).

16. The principle of minimizing the interest cost of the national debt should:
    a. never be adhered to as a guide to debt management policy.
    b. should be the primary guide to debt management policy.
    c. be followed only when it will not worsen recessionary or inflationary forces.
    d. None of the above.

17. The best way of financing a budget deficit:
    a. is to print money.
    b. is to borrow from nonbank sources.
    c. is to borrow from commercial banks.
    d. depends upon the state of the economy.

18. Government activity of any sort should not be undertaken unless:
    a. there are taxes to finance the activity.
    b. it can be paid for in a short period of time.
    c. the present value of the net benefits exceed the present value of the costs.
    d. Both (b) and (c).

19. The best way for the government to finance war expenditures is to:
    a. borrow from the private sector.
    b. create money.
    c. increases taxes.
    d. All of the above since they all transfer resources from private production to war production.
    e. None of the above since they all would create inflation.

20. The current account of a three-account federal budget would:
    a. include spending for investment goods and the debt incurred to finance these goods.
    b. include spending programs designed to stabilize the economy.
    c. be financed by the government incurring debt.
    d. always be kept in balance.

21. Which of the following are ways for the government to pay for its expenditures?
    a. Tax financing.
    b. Debt financing.
    c. Money creation.
    d. All of the above.

22. A government budget deficit due to discretionary decisions by Congress is called a
    a. monetary deficit.
    b. cyclical deficit.
    c. structural deficit.
    d. foreign trade deficit.

23. Which of the following would be an appropriate reason to finance government spending through borrowing?
    a. to provide public investments.
    b. to repay interest on past deficits.
    c. to stabilize the economy.
    d. a and c.

24. By the mid 1990's the public-held federal debt had reached a level of approximately.
    a. $285 Billion.
    b. $510 Billion.
    c. $1 Trillion.
    d. $3.5 Trillion.

25. What is a deficit caused by an economy operating at less than full employment called?
    a. structural deficit.
    b. cyclical deficit.
    c. frictional deficit.
    d. fiscal deficit.

PROBLEMS

1. Suppose that the economy is at less than full employment and that the government runs a deficit. Using supply and demand curves, show what happens to the rate of interest if the government finances the deficit by borrowing.

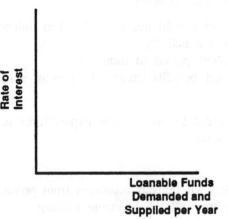

a. The rate of interest _____.
b. The demand for loanable funds _____.
c. The quantity of loanable funds supplied _____.

2. Suppose the economy is suffering from severe inflation. The government then decides to refinance the national debt in order to combat the inflationary forces. Using supply and demand curves, trace the changes in interest rates and in quantities of funds loaned in both the long-term and the short-term markets as a result of the refinancing operation.

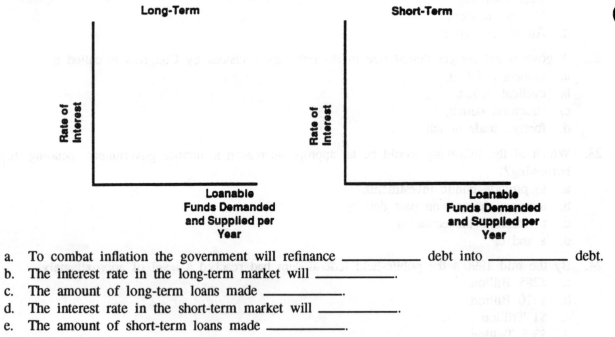

a. To combat inflation the government will refinance _____ debt into _____ debt.
b. The interest rate in the long-term market will _____.
c. The amount of long-term loans made _____.
d. The interest rate in the short-term market will _____.
e. The amount of short-term loans made _____.

3. On the graph below, indicate the effect of a federal tax surplus assuming that the original equilibrium is at price level p_1 and output level q_1.

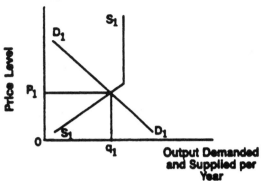

a. A tax surplus will cause aggregate demand to _____.

b. A tax surplus will cause a(n) _____ in the price level and in output.

Now illustrate on the same graph the effect of a federal budget deficit.

c. A budget will cause aggregate demand to _____.

d. A budget deficit will cause a(n) _____ in the price level and in output.

ANSWERS TO SELF-TEST

PUZZLE

Across	Down
2. Monetizing	1. Deficit
4. Investment	2. Management
7. Balanced	3. Investments
9. Primary	5. Recurrent
10. Debt	6. Secondary
12. Stabilization	8. Current
13. Surplus	11. Fiscal

TRUE-FALSE QUESTIONS

1. F	6. F	11. T	16. F	21. T
2. T	7. T	12. T	17. T	22. F
3. T	8. T	13. F	18. F	23. T
4. F	9. T	14. F	19. T	24. T
5. T	10. F	15. F	20. T	25. T

MULTIPLE-CHOICE QUESTIONS

1. b	6. e	11. b	16. c	21. d
2. c	7. a	12. d	17. d	22. c
3. d	8. d	13. b	18. c	23. d
4. a	9. a	14. a	19. c	24. d
5. a	10. d	15. e	20. d	25. b

PROBLEMS

1.

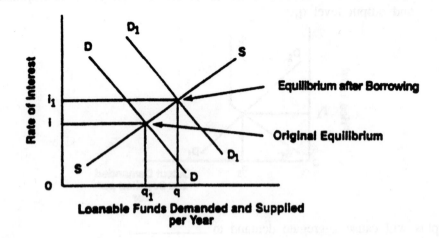

a. rises
b. increases
c. increases

2.

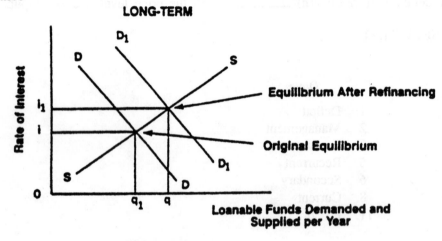

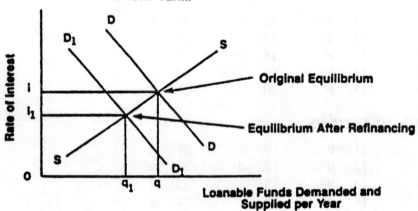

a. short-term, long-term
b. rise
c. rise
d. fall
e. fall

3.

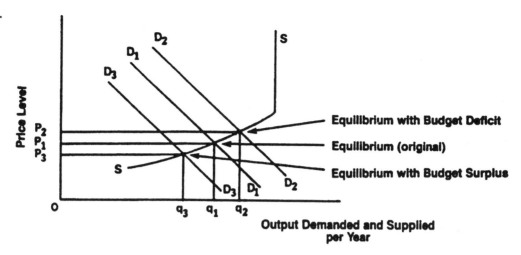

a. fall
b. reduction
c. rise
d. increase